FRAGRANCE

Also by Edwin T. Morris:

THE GARDENS OF CHINA: *History, Art, and Meanings*

FRAGRANCE

THE STORY OF PERFUME
FROM CLEOPATRA
TO CHANEL

Edwin T. Morris

E. T. MORRIS & CO.
PRODUCTS OF NATURE AND OF ART
GREENWICH, CT • NEW YORK, NY

To my children,
Jeffrey, Jerome, Simon, and Christine

Contents

ACKNOWLEDGMENTS

Perfumery is an ongoing craft and my information and feel for the industry has come from visiting factories and fields as well as from libraries and museums. I would like to thank the countless individuals and their companies in the essential oil, retail perfume and cosmetics, and art glass industries who have shared their knowledge, experience, and enthusiasm with me. In particular I would like to mention, in the United States, Henry G. Walter, Jr., of International Flavors and Fragrances Incorporated and the Vetlesen Foundation; Marc Parrilli of Berjé, Incorporated; Edward Davidson, Nigel Priest, James Bell, and Sharon Maes of Roure Bertrand Dupont, Incorporated; Thomas Pastre of Creatique; Dr. Brian Lawrence of the Avoca Division of R. J. Reynolds and Company; Dr. Arthur O. Tucker of the Department of Agricultural and Natural Resources, Dover State College; Hazel Bishop, Jack Rittenberg, Lilian Bartok, Marty Bronson, and Theresa Reilly of the Fashion Institute of Technology; Florence Wall; Fernando Aleu, M.D., and Annette Green of the Fragrance Foundation; Stanley E. Allured, Jean and Nancy Allured of Allured Publications; Frank Anderson; Mark Rasmussen; Paul Bedoukian of Bedoukian Research; Dr. Richard Evans Schultes, Director of the Economic Herbarium, Harvard University; Dr. Fred W. Stone, Firminich Incorporated; Dr. Seymour Lemberg, James Rogers, Rayda Vega, and Robert Doris of Fritzsche Dodge and Olcott Incorporated; Christian Marchandise and Didier Poursain, Saint Gobain Desjonquères (U.S.A.); Suzanne Biaillôt and her staff at Guerlain Incorporated; Steven Kany at Pfizer Corporation, and Thomas De Long and Bernard Lee at Coty Division of Pfizer; Suzanne Urban and her staff at Chanel Incorporated; Henri-Michel and Colette Hoffmann; Dr. Webster Hudgins of Allied Chemical; Frederic Rosengarten, Jr., Robert Dugrenier and the staff of Catherine Barré at Brosse U.S.A., Incorporated; Dr. Jan Buchel, Pepsico Research and Technical Services; Bernard P. Champon, Sr., and Lawrence De Wald of L. A. Champon and Company Incorporated; Stephen R. Manheimer of J. Manheimer Incorporated; Frank Fischetti, Jr., of Mero Incorporated; Gerald Nunziata of Penick Corporation; Dr. H. K. Palta; Dr. Braja Mookherjee and numerous other persons in the various divisions of International Flavors and Fragrances; Dr. Hu Hsiu-ying of the Arnold Arboretum; Harry C. McDaniel, the Procter and Gamble Company; James Dellas, Florasynth, Incorporated; Enrico Donati, Houbigant Incorporated; R. M. Hughes and Traude Baumann, Dragoco Corporation; Philip Kemelor; Madeleine Morrissey, Dana Perfumes Corporation; Michael Blumenfeld, Bloomingdale's; and Roberta Nugent, Roman Kaiser, and Ken Purzycki of the Givaudan Corporation.

Among those involved in the story of fragrance in France particular thanks go to Marylène Delbourg-Delphis, Analyses Conseils Informations; George Vindry and Joëlle Dejardin of the Musée International de la Parfumerie; Dr. Paul Teisseire, Benjamin Mazoyer-Lagrange, André Galfré, and Marie Christine Samarise at Roure Bertrand Dupont; Louis Peyron and Iran Gérard, Lautier Aromatiques; Agnès Demeilliers, Gilbert Sicre, Roger Schwob, and René Cornon of the Société Technique des Parfumeurs de France; Maurice Vinot of the Institut National des Recherches Agricoles; André Berthon of Pierre Chauvet S.A.; Bernard Meyer-Warnod of Camilli, Albert et Laloue; Daniel Joulain and Yves Tollard d'Audiffret of Robertet; Jacques Hetru and Jean-Jacques Bernard of Pochet et du Courval and Jean Marie Daumas, fragrance journalist of Grasse.

In England, I would like to acknowledge the assistance of Dr. Joseph Needham, Dr. Lu Gwei-djen, and Francesca Bray of the East Asia History of Science Library at Cambridge; Edmund Launert of the British Museum, Clinton L. Green of the Tropical Products Institute, and Rosemary C. R. Angel of the Museum of Economic Botany, the Royal Botanic Gardens, Kew.

In other countries, I would like to mention the help of Christa Brandt and Else Ziegenbein of Dragoco Gerberding and Company, Federal Republic of Germany, publishers of the *Dragoco Report*; Francesco Misitano of Misitano e Stracuzzi in Italy and of Aripe, in Brazil; and Dr. Xu Siang-hao of the South China Agricultural College, Guangzhou (Canton), China.

The following persons in cultural institutions have made their collections available for research: the curators and staff of the Department of European Sculpture and Decorative Arts—in particular, Jessie McNab, Lita Semerad of the Operations Department, Peter Dorman and Christine Lilyquist of the Egyptian Department, Jean Mailey of the Textile Study Room, Carolyn Kane of the Islamic Department, Dr. Maxwell Anderson of the Department of Greek and Roman Art, Mary Lawrence of the Department of Twentieth Century Art, and Paul Ettesvold of the Costume Institute, all of The Metropolitan Museum of Art, New York; Charles Long, Lothian Lynas, Jane Brennan, Rose Li, and the staff of the Library; Ann Botshon and Ann Schwartz of *Garden Magazine*; Allen Rokach, Marcia Stevens, and Kerry Walter at the New York Botanical Garden; Gerard McKiernan of the Carnegie Museum of Natural History; Professor Gary Ledyard and Jack Jacoby, Librarian, Department of East Asian Languages and Cultures, Columbia University; and Elain Dee, Lillian Clagett, and Katherine Martinez of the Copper-Hewitt Museum.

I would also like to express my gratitude for the support of the National Endowment for the Humanities, which funded several months of research into the essential oils, as well as the encouragement of my parents, Mr. and Mrs. Edwin Morris; my parents-in-law, Mr. and Mrs. Alexander Roth; Charles Roth of Roth Advertising; my students at the New York Botanical Garden and at the Fashion Institute of Technology, and my editor at Scribners, Megan Schembre.

Introduction

When I first became interested in the history of perfumes of fragrance, I felt embarrassed, as if I were researching trivia or had become the archivist of idleness. And really, were not perfumes and scents merely a pleasant extravagance for women to indulge in during their leisure hours? For most of us, scents are not necessities; they fit into the category of "frills," and our biggest scent-buying time is during the holidays, when we spend our money a little recklessly.

But despite the reservations I may have entertained at first, the subject of the aromatic plants, their uses and applications, and the wizardry of the sense of olfaction proved so intriguing that I could not put my investigations aside. In time, however, I came to feel less apologetic about this seemingly insignificant topic of research as I realized how influential smells can be on our behavior and how our ancestors put enormous store in products of fragrance, going to any length to procure them. They ransacked nature in search of beautiful and different aromas despite wars, revolutions, plagues, and pestilence.

Great strides in chemistry were made as technical minds grappled with the means to extract and preserve these essences, and traders trudged across deserts and ploughed uncharted seas to find them. Once procured, these aromatics became essential parts of religious rituals, stimulated romance, enhanced imagination, and dispelled whatever foul miasmas may have lurked in their environments.

The more I studied the historical records, the more I saw that in all major civilizations fragrance was a cultural need associated with magic, pleasure, and even healing and therapy. No one would doubt the importance of a book written on the history of medicine or pharmacy, and yet perfumes were looked upon for millennia as cures. As the Chinese put it, "Every perfume is a medicine." These beliefs were not too far wide of the mark. Perfume oils are powerful germicides. In France there is a movement that has developed in the last forty years called "aromatherapy." Scents can both stimulate and calm. There is an historical justification for the fact that even today perfumes are still sold in pharmacies.

Aromaticity has played a great part in the rise of the sciences. The father of botany, Carolus Linnaeus (1707–1778), was one of the first to map out a system of odor classification, which was a great tool in classifying plants. Botanists know that flowers create scents not as idle recreation but as an important link to survival: Understanding these scents leads to an understanding of their relation to the insects that pollinate the blooms. Today naturalists are studying how to frustrate pests (such as the gypsy moth) to valuable crops by spraying the fields with olfactory cues that confuse the mating pattern.

The study of fragrance has vital links to chemistry as well. Joseph Needham, an historian of science, has said, "The olfactory sense has always been one of the most important tools to the chemist."[1] The desire to ascertain and duplicate the perfumes of nature has been a considerable spur to the development of modern organic chemistry. In 1939, Leopold Ruzicka (1887–1976) was awarded the Nobel Prize in chemistry for his work in understanding the higher cyclic terpenes, found in essential oils.

The study of scent permeates literature as well. Much of the pleasure of literature is in imagining the scenes described, but we can also imagine the scents described. In the Bible, the beloved of Solomon was described as coming out of the wilderness "perfumed with myrrh and frankincense, with all the powders of the merchant" (Song of Solomon, 3.6). After the Babylonian exile, the Temple of Jerusalem was rededicated amid clouds of incense. These scents were real and are identifiable today.

Shakespeare spoke of the "forward, not permanent, sweet, not lasting," perfume of violets in *Hamlet*, and in his Fifth Sonnet of a "summer's distillation left a liquid prisoner pent in walls of glass." The scents of all the extracts which could be produced in his time, as well as of the herbs and flowers grown, are mentioned in his work.

In the nineteenth century, Baudelaire seemed to write with perfumed ink, an approach followed later by subsequent poets and novelists in France.

In economic history, "spices," the ancient catchall phrase for any aromatic, were responsible for the creation of the Silk Route to China and the overland and sea routes to the East and its Spice Islands. Like jewels, small amounts of these substances made a great impact.

Nevertheless there is still something frivolous and ephemeral about the story of perfumes that lends it an air of pleasure and delight. But even this *petite histoire* can give us some real insight into the larger movements of history. Napoleon carried with him whole kilos of eau de cologne on all his campaigns, and in the early Victorian age, manufacturers of textiles in Europe found that their paisley designs would not sell unless they also had the patchouli fragrance of the Indian originals. From these examples we learn about the very development of style; Napoleon was the prototype of the self-made man of the new era of the bourgeoisie, the mark of which was fastidiousness in matters of hygiene and personal cleanliness, and modern market research tells us that it is not merely printed fabrics but nearly every product that must be fragranced for consumer acceptance.

So then, without further hesitation, let us follow our noses through the unexpected and intriguing world of scent. First we will define some of the common concepts and important materials of perfumery and then examine the olfactory sense, which detects and enjoys these materials. Next we will delve into the long history of one of the world's oldest industries. We will see how, one by one, mankind acquires an ever richer palette of raw materials and the means of using them. In the chapter after that we will look at the supplies of the chief fragrance materials today, find out why they are costly, and what romantic lands they come from. We will ask how do rose essences leave the plant and find themselves in a flacon of perfume; where do synthetic fragrances come from; what are the animal essences that add depth to a perfume blend? The final section will look at the many activities of the modern perfume industry: the training of the creative perfumer, the research behind the scenes, new applications of scent, and the splash and myth-making of perfume marketing. In America alone, sales of fragrance reach a billion and a half dollars a year. The use of fragrance is extensive in Europe and growing daily in Asia, whose culture has long been interested in scent.

By the last page we will have a good overview of the materials, our own noses, the long history of aromatics in culture and in the evolution of styles, and the modern trade that produces such a panoply of products. Thus we will be really able to savor the art, the history, the magic, and the technology that have come together and are ready to spring from the next bottle of perfume or cologne we open and inhale.

SCENT
AND SMELL

The Materials,
the Essential Oils

What is a perfume? The word "perfume" comes from two Latin words, *per*, "through," and *fumum*, "smoke," betraying the origins of all perfumery: incense. Today, however, a "perfume" implies a mixture of ethyl alcohol (the solvent or extender) with one or possibly hundreds of essential oils, which are responsible for the scent. The ratio is usually eight parts alcohol to two parts essential oils, although it may become as high as seven to three. An *eau de toilette* ("toilet water") is a much thinner dilution of the same materials, containing approximately only five percent of essential oils. A "cologne" for men or women, or an "after-shave lotion" for men, is a further dilution, about three percent. However, here again there is no fixed rule in international perfumery, and the product may be made even more odorous by doubling the percentage of perfume oils.

"Essential oils" are the very essence of perfumery. We shall explore these materials in depth later on, but for now let us say that they are oils (hence not miscible in water) that the human organism perceives as either fragrance or flavor. These oils come from natural sources (chiefly plants), although they can be synthesized from petroleum and other sources, and they have the property of becoming gaseous at ordinary room temperatures. They are called essential oils after the Latin word *essentia*, meaning a liquid that easily becomes a gaseous essence. Because they vaporize so easily, the essential oils have also been called "volatile" oils (from the Latin *volare*, "to fly") or even "spirits" by the old apothecaries, as in the expression "spirits of turpentine," meaning the essential oil of pine. The Germans call them *ätherische öle* ("ethereal oils") for the same reason: We can perceive them although they may no longer be visible as liquids. These essences are diffused through the tissues of a plant, such as in the petals of a flower, and they are chiefly extracted for perfumery use through distillation.

Sometimes one will encounter the term "perfumer's alcohol," or "perfumery-grade alcohol." This alcohol, ethanol, is the all-important perfumer's diluent and fragrance carrier. It comes primarily from the distillation of wine to produce grape spirit (brandy), the earliest perfumery alcohol. Wine distillate, however, is expensive and retains a certain bouquet of the grapes, which interferes with most scents except for a few colognes, where it adds a desirable fruit note. So fermented grains such as rice, wheat, and sorghum, the starches in sugar beets, manioc, potatoes, and corn, and the sugar in molasses are used instead. Ethyl alcohol can also be obtained from the fractional distillation of petroleum. Since the United States has always had great reserves of that fuel, it has been the source of most American alcohol for perfumery. England, which traditionally has had tropical colonies rich in sugar cane, has used the alcohol from that source a great deal. The French have had to grow sugar beets for alcohol production since the British blockade of Europe at the time of the Napoleonic wars; they claim to detect a slightly rummy note in the alcohol from molasses. One of the finest carriers of a perfume is highly rectified rice alcohol, but if it is not highly rectified, the same oiliness one may notice in rice wine will appear in the perfumery alcohol.

If natural alcohol were used to carry the essential oils, as was the case for hundreds of years, a perfume or cologne would be no different from a tincture or extract, such as vanilla extract. The technologists who perfected brandies and herbal liqueurs were often the same ones who created perfumes and toilet waters. Today, however, civilized life being what it is, most governments have insisted that perfumery alcohol be denatured, that is, made unfit for consumption. Common denaturants are wood (methyl) alcohol, propyl alcohol, or diethyl phthalate, which are all toxic, or brucine sulfate, which is one of the most bitter of all substances. Some of these denaturants, even when the purest grades are used, can modify a composition very slightly and present difficulties to the modern perfumer that were unknown in earlier ages.

The alcohol used in perfumery not only mixes with essential oils but with water as well. Naturally, adding water reduces the price of the alcohol, which in America costs well below ten dollars per gallon. If too much is added (approaching fifty percent), the oils may come out of solution. Some water, however, is desirable in perfumery alcohol because it prolongs the persistence of the perfume on the skin, water being more viscous than alcohol. For the same reason, sometimes cologne alcohol will also contain some glycerin.

Perfumes are usually sold in bottles with conventional friction stoppers, but the more dilute fragrance blends are usually sold in a bottle to which a pump has been added to release a fine spray of the mix. Aerosols can also be used, but restrictions have been placed on the use of fluorocarbons as propellants.

Another vehicle for scent is a "pomade," or "cream," old names for the gamut of products we know as "cosmetics." We think primarily of cosmetics as emollients used to soften the skin and consider them carriers of fragrance only as an afterthought. The reverse, however, has been the case for most of the history of perfumery: The fats, oils, and waxes of a cosmetic were first and foremost carriers of fragrant oils and were considered fragrance products. One of the most classic cosmetics, cold cream, contains a fragrance content that is the same as that of an eau de toilette: five percent. The rest of the formula is a blend of lanolin, mineral oil, beeswax, lard, petroleum jelly, or other fats and oils according to various formulations and emulsified with water. Most cold creams carry a simple rose scent. Although for some consumers, cosmetics may be vehicles of scent only subliminally, their perfume content has a great deal to do with their sales success. Even "unscented" cosmetics usually require some scenting to overcome the fatty odor of the base raw materials.

A "stick perfume" is simply an essential oil dissolved in solid wax,

thus even lipstick is a perfume product with added dyes. Adding a wick
to such a blend of essential oils and waxes produces a "scented candle,"
a scent-releasing lamp, an ancient artifact.

Soaps and soap products such as shampoos are also important fragrance items because, like cosmetics, they are principally composed of
fats and oils with which essential oils will blend with success. Soap
manufacture began when an alkali (from the Arabic words *al qili*, "ashes
of the soapwort" [*Saponeria officinalis*], a marsh plant whose burnt
leaves served as the chemical lye of modern soap manufacture) was
added to lard or tallow. The Romans used a clay as a cleanser, but the
Arabs developed true soapmaking and introduced it to the Europeans
by the time of the Crusades. Latin Europe—Italy, France, and Spain—
pioneered in the use of soap, and the familiar "cake" of soap was in
regular production there by the eighteenth century.

The cleansing action of soap is an amazing and complicated affair.
The molecule of soap has both a polar and a non-polar end; this allows
it to first hold the greases that make up and contain dirt and then let
them be washed away by water. This behavior of the soap molecule
will keep the oils from coalescing as they would, say, if a salad dressing
were allowed to stand for a while. The oils will remain trapped by the
lather until it is rinsed away. Wonderful as soap is, it retains the odor
of fat and from its earliest days has been perfumed. Today almost all
the *grands parfums* are presented in soap form, but adjustments of great
delicacy have to be made in the formula of the perfume in order to
permit the essential oils to interact harmoniously with the fatty acids.
Shampoos and liquid soaps are simply dilute applications of the same
principle, but the fragrance is still critical. Yardley's Lavender and Colgate's Cashmere Bouquet are two famous fragrances carried in soap
form.

A bath oil is a combination of fifteen percent essential oil with mineral
oil, lanolin, or other fatty oils of plant origin. Estée Lauder's Youth
Dew appeared in 1953 in this format and broke sales records. The
scent was attractive in itself; Mrs. Lauder made it much richer in oils
than most other fragrances of the time; and the idea of using the bath
as a vehicle tempted many women to use a fragrance daily, whereas
they might have used a daily perfume. Bath salts are essential oils added
to sodium bicarbonate (baking soda) and sodium carbonate.

Powder is another scent carrier. It consists of essential oils mixed
with talc, a soft mineral that has been ground and purified and some-

Guests at an Egyptian banquet wearing the bit, *the scented cones of animal fats worn on the head. These were impregnated with gum resins from the land of Punt (Somalia). Before the distillation of alcohol, fatty oils from plant or animal sources were the first solvents for perfumes. In Egypt, where the hot, dry climate could easily produce drying and cracking of the skin, cosmetic substances such as lard, olive oil, and castor oil served as an emollient for the skin as well as a vehicle for the release of fragrance. Today cosmetics are still fatty oils scented with essential oils. Courtesy of The Metropolitan Museum of Art*

times supplemented with china clay and starches. The whole is then sifted through silk screens. In the eighteenth century, the white wigs fashionable at the court of Versailles were perfumed with ground orrisroot (from *Iris germanica, var. pallida* or *florentina*). The root contains starches interspersed with a fine, violetlike essential oil.

We expect soap and powder to be used as fragrance products, but leather may come as a surprise. The animal proteins that make up

This poster, attributed to Jules Chéret, uses the prestige of the Divine Sarah to advertise a rice powder, a fragranced product. The Belle Epoque, epitomized by Sarah Bernhardt, was a period of many innovative fragrances; she was an early patron of Rèné Lalique, the jeweler-turned-glassmaker. Courtesy of The Museum of Grasse

leather are a wonderful medium for the adsorption of essential-oil molecules. They are so large that they entrap the smaller, scented molecules in their orbit, like planets caught in the pull of the sun. Human hair is also proteinous and hence a wonderful carrier of scent. This is why men have traditionally applied scented pomades to the beard and women to their tresses. Furs, too, retain the scent of their owner for years. Leather has an innately attractive "animal" odor which always remains discernible. But leather goods have always been associated with perfumery because the traditional means of tanning the hides necessitated immersion in vats of urine. This is why counteracting any residues of that odor has preoccupied perfumers since the ninth century of our era. The Arabs produced exquisite glove scents from attar of rose, musk, and citrus oils, and Muslim Spain became heir to these formulas. Even today a type of perfume is known as *Peau d'Espagne*. At a later date the Russians utilized the essential oils found in birch tar in their great birch forests to produce the fragrant "Russian leather" (*cuir de Russie*) odor. In the Middle Ages the guild of the glovers was just as avid for the musk and sandalwood from the East as were the perfumers and apothecaries. Although urine is not the only tanning agent today, many fine leathers are still scented.

* * *

What is incense, mankind's first perfume? There are two kinds of incense—Western and Eastern—each with a distinct character and composition. Western incense, which is still used in the sacred rituals of the Catholic and orthodox churches, is composed of gum resins exuded from the bark of small trees. These are combinations of essential oils (the resin half) and gums, the latter contributing the stickiness. Everyone who has handled a Christmas tree to find his or her hands coated with a sweet-smelling, tacky gum has had contact with gum resins. These are secreted by pines and other trees and bushes to protect the plant from infection after laceration of the bark. Often, in dry climates, these resins will harden and can be scraped off the bark with a knife. In this form they will travel without deterioration, preserved by a natural packaging. When these dry grains of incense are sprinkled over a burning coal, the gum melts and releases the aromatic resin. The perfumes of frankincense and myrrh that are still burned in the great cathedrals in Latin Europe make a heavenly scent, especially when they are inhaled along with the odor of beeswax candles and altar flowers. Incense was such heady stuff that the early Christians hemmed and hawed before incorporating such pagan trappings into their rites, and it was one of the first things banned by the reformers of the sixteenth century.

East Asian incense is slightly more processed than ecclesiastical incense and usually is made of more ingredients than frankincense and myrrh, which, with the addition of gum benjamin (benzoin) and rosemary, are the chief constituents of Western church incense. Frankincense and myrrh were exported from Arabia toward the east as well as north and west, but in addition, Indian, Chinese, and Japanese perfumers made use of sandalwood, agarwood, patchouli, and vetiver. The botanicals were ground in a large mortar and pestle in which water was placed, thus making a paste. Sometimes a dash of saltpeter was added; this is potassium nitrate, an efflorescence that appeared over sewers and gave a steady burn to the incense mix. The Indians then daubed this paste onto a sliver of bamboo and the stick was known as an *agarbatti*; the Chinese mastered the trick of extruding the paste through tiny holes, like noodles, thereby creating strands of straight or spiraled incense, air-dried and hardened for use in the temples. The Chinese often burned incense in such sanctuaries in conjunction with another pyrotechnic, fireworks, which made their religious services somewhat more riotous than those in the West.

What Are Essential Oils?

In taking stock of the gamut of fragrance-bearing artifacts, we have seen how essential oils are the common denominator in all of them. At this point let us examine in greater depth the properties and sources of these amazing oils.

The essential oils are truly amazing, for even the minutest quantity is perceivable to us as a fragrance or flavor. Musk can be detected in amounts as small as 0.000,000,000,000,032 ounce, and vanilla can be noticed when present at two millionths of a milligram per cubic millimeter in the air. This is the meaning of "essential." They are also truly "oils" for they do not mix with water, which is a polar substance, but they will mix with alcohol and the fatty oils. When essential oils are placed in a Florentine flask with water, they either swim to the top or slip to the bottom, depending upon their own specific gravities.

The volatile oils derive from a limited number of animals, the two fossil fuels—petroleum and coal—by synthesis, and from a great number of plants.

The animal sources are easy to inventory: Musk derives from the musk deer (*Moschus mochiferus*), a shy denizen of the rhododendron and birch thickets of western China. Fully grown males weigh only ten kilograms, and it is the male deer that carries in front of the abdomen a sac that secretes a sexual signal, similar in function to the spray of a tomcat but of greater sweetness. Hunters, noticing an unearthly fragrance throughout the forest, eventually isolated the source of this odor, and the minuscule deer has been hunted ever since. After killing the deer, they removed the sac and dried and sold it.

The sperm whale manufactures the precious ambergris. This great mammal (*Physeter catodon*) lives on a diet of cuttlefish, a kind of squid that contains a sharp bone, the cuttlebone, which is used in bird cages for sharpening the beaks of parakeets. Ambergris is secreted to protect the intestinal lining of the whale from this abrasive. As an oil, it will float, and from time to time it would become caught in the nets of fishermen plying the Indian Ocean. The Arabs appreciated its sweet odor and its great fixative qualities; it is able to delay the rate of volatility of other oils with which it is mixed. Today both musk and ambergris can be synthesized, and the perfume trade has voluntarily refused to purchase ambergris out of consideration for the survival of the sperm whale.

The essential oil "swims" on the surface of the condensed water of distillation, still clouded by minute drops of oil that have not yet come out of solution. Photo by Allen Rokach

The essential oil in the plant: glands of lavender oil, as revealed by the scanning electron microscope. Courtesy of John Innes Institute, Norwich, U.K.

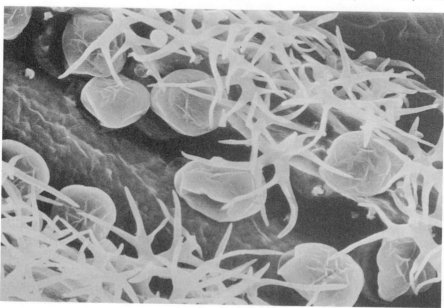

Civet is a glandular secretion of both male and female civet cats (*Viverra civetta*), an East African cat that grows no more than four feet long. Near the genitalia a fatty substance is formed that can be removed from captive cats about twice a week. It has a revoltingly fecal odor but becomes both extremely agreeable and strongly fixative when blended with other essences.

The last of the commercial animal essences is castoreum, from both Russian and Canadian beavers (*Castor faber*). This collects in two abdominal sacs in both males and females. In extreme dilution, castoreum is not without charm, but it is mainly used as a fixative in very strong perfumes. The fixating qualities that mark all of these animal essences is a function of their high molecular weight, which impedes the loss of the molecules to the air.

The aromatic chemicals produced by the coal-tar and petroleum industries are vastly greater in number than those found in the animal kingdom. Most synthetic aromatic oils are extremely cheap compared to natural ones, hence the reason for their use; but others are complicated final products of extensive chemical building and manipulation and sell for hundreds of dollars for a few pounds. Too many aroma chemicals will produce a somewhat harsh odor, but their incorporation with natural materials can give them a bloom they would ordinarily lack.

Another important source of what can be called "semi-synthetics" are natural oils which are fractionally distilled for the extraction of a certain molecule; thus cheaper oils can be "mined" for more desirable aromatic constituents, and they can also be used as starting points for transformation into other organic compounds. As civilization evolves, the desire for fragrances continues to accelerate across the globe; the supply of natural materials alone is insufficient for even half of this demand.

However, this same upsurge of demand has also caused more cultivation of aromatic plants than ever before in history. The softness of the plant odors and the great range of their minute but important trace elements make them an indispensable part of fine perfumery. The human olfactory sense is so well honed that it can detect the presence or absence of natural scents in a composition and prefers those which include them. This attraction to natural essential oils makes them a desirable investment for the agriculturalist, whereas the natural dyes have become almost obsolete commercially. For centuries these essential oil-bearing plants have been the source of ninety-eight percent of all perfumery. Even today perfumers retain the categories derived from the plants in describing odor chemicals: They may be "rosy," "jasminelike," or "mossy," no matter what their actual origin.

No one plant family can claim a monopoly of essential-oil species; they are scattered throughout a great number of families although especially numerous in the rose, mint, myrtle, laurel, and carrot families (*Rosaceae, Labiatae, Myrtaceae, Lauraceae,* and *Umbelliferae*). Nor are they to be found in one specialized part of any plant. Obviously the floral parts are most likely to harbor volatile oils to release into the empyrean and attract pollinators, but the roots, leaves, fruits, seeds, and branches may be equally endowed.

Whenever you press a part of a plant tissue and detect an odor, you are in the presence of an essential oil. The floral parts of jasmine, orange blossoms, violets, tuberoses, carnations, honeysuckle, lilies, saffron crocuses, jonquils, narcissus, mimosa, and ylang-ylang bear essential oils; rosemary, patchouli, mint, rosy-leaved geraniums, camphor, and cloves bear leaves with aromatic oils; the roots of vetiver, valerian, and angelica are aromatic. The rhizomes of ginger and orrisroot, the twigs of the petitgrain citrus, the peels of oranges, lemons, tangerines, bergamot, and grapefruits, and the fruits of coriander, nutmeg, anise, and fennel contain these oils. Aromatic gum resins ooze from the bark of *Boswellia* and *Commiphora* plants to produce the classical incense gums of the West, and similar exudations can be found on pines, cedars, and other evergreens. Further on we shall study the nuances of each natural crop; commercially, about one hundred are utilized in the industry.

What explains the presence of these oils in plants? Insofar as the life of the plant itself is concerned without consideration of its relation to the outside world, there is no simple answer. For example, we know that the plant will not reabsorb the essential oils it has formed in a leaf before shedding it in the fall. Sugars and starches, however, are returned to the main body of the plant prior to the shedding of leaves: hence some botanists concluded that the essential oils such as latex, gums, and alkaloids were "waste products" of the plant's metabolism. Modern research tends to reject this conclusion: The oils seem to possess components that can serve as energy sources during a deficiency resulting from an interruption of the normal assimilation of carbon dioxide. They may also serve as hydrogen donors in certain reactions. Whatever their purpose within the plant, they clearly serve an important role in its survival vis-à-vis its environment.

It is this role as monitor of the plant's condition in the environment that explains why so many essential oils are located at the periphery of the plant's structure, although the oils may be compounded deeper within the living cytoplasm of the plant itself. In roses the scent glands appear in the papilliform cells of the outer epidermis of the petals. In mints, lavender, thyme, and other labiates, the oils are formed on epidermal hairs. In the fruits of umbellifers, they occur in canals known as vittae. Thus positioned, they can call to pollinators or stand sentinel against predators.

These oils must be somewhat segregated from other plant tissues because they can be extremely toxic. Pine oil, for example, can damage plant tissue in as small a proportion as one to fifty thousand parts. This toxicity will keep away predators, but it must not harm the plant that compounds it. This segregation is also noticeable in the case of rubber latex and of alkaloids, which are of only secondary importance to the plant, although extremely important to man.

If the ordinary metabolic requirements of a plant have been met, essential-oil production can be considerable. The gas plant (*Dictamnus alba*) secretes so much volatile oil on hot days that it can actually be ignited. The peel of an orange, when pressed near a candle, will similarly combust. This "shield" of oils emitted into the air serves to ward off grazing animals for the oil burns the mouth and thus protects the plant. The goats that have been such a scourge to the forests around the Mediterranean have spared many of the pungent herbs of the *maquis* of Provence and Corsica, such as the *serpolet* (wild thyme) and *origan* (wild marjoram). Citronella and camphor oil repel certain insects, and sandalwood is impervious to termites. Sage, clary sage, wormwood, tansy, and thuja (yellow cedar) all contain thujone, which is so powerful against parasites that it has been used as an anthelmintic in medicine.

These essences, manufactured so abundantly by the plant to ward off pests, are also powerful against microbial threats. Oils have been found effective in controlling staphylococcus and the tuberculin bacillus. Given the germ-killing power of carbolic acid as 1.0, these oils have been shown to have the following germicidal strength:

Oil of thyme	12.2	Oil of rue	6.4
Oil of clove	9.2	Oil of rosemary	5.4
Oil of cinnamon	7.8	Oil of lavender	4.4
Oil of rose	7.0	Oil of ylang-ylang	2.8

Synthetic oils and isolates also demonstrate this antiseptic value. These powers were first surmised in the latter half of the last century, when the perfumery workers at Grasse were found to have a lower rate of cholera and tuberculosis than the rest of the European population.

In addition, essential oils have shown startling fungitoxic properties. Oil of clove is toxic to specific growths, and oil of geranium is effective against a broad range of fungi. *Cymbopogon* grasses, an Indian genus of aromatic grasses, have been found effective against *Helminthosporium oryzae*, a source of food poisoning, *Aspergillus niger*, a cause of seborrheic dermatitis of the scalp, *Absidia ramosa*, the cause of otitis, and *Trichoderma viride*, another cause of dermatitis. Man has long guessed that these oils that the plant secreted to protect itself from insect, fungal, and microbial dangers could serve him as well. Thus it is that the story of perfumery is intimately linked to the story of pharmacy. Our ancestors could not formulate the germ theory of disease, but they assumed that whatever smelled clean and healthy must be of use in hygiene.

So much for the oils as armaments; let us now turn to the role of the oils in the work of pollination and the role of perfumes in the very survival of the species.

Flowers that exude a heavy, languorous sweetness, and which the chemists call the indolic type, are communicating with the moth and depend on it for pollination. Thus the romantic scents of jasmine, lilies, hyacinths, and honeysuckle. Despised as he is among men, the moth is the true aristocrat of scent. It is this heady floral type of fragrance that is the most popular among women. White Shoulders, Chloe, Pavlova, and Je Reviens are languorous scents that would meet with a moth's approval. Floral fragrances are rich in night-blooming flowers. Nature drains their blooms of the chlorophylls, anthocyanins, xantophylls, and carotene that color other flowers because these pigments would be useless to moths, who fly by night. The whiteness of their surface reflects the moonlight and starlight, which, along with the flowers' perfume, guides the moth on his *vol de nuit*. It is a moth that takes the world's trophy for olfaction; the Chinese Emperor moth can detect a stimulus it can recognize six miles downwind. The silkworm moth (*Bombyx mori*) is so odor conscious that if an off odor reaches its receptors, it will not spin. Moths generate a scent used in communication across the sexes, which we will consider in the next chapter in the section on the physiology of odor perception. Some flowers have been found to mimic these insect pheromones, as these scent packets are called. It is among the white flowers, those that chiefly address themselves to the moth world, that we find the greatest number of aromatic blooms—fifteen percent.

The next category to claim large percentages of odorous flowers are the reds and pinks, with nine percent. These tones are favored by other pollinators, the day-flying butterflies. The bees, too, can perceive color as well as scent, picked up by their antennae, but they prefer yellow, lavender, and blue flowers. These insects, like the moths, have great olfactory acuity. They possess pore plates, a sophisticated apparatus for odor reception, and a brain and nervous system developed enough to process the information received. Bees can even be trained to recognize a wide variety of odors: Out of a total of 1,816 pairs of aromas, the bee could clearly differentiate over ninety-five percent of them. This olfactory sense works both in determining targets and in communicating this target selection to other members of the hive. This is why apiculturists can market an all-clover or all-buckwheat honey despite the fact that many flowers are within range.

From the refined moth and the clever bee, we must descend to consider some exhalations of the plant world that are not so highly pitched. Some flowers produce oils that mimic the food sources of such lowly creatures as flies and dung beetles. The world's largest flower, the Sumatran *Amorphophallus*, breaks forth from the ground in a phallic shape the height of a man, bathing the jungle with the odor of rotting flesh. Needless to say, this has not been tapped for perfumery but it is attractive to its pollinators, the flies.

The Chemical Nature of the Essential Oils

Once man has been able to extract these precious globules of essential oils, created in the chemical lab of nature to protect and prolong the life of the plant, the physical properties of the oils can be examined. The essential oils, compounded from simpler starches and sugars, will not mix with water, but with alcohol. There are exceptions to every rule, however, and it should be noted that some oils have a slight water solubility. Rose oil, for instance, will remain within the waters of distillation after most of the oil has separated out and confer a decided rosiness to the water when smelled or drunk. This is the "rosewater" of pastry cooks.

Another physical characteristic of the volatile oils is that they are optically active. This means that when a beam of polarized light is shot through an essential oil derived from a plant, it will be twisted, or refracted, to the left, or sometimes to the right, but it will not remain in the same line. Since this activity is characteristic of natural oils, a polarimeter is a tool that can be used to differentiate between natural or synthetic oils. Synthetic camphor, such as is used in mothballs, will not deflect the beam of polarized light, whereas natural camphor will twist it to the right. The essential oils have high refractive indices.

Another attribute, already alluded to in the various names for the oils, is their habit of passing from the liquid to the gaseous phase at relatively low temperatures. Thus, unlike the fatty oils, they will not leave a grease mark on paper. A mark may remain for a few minutes, but the oils will rapidly rise into the air. Again, unlike the fixed or fatty oils, they are non-nutritive, and they cannot be made into soap. Olive oil, almond oil, and safflower oil were among the earliest vehicles for scent, but all the fatty oils have the property of becoming rancid in a few months if not refrigerated. The essential oils have an almost eternal shelf life as far as this form of deterioration is concerned; their germicidal qualities render them impervious to fungal or bacterial decay. However, they will become gummy (polymerize) and darken if exposed to the air for a long time.

What is the chemical nature of these perfume oils? The physical characteristics are similar across the board, but we find an enormous variety in these substances when it comes to chemical composition. Many types of compounds known to organic chemistry can be discovered in the essential oils: hydrocarbons, alcohols, aldehydes, ketones, acids, terpene alcohols, esters, phenols, phenolethers, lactones, and sulfides. For example, benzaldehyde is found in oil of bitter almond, cinnamaldehyde in oil of cinnamon, benzyl alcohol in oil of jasmine, and phenylethyl alcohol in oil of rose; tiglic acid is found in oil of star anise, and various lactones are in the chemical make-up of cold-pressed citrus oils. Aldehydes are so reactive, so pungent on the nerve sites of the nose, that they are the only chemical group that gives a name to a type of fragrance, the "aldehydic," with its strong, quick top note.

The terpenes are the most common constituents of the essential oils. In 1887 the chemist Otto Wallach (1847–1931) discovered that these hydrocarbons were multiples of a unit $C_5 H_3$, called the isoprene unit;

isoprene is a liquid hydrocarbon obtained by heating rubber. Mono-terpenes are a doubling of the unit, $C_{10}H_6$, and sesquiterpenes (from the Latin prefix *sesqui*, meaning "one and a half") represent the unit raised one and a half times, thus $C_{15}H_{24}$. Monoterpenes can be acyclic, such as geraniol, the scent characteristic of the rosy-leafed geranium, or nerol, found in the citrus oil, neroli, or they can be monocyclic. Menthol is monocyclic, one of the oils to exist in the solid state (as crystals). Camphor, which is also solid in the pure state, is a bicyclic monoterpene. The sesquiterpenes, however, are mostly liquids, and their long molecules may be acyclic, monocyclic, bicyclic, or tricyclic. The sesquiterpenes have greater weight and less volatility, but quan-titatively the lower terpenes are the most representative of the essential oils.

Phenols, consisting of an aromatic benzene ring with an $-OH$ group attached, also occur in essential oils. Eugenol, found in oil of clove (from the early botanical name for the clove tree, *Eugenia aromatica*), and thymol (from *Thymus vulgaris*, thyme) are two important phenols found in essential oils. Thymol will also crystallize when isolated. Methyl salicylate is another constituent of the essential oils that has the aromatic ring structure in its molecule. It is almost the entire component of oil of wintergreen and is also encountered by children when they chew on a twig of the black birch. Methyl salicylate is the common winter-green lifesaver flavor. This clean scent is popular in America, but to Europeans it is reminiscent of cleaning solutions.

These terpenoid phenols have been found to develop in the plant from the metabolism of acetate, and the cyclic terpenes from the iso-prene pathway. Radioactively tagged carbon molecules have been watched as they become part of ever more complex molecules in the plant; this is how we understand their genesis.

The greatest laboratory tool for analyzing which of these components are contained in which oils, and to what extent, is the gas chromatograph (GC) or, as it is sometimes called, the gas liquid chromatograph (GLC). What took organic chemists days of elaborate deductive experiments in the 1940s can now be determined in a few hours, automatically. In the GC printout, each molecule appears as a peak, so its presence in an oil, and the amount, can be readily determined. A porthole also allows the chemist-perfumer to assay each component olfactorily as it comes out. The more volatile fractions appear first, the heavier ses-quiterpenes afterward.

Research into the chemistry of the essential oils is one of the main

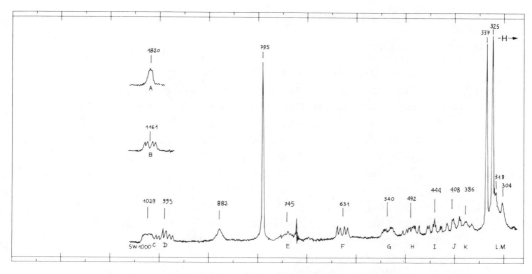

The gas chromatograph (G.C.), or gas liquid chromatograph (G.L.C.), has enabled accurate identification of the constituent molecules of an essential oil. Here, in a printout, various components of patchouli oil appear as quantifiable peaks. Courtesy of Recherches, July, 1974, Roure, Bertrand Dupont, Grasse

efforts of the modern perfume industry. In order to widen the perfumer's palette, researchers seek to learn more about the components of the natural oils, how to extract selected elements in them, how to duplicate them synthetically, and how to create new odor chemicals.

Extracting the Essential Oils

We have now discovered the sources of the volatile oils as well as their functions in nature, and we have obtained some idea of both physical and chemical characteristics. One question remains: How are the essential oils obtained from nature for man's uses?

Nearly eighty percent of the natural oils are produced by the still; this apparatus allows the extraction of both the pure alcohol and the pure oils that are the basis of the familiar perfumes and colognes of today. Without the still, perfumes would mean only unguents and cosmetics. Central as the still is, however, there are other extractive tools as well, and we shall consider each process: the use of solvents for extraction; enfleurage; maceration; and cold-pressing.

DISTILLATION

Few urban dwellers have had any contact with stills. Images arise of backwoods "moonshiners" at the mention of the word. Actually such "moonshining" stills are the simplest type that are used in extracting essential oils, a tool whose origins go back to the alchemists of the second and third centuries A.D., but which reached final form by the thirteenth century, when the trick of water cooling was mastered. The principle is simple: Plant material is placed in the body of the still with water and a still head is bolted over the tank. The head is molded into the "gooseneck" (in French a "swan's neck," or *col de cygne*), which is tapered into a leadoff pipe that is cooled to condense the vapors that rise from the boiling pot. The vapors are both essential-oil gases and water vapor, but as they come over, cool, and drop into the Florentine flask that collects them, water and oil separate. Most oils swim on top of the water, but oil of clove and anise drops to the bottom. In the words of the *Emerald Tablet*, one of the earliest texts of alchemy, this is the basic operation by which "you must separate the subtle from the gross, skillfully and with art."

The boiling points of most of the constituents of the essential oils range from between 150° and 300°C. Were they to be boiled in the still at such temperatures, they would either decompose or become a gummy mass, but distillation takes advantage of a phenomenon known as "Dalton's Law of Partial Pressure," which states that when two volatile liquids that are not mutually soluble are boiled together, they will do so at a temperature lower than the boiling point of either one. The distillers can thus remove the oils from the gross botanicals in the water at a temperature lower than the boiling point of water (100°C., 212°F.). At such a temperature, the oil collected in the condenser has not been changed markedly from the oil as detected in the leaves or flowers of the plant, although there are some minor differences, sometimes even for the better as far as our sensibilities are concerned. Some plants cannot stand even that amount of heat. The subtle changes identify a distilled oil as an artifact of man's, not wholly a reproduction of the oil in the plant. The distiller knows that when the temperature gauge on the still reads 100°C., it is the end of the volatile oils in the batch and the operation can cease.

There are three types of distillation, differing only in the degree of contact between the plant material and the water. The first is the ancient,

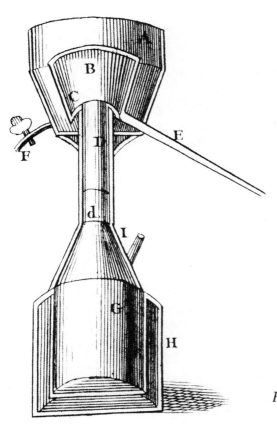

simple "water distilling," where the charge is immersed in a tub of water and the gooseneck used to lead off the vapors; the pipe that issues from it is cooled. The charge is loaded into the body of the still; the gooseneck is fitted on over a gasket and lag-bolted down. Cooling waters are run over the condenser pipe, and the fire is stoked up for the ten, twelve, or twenty-four hours that the job will require. This most simple form of hydrodistillation is cheap, requiring few and inexpensive components, portable—it can be set up close to the place of harvest—and has certain technical benefits. For some kinds of plant materials (rose petals are a good example), the material would become a compact lump if subjected to the more sophisticated steam method of distilling. Cinnamon sticks and camphor chips also benefit from the roiling action of the water over heat. No part of the plant tissue will remain dry and untapped by the water, and all the oils can be removed. The disadvantages of this method are that it is slow and some materials deteriorate from prolonged boiling, and if the flames from the heat source lick around the bottom of the tank and heat a piece of material that has not become wetted, a burnt odor might appear in the final oil.

The second means is that of distilling with both water and steam in the body of the still. The plant charge is set on a grill over the water so that although there is water in the still, the steam alone is in contact with the plant material. This method is suited to leafy, herbal material, but it must be evenly arranged on the grille; otherwise there will be channeling, the formation of "rat holes" in the charge, and not all the oil will be extracted.

The third method is the most modern, namely, steam distillation. In this case there is no water at all in the body of the tank; the boiling pot, only a coil from which issues live steam, is heated outside by a separate steam boiler. The steam may be saturated or slightly super-heated; usually it is generated at a pressure of forty or fifty pounds. The steam that condenses on the plant charge helps facilitate the removal of the oil from the tissue, and a drain at the bottom of the tank permits the removal of an excess of condensing water. The use of only "dry" or superheated steam tends to remove the moisture in the plant material before the oils are all out and seal in the remaining oils, imprisoned by the shrinking plant tissue. So *some* wet steam must be used for the success of this technique. This, the most modern distillation method, is extremely rapid, and its very speed minimizes the decomposition of delicate components of the oils (such as esters). If the plant material on the tray above the steam source has been carefully arranged, a high-quality oil will be produced and at a more rapid rate than by any other process.

Traditionally stills have been made of copper, lined with lead-free tin. The copper is malleable and therefore capable of being molded into the graceful gooseneck. The oils would take on a blue-green color from the copper were it allowed to touch the oils directly. Sheet aluminum has been used, but it is unsuitable for the distilling of oils such as wintergreen and thyme, which contain phenols, for phenol molecules attack aluminum. All essential oils deteriorate plastics. Stainless steel is expensive, and too expensive for many farmers, but it does not react at all with the oils. Mild steel is acceptable except for lime, clove, bay, and pimento, which are acidic and will cause corrosion. Not all rusting in the tank need be deleterious for it is not likely to be carried over into the oil, although this can occur when the gooseneck is not corrosion-proof. Economic necessity has forced some farmers to employ wooden stills, which, when stoutly made, can produce a passable oil. But once an oil has been run through such a still, nothing else can be used in it, be it camphor, mint, or lavender, for it will retain fumes from the first batch forever. Concrete stills suffer from the same limitation.

The original still was simply a tank capped by a gooseneck set over a flame. The distillate (from the Latin *stilla*, "a drop") was collected in a flask at the leadoff end of the gooseneck, and the oil pooled up (or below) the distilled water that also came over. The classical word for such a collecting flask was the "Florentine flask," named for the city that led in the distilling of essences during the Renaissance. Another extension of this basic apparatus was the setting of a water-cooler around the gooseneck drain, which was made in a serpentine. The drain was shaped and then immersed in a tub of cold water. This helped condense the vapors.

Proper cooling is essential for the retrieval of the oil; otherwise the essences will "reflux" and drop back into the tank. The stills being made today have a cooler that can conserve the heat absorbed from the pipe leading out of the gooseneck and use it to heat the original tank, thus saving fuel: the old cognac-makers' trick of *réchauffage*.

A good still should have a baffle to prevent any plant material that might be wafted upward by the heat of the process from becoming lodged in the gooseneck or in the coils that issue out from it. Pressure would begin to build up in the still, and eventually the whole unit would explode in a mass of expanding steam and ripping metal. Perfumery has had its martyrs.

Distilling can also be carried out at a lower temperature by using a pump to reduce pressure and thus preserve some of the heat-sensitive constituents, but this is high technology, not the kind of equipment that can be set up in a field of citronella grass. But when the material can be transported without damage, such as agarwood or dried patchouli leaves, it can be given the best treatment. A number of tropical crops were regularly shipped to Europe and the United States for high-tech distilling before World War I, but the U-2 boats put an end to that. The result was to stimulate better on-site distillation.

Plant material often needs preparation before the distillation can begin. The tissue in which the oils are contained must be rent to expose the oil glands to the steam or boiling water. Seeds such as coriander or fennel are crushed; roots (vetiver or orris) are chopped into short lengths; but petals and leaves do not need this pretreatment, called "comminution."

Sometimes the distiller may find it necessary to re-distill, a process known as "cohobation" (from the Arabic *qohba*, "a dark color"). This is most often required in the extraction of oil of rose, for the oil has a small solubility in water and must be wrung out of the distilled waters by a second distillation.

Standing by a still, it is easy to appreciate the wonder distillation engendered in the imaginations of early technologists. A mass of leaves, roots, or seeds went into the still, and at the final term of the process, only the purest drops of the clear essence can be seen to collect in the Florentine flask. The botanical material was subject to every kind of deterioration, and yet the quintessence extracted seems to defy decay.

Most essential-oil–bearing plants can be distilled, but not all. In fact, some of the most desirable scent plants such as the moth-pollinated white florals could not withstand the chemical violence of boiling water and steam. Some constituents of jasmine and narcissus, for example, are so volatile that they do not condense and would be lost in the air; others would be destroyed by the heat, even at the reduced temperature of distillation under a vacuum. Jonquil and violet perfumes were available to aristocrats of the seventeenth and eighteenth centuries, but they had to be extracted by the laborious method of enfleurage, which we will describe shortly. Solvent extraction, however, which we will consider here, has enabled large-scale extraction of delicate fragrance materials at reasonable costs. A final product called an "absolute," remarkably like the scent of the blossom itself, can be obtained by this method. This does not mean that absolutes are cheap—far from it; many cost thousands of dollars a pound. But these floral essences are so intense that that one pound of absolute will give a perceptible jasmine or honeysuckle perfume to myriad bottles of perfume. The technique of solvent extraction was first observed in the petroleum plants of Pennsylvania and applied to perfumery by Robiquet in 1835.

SOLVENT EXTRACTION

The process unfolds in the following sequence. The flowers are first picked at optimal conditions, even before the warmth of the sun has dispelled any of the volatile esters. Then, as soon as possible, the harvest is taken to the extraction plant and loaded into tanks of 500–1,500 liter capacity. These are hermetically sealed and the solvent is sent percolating through. This process is very much like a dry cleaning of the flowers, but only the fragrant oils are being removed, not dirt and grease. The solvent is also different from that the dry cleaner uses, carbon tetrachloride, which is powerfully odorous itself and unsuitable for perfume work. The solvent employed here must be miscible with the oils and have a low boiling point since the petals are sensitive to heat. Benzene, with a boiling point of 80.1°C., and petroleum ether (isomeric hexane), with a boiling point of between 60 and 80°C., meet these requirements, and each has been used.

Benzene, however, has been identified as a carcinogen and is no longer in general use. There would be no danger of cancer through

Preparing oakmoss for immersion in vats of solvent, Grasse. Courtesy of Allen Rokach

use of material extracted through benzene, but there would be danger to the workers who would have to handle it.

The petroleum ether which is now extensively used must be of the highest purity; it must often be re-distilled before reaching sufficient dryness for extraction work. This adds to the cost of this elaborate means of processing perfume oils.

Solvent can be made to submerge the flowers or to agitate them by rotation, constantly dousing the charge—the most successful process. The essential oils from the plant material dissolve into the benzene or petroleum ether, but so do the plant paraffins, the waxes that can be

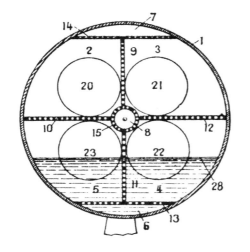

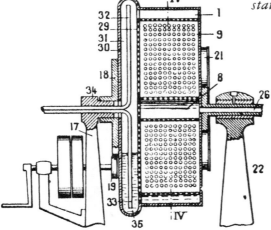

1, rotary drum; 2 to 8, compartments; 9 to 15 and 29, perforations; 16, rotary axis; 17, stationary bearing supporting column; 18, 19, transmission gears; 20 to 23, manhole covers for charging and discharging of corresponding compartments (2 to 5); 32, 33, stationary pipes; 32, gas entrainment tube; 33, siphon; 26, steam inlet.

A rotary extractor for immersion of botanical materials in solvent, from a 1923 French patent drawing.

observed on the surface of a flower and serve to protect it from rain and wind. Some of the pigments found in the flower also come into solution. One would not ever suspect the jasmine flower to contain any pigments by looking at it, but when thousands of flowers have been collected and the components concentrated, one finds that the floral wax is bright orange.

Once the oils are out of the plant and into the solution, the next step is to remove the solvent; this is easily done by evaporating it off under reduced pressure. At this stage we have what is called a floral "concrete"; it is solid due to the presence of the plant paraffins, and intensely odorous from the essential oils. The waxes have no odor value of their own and must be removed. The concrete is put in a cylinder flooded with ethyl alcohol and beaten with spatulas for over twenty-four hours. This apparatus is called a *batteuse* (beater) in the French trade. The oils pass into the alcohol, and when the mixture is removed and chilled, the waxes solidify and can be removed by simply pouring the liquid through a filter. What remains is a tincture: essential oils in alcohol. The final step is to remove the alcohol that has served to extract the oil by distilling it off under a vacuum to maintain the low temperatures so necessary to the conservation of these delicate floral essences. Solvent extraction is perfectly suited to jasmine, violets, hyacinths, carnations, boronia, oakmoss, and Spanish broom. Almost any botanical can be extracted in this way, but if distillation would serve as well, it would be considered first because of the price.

ENFLEURAGE

The third means of extraction is of such antiquity that its principles were known to the Egyptians; it still continues to be one of the tricks of this most ancient of trades: enfleurage. We have all noticed how in the refrigerator butter picks up the odor of scallions or garlic if set near them. The Egyptians, instead of cursing fate for the change of odor in their butter, turned calamity into opportunity by using animal fats to capture some of the odors of nature they desired. Lard was the cheapest and most easily obtained fat, but because it can become runny at warm temperatures (33° to 41°C.), tallow (beef fat), with a higher melting point (44° to 50°C.), was added. This suet is from the conjunctive tissue of the bull and has a grainy, firm texture with a slight fatty odor. Today the French perfume houses (for enfleurage is done only in Grasse) use lard and tallow in a two to one ratio. A little tincture

The carnation (Dianthus cary-ophyllata) *contains eugenol, which bears the same molecule found in oil of clove although the two plants are in distinctly separate botanical families; thus the carnation has been known as "clove pink." The floral oil is removed by solvent extraction as a by-product of the cut-flower industry.*

of benzoin is added to preserve the fats and a little rose essence to mask some of the odor of the fats.

The fats are slowly cooked with a small amount of alum in a waterbath (the French *bain-marie*, named after Maria Prophetissima, who invented distillation in the third century). The impurities come to the top and are skimmed off. Only lard from healthy pork can be used; it must be perfectly clean, free from all blood vessels and skin. After heating, the liquid fat is poured through a filter and left to cool. Any water in the mix will separate out.

Traditionally the manufacturers of perfumes in France would prepare their fats for enfleurage during the cold season of the year, before the floral crops had appeared. The hog fat and suet from cattle were diced and washed in water and, after heating and filtering, poured into wooded cases lined with tin plates and with a capacity of up to four hundred kilograms. The utmost cleanliness was needed during these operations to prevent rancidity; contact with heavy metals had to be watched as well to prevent deposition of metallic salts. At one time petroleum jelly was introduced because it never becomes rancid, but it lacked the adsorbtive power of hog and beef fat. Thus these solvents, the same ones used by the ancient Egyptians, continue to be used in enfleurage today.

The manner of deploying them is as follows: The cases of prepared fat are taken out of the cellars at the onset of the flowering season, and a layer of the fat is applied by spatula to both sides of a glass plate that fits into a wooden frame twenty inches long by sixteen inches wide, called a *châssis*. Each frame fits on top of another with a space of about two inches between plates, thus locking in the odorous essences released by the flowers, which are set on each pane of glass. The Egyptians utilized mints, lilies, and pine, but today enfleurage is reserved for two plants alone: jasmine and tuberose flowers. The flowers are carefully placed by hand on top of the congealed fat, which has been combed to present greater surface area for adsorbing the exhalations of the flowers.

The flowers must be perfectly dry or else the fatty *corps* may become rancid, and they must be healthy or an odor of decay will be imparted to the fat. Three kilograms of jasmine can be used per kilogram of fat and a little less for the tuberose, a plant with a larger floral structure. These flowers are treated by this method because they continue to create fragrance after picking, whereas roses, violets, orange blossoms, mimosa, and other flowers will yield only as much oil as they contained at the moment of picking. This is due to hydrolysis of the glucosides. The production lasts for forty-eight hours in the case of tuberoses and twenty-four hours for jasmines. When the time has come for removal (*défleurage*), the frame is held in both hands and turned over, dumping most of the flowers. Those that remain in the fat are picked off with little sticks. The use of a vacuum to remove the white flowers has been tried but without success.

After the fat of each frame has become permeated with the scent of the flowers, it is scraped off the glass (*raclage*) and combined with the fat from all the other *châssis*, and the whole is gently warmed until it melts. The liquid fat is filtered through gauze and left to cool. The next step is exactly like that in solvent extraction whereby the mixture is charged into a beater containing ethyl alcohol. For several days the mix is beaten, just as with the floral concretes. The essential oil from the flowers passes into the alcohol, and the fat is filtered out by chilling. This stage is known as the *extrait*, and many perfumers prefer to stop the process right there. Others prefer the semisolid *absolute d'enfleurage*,

Maceration was a means of extracting oils into fatty oils, such as olive oil or almond oil, or heated animal fats, such as lard and suet. The result was a scented cosmetic pomade. The process was known to the Egyptians and used until the 1920s. This illustration is from Charles Piesse's The Art of Perfumery, *1891.*

which is prepared by distilling off the alcohol under a vacuum—the same process as used in obtaining the absolute. This absolute of enfleurage is a dark and semisolid product. An *absolute de châssis* can be prepared by saving the flowers that have been dumped out of the wooden frames and treating them with hexane in the manner of solvent extraction. The blossoms retain some perfume that has not been dissolved into the fat, and it can be saved in this way, although the scent is not as fine as the absolute of enfleurage. When added to synthetic jasmine compounds, it gives them a soft fullness they would lack otherwise.

Enfleurage can easily be tried at home; the only difficulty is in wringing the essential oil out of the fat for most kitchen chemists cannot obtain pure ethyl alcohol without a permit. But you can make a fine hand cream by placing jasmine and tuberose flowers (which are easy to grow) into a large, wide-mouthed jar such as is used to hold mayonnaise for restaurants. Prepare the jar by coating the bottom and sides with a mixture of warm liquid lard and suet. Only unsalted fats should be used. The flowers will adhere to the fat, which will congeal on the jar surfaces if it is put in a cool place. Cap the jar to contain the essences and keep the whole in the refrigerator if necessary. At first the thick lard odor will seem so strong that nothing would seem able to dissipate it, but within a short time a remarkable transformation will take place and the fat will bear an exquisite fragrance. As the flowers show signs of wilting, remove them and replenish the jar with new stock. By the end of a month the pomade can be scraped out and stored under refrigeration as an emollient cream with a powerful floral note.

The elaborate process described above was brought to perfection by the French craftspeople of the early nineteenth century. Today, these elaborate techniques are no longer profitable in an industrial society. However, a small amount of plant material is still treated to the enfleurage process at Grasse.

Maceration is another process that also harkened back to ancient Egypt, but which, by 1920, had become abandoned by the perfume industry. It too utilized animal fats. Plant material was immersed in double boilers of hot lard and beef suet (in nearly equal amounts) at temperatures between 50° and 70°C. and stirred by hand with long wooden spatulas for about two hours. The most popular material for this process was orange blossom, but roses were also treated in this way; neither of them suffers a loss of odor quality in processes involving high heats. A *scourtin*, or press bag, like that used by winemakers, removed the scent-saturated oil from the blooms, and by the turn of the century a centrifuge was used. The odor from maceration was very agreeable and suited the manufacture of cosmetics and soaps. If the oils were desired free of the fats, they could be removed exactly as in the enfleurage process.

Today the large copper-plated vats set in the *bains-marie* at Grasse are a relic of perfumery's past. Tourists file by but no longer do women stand over the hot kettles for hours with their great stirrers. Maceration served the Egyptians well when they wanted to obtain the fine fragrance of gum frankincense, gum myrrh, and pine resin without burning them as incense. Before the isolation of alcohol from wine was perfected, these fats were the best solvents for these essences.

EXPRESSION

Distillation retrieves most of the natural essential oils for man's uses; solvent extraction and enfleurage retrieve delicate floral oils that heat would harm, but there is only one technique that can properly extract the oils in the skins of the plants in the citrus family: expression. This is the one case where essential-oil retrieval resembles the pressing of fatty oils such as olive, sesame seed, and peanut oils. Because steam exerts a deleterious effect on most peel oils, most citrus oils—orange, grapefruit, lemon, tangerine, bergamot—are the results of a cold-pressing, not distillation. The oils lie in glands deposited throughout the outer peel of the fruit, but below the colored skin (the flavedo) lies a white, spongy zone (the albedo). After the peel has been squeezed under a spray of water, the oil does not simply rise to the top but becomes trapped in a blanketlike emulsion composed of albedo, with its pectin and cellulose, water, and essential oils. This slurry is screened and centrifuged at 16,000 to 18,000 rpm). Waxes from the fruit skin must be removed by chilling the oil and letting the wax drop to the bottom of the settling tanks. At $-10°F.$, it will take orange oil five days to precipitate its wax, but at $25°F.$, it may take three weeks. The oil is given a final filtering before being decanted and stored.

The orange is a native of China, brought westward by the Arabs. Sicily and Spain, both parts of Europe that were long under direct Arab control, developed the first citrus plantations and were the first areas to utilize the fragrant peel oil. Sicilian oil, because of the arid climate, is one of the most exquisite and fragrant oils, although from the standpoint of juice, the Sicilian orange is less productive than those of more humid regions.

In Sicily before modern presses became available, the traditional means of extracting the oil was the sponge method. A sharp spoon encircled the orange half, removing the fruit. The peels were placed in water and then pressed between a convex projection and a sponge. As the sponge became saturated with oils, it was periodically wrung into a bowl beneath the worker. The tissues of the sponge served as a filter, trapping bits of the spongy albedo. Absolute cleanliness was maintained to prevent any contamination of the oil. This produced a fine-grade oil, but the technique has died out because machine extraction is cheaper. Today a machine presses the peels that have first been removed from the fruit. The oil is then pressed through wool filters. This is known locally as the *sfumatrice* method, and the oils are nearly as fine as those produced by the ancient sponge method.

There is another means whereby the whole fruit is charged into a machine that tears away the peel and releases the oils but without breaking into the deeper layers where the acid fruit juices are located. This *pellatrice* method is suited to Sicily because in arid climates citrus trees protect their fruit against dehydration by creating an extra-thick layer of albedo. A *pellatrice* obviously is more suitable for thicker peels,

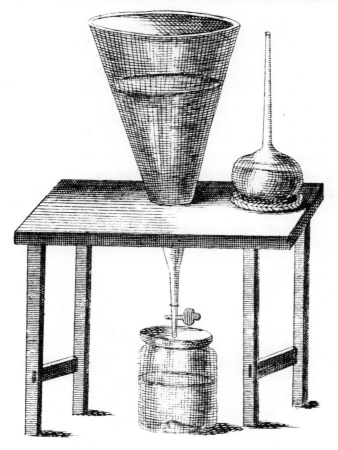

Most citrus oils are cold-pressed from the rinds of fruits such as oranges, lemons, limes, and grapefruits, but the oil must be filtered to remove particles of the peel that remain suspended in the oil. The operation today still resembles this illustration from Poncelet, La Chymie du Goût et de l'Odorat, *1766. From the collection of Florence Wall*

but the machine can be adapted for the almost paper-thin skins of the Florida crops. However, most of the American citrus oils are pressed rather than scarified, using a variety of methods: screw presses, roll presses, or squeezing cups contoured to the surface of the fruit. Centrifuging is the final step no matter which means of expression is chosen. Limes are the exception to the rule of cold-pressing citrus oils. West Indian lime oil can be distilled, and it is one of the key flavors in carbonated beverages such as Coca Cola, Pepsi Cola, and 7-Up as well as a component in the after-shave lotions.

The ancient practice of *écuelle* (from the Latin *scutella*, "dish") was developed in the south of France and has been used both there and in the West Indies as another means of obtaining lime oil. A shallow bowl with a funnel tube at the center is studded with nails that puncture the skin and the fruit. The ecuelle method is now only a part of the history of perfumery, for the cost of labor is not compensated by the small amount of oil retrieved.

Now that we have discovered the sources and properties of those materials that cause or contain aromas, let us consider another half of the equation: the nature of the apparatus that receives the cues put out by essential oils, whether they are presented in an alcohol medium, a powder, or a cosmetic. We will now explore that least-understood of the five senses, the sense of smell.

The Importance of Olfaction, Key Sense in Scent

How Noses Work

The sense of smell has been called "the supersense," "the mystic sense," and "the forgotten sense." It's called the "supersense" because odor-related impressions can be stored with surprising vividness for very long periods of time. As Vladimir Nabokov observed in *Mary*, "Nothing revives the past as completely as a smell."[1] The nose can register these impressions when only the minutest traces of essential oils have been detected in a great volume of air. Smell is known as the "mystic sense" because it works invisibly and because the parts of the brain where odor memories are locked are associated with the deepest emotions.

And yet this sense has truly been forgotten by our culture. One does not need to discuss the importance of the eye before studying art history or the ear before reading the story of the great composers, but the materials and art of perfumery do demand more information than is generally known about olfaction. Up till recently it would have been difficult to learn much about this sense. Our culture has had a puritanical skittishness about smelling that has affected such things as scientific research allocations and even the way we have hybridized plants—for looks, not for scent. The cause is to be encountered in a residual puritanism allied in the nineteenth century to the germ theory of disease. Children were taught a horror of their bodily functions; smells were "animalistic," and even breast-feeding, an olfactory delight for both mother and child, was hastily jettisoned in favor of sterile and odorless rubber nipples and glass bottles. In that milieu, smells just did not have a chance.

But what has been true of our culture in the recent past has not always been true. Museums are filled with scent artifacts from the great civilizations of the past: incense burners, flasks, unguent jars, vials, and philtres. Nor have all the members of our own society been able to live without full use of this sense. Olfaction can have no better praise than these words of Helen Keller:

> Smell is a potent wizard that transports us across thousands of miles and all the years we have lived. The odors of fruits waft me to my southern home, to my childhood frolics in the peach orchard. Other odors, instantaneous and fleeting, cause my heart to dilate joyously or contract with remembered grief. Even as I think of smells, my nose is full of scents that start awake sweet memories of summers gone and ripening fields far away.[2]

But now our culture is retreating from puritanism and coming to an appreciation of scent. Researchers such as John Amoore of the United States Department of Agriculture, Dr. Robert I. Henkin of Georgetown's Center for Molecular Nutrition and Sensory Dysfunction, and the physiologists and chemists R. W. Moncrieff and R. H. Wright have uncovered an almost ESP-like quality of the great information processor and storer, the sense of smell, our chemical sense of touch. Let us examine some of the findings of their researches.

Joan Rivers, when asked how she liked men to smell, replied, "With their noses."[3] How do noses work—men's *and* women's? Human noses, unique among animals, are distinct from the rest of the structure of the face. This external nose juts out into the gaseous seas that we inhabit and draws in air through the nostrils. Both individuals and races exhibit much variation in nose shape, but these differences do not affect odor perceptiveness as the sensing is from within. About five hundred cubic feet of atmospheric air is received in our lungs every twenty-four hours, and yet, due to the structure of the inner nose, only two percent of it is shunted up across the two olfactory sensing surfaces. But this is enough for us to monitor the air we breathe. These surfaces, each about the size of a dime, are located in our upper nose, are yellowish in color and bathed in mucus. Within each one, five million cells pick up stimuli and relay this as information to the brain. An amazingly complex information system is compressed into the scant three inches between receptor sites and brain.

These cells are unique in the nervous system for they are the only nerve cells in the body that regenerate themselves; also, unlike the cells of other sensory systems, one neural unit both receives and transmits impulses to the brain. Each receptor cell has six to twelve filaments, or cilia, which, in powerful movements, comb the air that is sent over them—our human equivalent of insect antennae that pick up such delicate stimuli. This region of the cell, which prods and explores the air sent to it by the surrounding world, is linked to another part connected to the brain. The section of the brain thus linked is the limbic area, associated with emotion, sexuality, and nourishment. Two olfactory bulbs relay information to the amygdala in this limbus region; damage to the amygdala has been found to affect memory recall and to cause eating and sexual dysfunction. The nerve fibers of the olfactory system go directly to this part of the brain instead of passing through the switching station, the dorsal thalamus, as is true of other senses, thereby accounting for the immediacy of odor-related memories. Olfaction bypasses the thinking brain (the neocortex) in a way not true of sight or sound.

Just what happens at the sensitive interface between the scent and its perception? There are two main theories to explain how the brain can interpret smells. John Amoore finds a lock-and-key relationship between the shape of the molecule and the receptor site. He postulates variously shaped openings on the nerve endings at the receptor sites: circular, rod-shaped, keyhole-shaped, and wedge-shaped. His theory explains very well the phenomenon of different odors that come from different chiral forms of the same molecule. "Chirality" is a term from the Greek word for "hand" (*cheiros*) and is used to describe those molecules which, although the total number of carbon atoms is the same, have a shape that may be "left-handed" *(laevo-)* or "right-handed" *(dextro-)*. We have seen how certain natural oils will deflect a plane of polarized light, usually to the left, evidencing the "optical activity" of those oils. It is just as each of our hands has five fingers but one hand cannot be set on top of the other without first turning it over if the fingers are to exactly align with each other. Different chiral forms of the same molecules often, though not always, have differing odors, thus supporting Amoore's theory that molecular architecture has a bearing on odor recognition.

However, R. H. Wright of British Columbia seeks to explain odor perception in terms of the vibrational frequency of the molecule, or by a possible combination of attributes, including shape, which can be made into a code just as the twenty-six letters of the alphabet can be combined into thousands of words. He argues that simple shape cannot account for the amazing specificity of stimulus recognition among a vast universe of smells: for example, the specificity of the silkworm to its mate or that of a perfumer to one specific jasmine from one particular locale. If this is the answer, we are still a long way from cracking the code, although both Amoore and Wright have been able to successfully predict certain responses from their theses.

In his book *The Chemical Senses*, the Scottish chemist R. W. Moncrieff has enumerated sixty-two statements that can be posited of the relationship between odorous chemicals and the nose that receives them. Chirality is one of the most important factors; others are that:

> Compounds of chemically different constitutions may still register as the same odor.
>
> Not one of the basic atomic elements is odorous per se under normal conditions, but it might be as part of a molecule.
>
> Fruity, fragrant odors characterize esters.
>
> Ketones generally have pleasant odors.
>
> Lactones have fragrant, esterlike odors.
>
> Compounds with nitrogen in them, such as those found in urine, frequently have "animal" odors, a note generally missing from compounds without nitrogen.
>
> Many nitriles have a bitter-almond odor.
>
> When a compound is volatile and chemically reactive, like the aldehydes, a strong odor often results.
>
> Some substances change their odor on dilution. Indole is an ex-

ample, for in small quantities it is a pleasant component of white-flower perfumes but in larger concentrations it can be perceived as the odor of putrefaction.

We tend to think of flavor as a sensation made on the tongue, outside the scope of the olfactory sense, but this is not so. The tongue is the receptor site for four perceptions alone: salt, sour, sweet, and bitter. All other "tastes" are really perfumes of oils contained in food and drink that are wafted up over the sensors from behind by the pumping of air caused by chewing and swallowing. The French word for flavor is *arome*, which is a true statement of the physiology of a flavor.

Although tongue and nose work together, the olfactory sense is the more powerful site of food recognition. For the tongue to perceive ethyl alcohol on its surface, a quantity that is sixty thousand times greater is needed than for the minute quantity that the nose can detect. All flavors, our herbs and spices included, are really perfumes taken in through the mouth. These essential oils serve to pique the brain and stimulate the secretion of digestive enzymes, and most of them are carminatives, which help dispel gas in the intestinal tract. But the olfactory sense that perceives them is the same as that which perceives a perfume, and the story of the spice trade is equally relevant to perfumery. All the spices can be used in a perfume blend once the essential oils have been liberated from the plant tissue. Reciprocally, perfume material such as jasmine absolute and orris oil find their way into flavored foods and beverages.

In order for us to perceive a scent, our nose requires that the material be volatile, which usually means that it has a high vapor pressure (a characteristic of most essential oils). This is not always applicable, however, for water has a high vapor pressure and musk a low rate of volatility. The materials must be soluble on the mucous surface of the receptor site.

If you wish to increase the perception of a perfume, sniff—this causes eddies of air to rise up and pass over the olfactory sites. To enhance the perception of a flavor, exhale—this causes air to flow over the same sites from the opposite direction.

"Masking" is the ability of one percept to dominate and negate another. Researchers have found that oil of pine and cedar are the most efficacious oils in covering disagreeable odors. Some percepts tend to neutralize each other, such as carbolic acid and the odor of putrefaction, the antiseptic, iodoform, and the plant exudate, Balsam of Peru. Some gases can anesthetize the nose; there is even a mild anesthetic that follows the perception of the odor of violets. Formaldehyde both anesthetizes and irritates the nasal receptors.

Odor researchers call an individual's inability to perceive a particular odor an "anosmia." One of the most common anosmias is a lack of perception of the urine odor. Many people have limited anosmias, and perfumers have to learn whether or not they themselves may have any unrecognized "blind spots." A "phantosmia" is a kind of olfactory hallucination—the perception of an odor when no such stimulus is actually in the environment—that sometimes accompanies damage to the brain. The olfactory system is one of the less tortuous of the human paths of sensation, and yet, as with any neurological unknown, research into its physiology remains slow and arduous.

Why Smell Evolved and How It Affects Us

From an evolutionary perspective, olfaction appeared early, when man's predecessors lived in the sea; it is a function suited to a fluid medium. Olfaction was the first "early warning" system to alert a fish to the presence of a predator or to guide it to a mate. The salmon are still directed by olfactory cues in their complex reproductive cycle. The olfactory system, well developed in fish, was shared by many reptiles and insects. As the vanguard of evolution left one fluid layer and entered another, the mantle of air, the olfactory sense continued apace. Moths, among the insects, hold pride of place in smelling ability, but bees, wasps, and ants also have a keen sense of smell. Although gypsy moths are much maligned, their olfactory refinement is spectacular: Odor cues of 0.000,000,000,000,004 ounce could be detected from one moth to another.

As man's antecedents moved from terra firma to an arboreal existence, the sense of smell declined. Primates such as monkeys lack the keen sense of smell that characterizes bears and dogs, who lead a life close to the ground. Tree-dwelling encouraged the development of the hand, while the eye and ear became primary distance monitors. By the time proto-man returned to a ground existence, the olfactory sense had achieved the status it conserves today—not quite as keen as in some animals but superior to others. The sensitivity of the male silkworm to his mate is only eight times greater than is our perception of musk.

SMELL AND SEX

Researchers have discovered much about the language of smell in animals, and this has led to the discovery that man, among the higher animals, shares such a language as well. "Pheromone" is the term used to designate the scent signals that one insect sends to another. It is a word coined in 1959 from two Greek words, *pherein*, "to bear along," and *hormōn*, "an excitement." Hormones are secreted within the organism, but pheromones are secreted into the environment, not indiscriminately but at the right time and place to the related sex of one's own species.

The effect of a pheromone from one insect to another is comepelling. Pheromones are absolutely irresistible sex attractants among moths. Indeed, a women's perfume has been created called Pheromone, borrowing the language of this odor research. But the pheromone principle that will send an insect into a frenzy of passion does not necessarily work in the same way with humans. Neither men nor monkeys exhibit the irresistible, automatic response to scent signals from the opposite sex, although each sex does secrete a characteristic odor perceptible to the other. So far in the higher animals there has been no definitive correlation between sexual odors and sexual activity. In monkeys it was found that simply nice odors, unrelated to the specifically monkey odor, encouraged sexual activity. Man has evolved so much that most of our responses to olfactory stimuli are learned, unlike the automatic passion induced by sexual emanations at regular periods of the year among the insects.

However, the links between sex and scent are certainly present, if in uncertain strengths. Men and children before puberty have difficulty in detecting the odor of exaltolide, a substance found in musk and civet that is chemically similar to testosterone. Women, however, are particularly sensitive to this odor just before ovulation, as much as one thousand times more sensitive than earlier in the menstrual cycle. The sex-linked sensitivity of certain women to musk-type perfumes was exploited in the 1970s when some of this research percolated down to ad agencies with perfumery accounts. In general, women have a slightly better sense of smell than men, doubtless harkening back to a time when survival of the species depended on her selection of a healthy mate; smell is a good indicator of health.

Not only does the presence of hormones influence our ability to smell, but the sense of smell influences our ability to produce hormones.

A fourth of those people who lose their sense of smell suffer from diminished libido. Dr. Robert Henkin of Georgetown University Medical School reports that women who have difficulty in menstruating are more apt to recover if they have an ability to smell. Those who have impaired olfactory ability show much less tendency to improve.

The power of sense of smell has also been observed in situations such as in a woman's dormitory. It was discovered that in such cases menstrual cycles tended to be synchronized and to be longer than usual. But when women were exposed to males more than three times a week, simply in odorous contact, the synchronicity was broken and the span of the period returned to the normal twenty-eight days. Men have reported less production of facial hair, a secondary sexual characteristic measured by dry weight, when they are kept in olfactory isolation from females than when in olfactory association. The French boarding-school syndrome, noted in medical literature around the turn of the century, showed that women isolated from men enter puberty at a later date than when they are in normal olfactory association.

Every individual has a unique odor to his or her skin. There are variances in each race and for both sexes. Researchers have noted that one of the most characteristic human odors resembles the agreeable yeast scent of baking bread. Most women describe the characteristic male smell as "musky," and males describe the female smell as "sweet." Men described the odor of women most captivating during ovulation, for there are distinct variances in amounts and intensities of odors exuded just as there are variances in our ability to receive odor (it is weaker early in the day and keener at evening). Even prepubertal children can determine whether garments were worn by males or females.

Mammals, including humans, emit scent-carried information through their apocrine glands. These are modified sebaceous glands, those glands that emit fats to keep hair and skin soft. Another olfactory agent is the eccrine gland, the sweat gland. Actually sweat, like water, is odorless. The smell associated with sweat is a secondary change wrought by the flora (bacteria) on the skin. The apocrines are small at birth but develop at puberty. There are many apocrines on the face, under the arms (except among Chinese and Koreans), on the chest, and in the genitoanal areas. Research psychologist Michael J. Russell of the University of California Medical Center, San Francisco, believes that a precopulatory odor cue is emitted by apocrines throughout the entire body, especially by those on the face. Hence the olfactory pleasure in kissing and caressing the face.

In terms of odor, sexuality among humans works in the following way: the woman exudes a scent that is most agreeable and strong during her fertile period. Stimulated by this, the male produces odor to the degree of his arousal, which in turn acts as an aphrodisiac to the woman. In 1886 the French psychological theorist Auguste Galopin expressed the view that "the purest marriage that can be contracted between a man and a woman is that engendered by olfaction." This may be a little extreme, but the link to sexuality is nevertheless real, and companies have even attempted, as with the Andron fragrance released by Jovan, to reproduce some of these sexual cues. This scent makes use of a substance that may be derived from a European wild boar and which smells like male sweat. The links of odor to sexuality, unclear as they may be, do exist. Dr. Henkin even speculates that a vapor of sufficient specificity may be developed that could forestall ovulation.

SMELL IN EVERYDAY LIFE

Smell begins early. Within a few days after birth, infants can distinguish their own mother's breast, and olfaction remains keen with us long after there has been diminution of sight and hearing.

Smell can protect our very lives. Since the olfactory receptors sit as faithful sentinels atop all the atmosphere that we inhale, they monitor it constantly for toxic fumes, for decreased air quality, for escaping gas, for the smell of "something burning," or for an off flavor indicative of spoiled meat or fish. The hedonic (pleasure) reaction, as it is called among odor researchers, helps cause saliva to flow and stimulates digestive juices, thus promoting metabolism of ingested foods—from the infant's first odorous nourishment at the breasts throughout life. Olfaction also monitors our selection of nutrients. Merchandisers have discovered that, consciously or not, the nose guides consumers as they shop. At Colgate College, Dr. Donald Laird gave shoppers three identical lots of nylon hosiery. One remained with its own chemical smell, another was masked with a fruit scent, and a third with a flower scent. Less than ten percent of the shoppers chose the unscented lot, describing the floral lot as softer although all three were identical—except for odor. Today the American perfume industry is only twenty percent concerned with pure perfumes; eighty percent of its revenues accrue from perfumed objects: plastics, fabrics and clothing, rubber tires, automobile interiors, tobacco, cleaners, and medicines. In the prolific world of soaps, market researchers give fragrance credit for being the key factor in a buyer's choice.

Because of our traditional apathy about odor, few parents encourage an olfactory examination of the world their children encounter; it is no wonder that researchers find a marked drop in the ability of children to detect odors by around the age of ten, the first age of great cultural conformity. Another great falling-off is found at the age of eighteen, a second entering into "maturity" as defined by society. Educators now know that audio-visual equipment is not just a treat given as an incentive for lazy students but is a distinct avenue for stimulating intelligence. Certain things will be known only if informed visually or audibly. But what about the nose? Pharmacists are taught to routinely examine materials by smell, and this should also extend to beginners in science. Training can produce wonders; conscious exposure to a variety of stimuli can develop a huge vocabulary of odor.

Since the limbic area of the brain evolved very early in the human species and is linked to primordial emotions, smell memories that are directly routed to this area tend to be sharp and intense. Visual and auditory memories begin to crumble within a few days, subject to the phenomenon known as "short-term memory," but researchers have found that there is almost no short-term memory with odors. Three months after subjects were presented with a series of smells, they could still recognize seventy percent of them. It has been found that when children were given olfactory information along with a word list, the list was recalled much more easily and better retained in memory than when given without the olfactory cues.

Our sense of smell is a supple and resilient faculty, springing agilely from one perception to another. Most people believe that they "can no longer smell anything" after they have been given five or six things to recognize, and yet have no lack of confidence about their ability to hear or see many percepts in a short period of time. A perfumer works a full day, and yet he or she is constantly attending to odor differences.

"Adaptation" is a way this sense has of protecting itself from potentially self-defeating situations. At first a smell is perceived, but soon afterward, if it does not go away, it is "censored" from conscious awareness. Usually a perfumer has to create a scent against a background of a rather odoriferous factory. This "background noise" fades into oblivion within a few minutes of entering the premises, enabling him to concentrate on new scents.

Lack of odor perception in those who have been born without it is not exceedingly troublesome, but it is perceived as an enormous handicap, liable to cause depression among those who have had it and lost it. Loss of smell can be related to a zinc deficiency, but it can also be caused by surgery, as when a brain tumor is removed. Sometimes smell can be restored by zinc therapy; placebos have at times affected the condition, and there have been spontaneous remissions as well. In a *New Yorker* article, one sufferer described what food was like without its aromaticity:

> Of course, I had to eat—I didn't want to die. But the regular food—it was all like garbage. I could drink a little cold milk. I could eat a little cold boiled potato. I could eat a white grape. I could eat a little vanilla ice cream. That stuff, it didn't taste good, but it didn't taste bad. It didn't have any taste at all. So I lived on that. No coffee—God forbid. Even a banana—I couldn't go near it.[4]

Without the aroma of the food or beverage the delight of eating or drinking had fled.

SMELL AND HEALING

If the lack of fragrance can be devastating, its presence can be restorative. An entirely new area of therapeutics has developed in France that goes by the name of *"l'aromathérapie."* Research has also been done in Italy in this area. It is new only in the sense that modern science is investigating the effects of essential oils upon the nervous system. The ancient Chinese were great consumers of spiceries from the South Sea archipelago (Nan Hai, modern Indonesia); these imports went under the title of "aromatic medicaments" (*hsiang yao*). This trade flourished from as early as the ninth century. In the fourteenth century a Persian follower of the great Hafiz described the tonic effect of perfumes in the following lines:

> *I do not feel like writing verses;*
> *but as I light my perfume-burner*
> *with myrrh, jasmine and incense,*
> *they suddenly burgeon from the heart,*
> *like flowers in a garden.*[5]

The first suggestion of the healing and depressive possibilities of aromatics to appear in modern scientific literature was in an article in

Perfumery has always been closely linked to healing and medicine. In the famous frontispiece to Adam Lonitzer's Herbal (Kreuterbuch) *of 1533, we see the harvesting, grinding and distillation of essential oil plants used by the apothecaries in their practice.*

The Medical Press and Circular in Great Britain in 1875, wherein W. S. Watson reported the exhilarating effect of odors on the mentally ill and recommended treatment with attar of roses for those who suffered from nervous stomachs and poor digestion.[6] Odors have a demonstrable effect on the emotions, and they can be measured by the changes of electrical charge on the skin. Bergamot, lemon, and lavender have been found to give courage and resolve, and vanilla and rose to tranquilize the nerves. As Professor Paolo Rovesti points out in his book *In Search of Perfumes Lost*, both anxiety and depression characterize our age, and

> The possibility of contributing new therapeutic solutions to these two now very common psychoneuroses is therefore of notable interest, especially in view of the fact that the essential oils used in aromatherapy, if in appropriate doses and applications, are harmless to the organism and do not give rise to any of the disturbances caused by chemical drugs. It must be said that ever since the remotest times the fumigations of certain aromatic plants have been employed as tranquilizers and antispasmodics in cases of erethism [irritability] and of high nervous tension and, conversely, as excitants against fainting fits and depressive states.[7]

We have all experienced the way in which a fine scent can stimulate our tone, brighten us, stoke once again our interests and ideas. Rousseau wrote that "smell is the sense of the imagination," and when the imagination is nourished, the nerves and hormonal secretions conducive to good health are not far behind.

Vinaigrettes were watch-like lockets used in the eighteenth and early nineteenth centuries to contain aromatic restoratives. A wad of cotton was soaked in vinegar and essential oils, to be inhaled in times of faintness the way smelling salts were used later—an early form of aromatherapy.

The Perfumer's Vocabulary

The nose of the perfumer-artist is no different physiologically from anyone else's; its only advantage is that it has been consciously trained, which renders it more sensitive than the finest gas chromatograph yet invented. For his job, the perfumer has to use a special language to describe and manipulate the odorous world.

Amoore discovered shapes that account for camphoraceous, musky, floral, minty, and ethereal odors. Later research led him to include the categories of putrid, sandalwood-like, watery, and urinous. Linnaeus had grouped odors into hircane (goaty), aromatic, alliaceous (garlicky), fragrant, ambrosial, nauseous, and aromatic. But neither of these efforts at classification is of sufficient specificity to please the perfumer. A great number of odor types have been evolved, and we shall give a representative list. These can be called "accords" for they usually represent a weaving together of several individual odors, much as a chord of music is a combination of certain constituent notes. The following terms serve to map out the main "continents" in the world of scent, and we will then indicate some of the divisions within them:

1) Floral scents
2) Green scents
3) Citrus scents
4) Oriental blends
5) Chypre types
6) Aldehydic scents
7) Leather/Animal

Looking into these categories more specifically, in the floral category we can have both single florals and bouquets. Single florals would include such languorous indolic types as jasmine, hyacinth, lilac, tuberose, honeysuckle, and gardenia; the fresher lily of the valley (*muguet*) and orange blossom; the distinct violet-type scent; carnation; and rose. Floral bouquets are scents that weave several florals together.

Green scents are characterized by the odor of a crushed green leaf. Included in this category we find pine and mint as well as the scent of herbs. Lavender is a link between herbal notes and a decided floralcy. Camphor, with its ringing clean scent, has a green character.

Citrus scents are the familiar lemon, orange, tangerine, and grapefruit-peel odors as well as the more exotic members of the citrus family, bergamot, neroli, and petitgrain.

Oriental blends represent heavy perfumes with a preponderance of animal notes and three important sub-groups: (a) spices, (b) incense resins, and (c) woods (such as the odors of sandalwood, cedar, and patchouli). The net effect of such notes in combination is intense and heady. Youth Dew, Opium, Tabu, and Shalimar are familiar oriental blends.

Chypre is the French for the island of Cyprus, birthplace of Venus, goddess of love. These perfumes take their names from Coty's Chypre, created in 1917. They are a congeries of gum labdanum and oakmoss, with their sweet, honeylike notes, bergamot, a fresh citrus odor, and a soft background of sandalwood. The net effect is that of a soft, warm, sweet scent, and Miss Dior, Femme, and Crêpe de Chine are classic chypre-type perfumes.

Aldehydic, or "modern," perfumes are those with the arresting top notes of the aldehydes, which are so reactive with the human sensorium.

Most people are familiar with the pungency of formaldehyde, but there are other aldehydes, many of equal strength but most with more pleasant smells. Chanel No. 5 is one of the famous aldehydic perfumes and one of the earliest. Je Reviens, Arpège, and Chamade also use these aldehydes.

Leather notes are caused by both the animal protein of the hides and the birch tar and other aromatics used in the tanning process. No leather extract is used in duplicating the scent of the fine gloves once produced by Spanish and Russian craftsmen, but the animal note inherent in the leather can almost be perfectly reproduced by the use of civet in a "leather" perfume composition. Animal notes lack the addition of the other aromatics (such as birch tar or rose oil) used in preparing hides, but have a similar warm, heavy, and persistent quality. Musk, ambergris, and civet are animal notes; they are caused by large molecules that volatilize only slowly.

These are common terms in perfumery language, understood by every worker in the field. However, there are some "sets" of odors that other perfumers would include in a list of general terms: maritime, mossy (like the soft odor of oakmoss, reminiscent of the odor of the forest floor), spiritous, vanillalike, metallic, fishy, sulfurous, burnt, spermous, anisic, fruity, ammonialike, waxy, putrid, or fecal. Sometimes another large category is included, that of fougère, a blend of lavender, green, and warm "amber" notes named after the French word for "fern." Houbigant's Fougère Royale is the classic type of fougère. The term is a little mystifying since very few ferns have any real odor except for a muted greenness.

All of the above categories can be combined; thus we have aldehydic florals and green chypres. The listing of such terms and the combination of them may seem a little overwhelming, but they really are not. What is overwhelming is the universe of smells and the wealth of fragrant works of art that have been composed by perfumers over the years. Each category tends to reduce that multiplicity a little and agglutinate several smells into one "set." These terms are conveniences, not dogma. Just as one artist may call a color "umber" and another "russet," both have a good idea of what the other means; the general nuance has been pinpointed.

An odor "tone" is used to describe whether a particular odor is "sharp" or piercing, or mild or "medium" or "low," meaning muffled, warm, and heavy.

The "tenacity" of a fragrance means its ability to last for a long time and to last without too much diminution. Fixatives with high molecular weight will prolong the tenacity of materials which of themselves are rather fleeting.

High vapor pressure and low molecular weight in a material can give great diffusive "lift" to a blend. Green and aldehydic materials have this "zing," or "blast."

Once a variety of individual odor chemicals has been compounded into a perfume, the end product should have "volume," like the "body" of a wine. An injudicious blend will come across as "thin."

In terms of mapping out the experience of a fragrance in time, perfumers utilize the following terms: "top note" (in French trade parlance, *note de tête*), middle note *(note de coeur)*, and dry-out note *(note de base)*. These refer to the time of sublimation, or the time it takes the sniffer to fully absorb the scent. The first microsecond of the percept is important and perhaps the key to the desire to purchase a particular fragrance, but this initial "Aha!" must be followed by sympathetic responses in the succeeding minutes, and even over several hours. The art of the perfumer is not unlike that of a musician, who must make a composition which will unfold with variety and interest over time.

A perfumer is also similar to a painter. He may work together many different odors as an artist does with colors. He may create a "representational" perfume, one that imitates the odor of a flower, a fine tobacco, leather, or a box of oriental tea. But there are also "abstract" perfumes, pure arabesques of olfaction that represent nothing but themselves. However, even a representation cannot be a simple imitation; something of the artist will mold and affect it. As an example of a representational perfume, the perfumer Edmond Roudnitska describes his creation Diorissimo (Christian Dior): "This is a pure lily-of-the-valley scent that also has the odor of the woods in which it is found and the indefinable atmosphere of the springtime." His Dior-Dior, Chanel No. 5, and Arpège are nonrepresentational perfumes.

Smell and Scent in Literature

Olfactory cues are especially noticeable in French literature. Charles Baudelaire (1821–1867) was the first to isolate the great power of scent in stirring imagination. Of himself, he wrote:

> *Comme d'autres esprits voguent sur la musique,*
> *Le mien, ô mon amour, nage sur ton parfum.*[8]

> As the spirits of certain people hover over music,
> Mine, o my love, swims upon your perfume.

Baudelaire observed how scent could unlock memory, presenting us today with "the past restored." These long-forgotten images come to us as we breathe in a scent "with intoxication and slow self-indulgence," *(Le Parfum)*. In a beautiful image, these memories, at the touch of a smell, begin to quiver like pupae in their cocoons, until they free their wings and take flight like butterflies with wings "tinted with blue, with rose, spangled with flecks of gold" *(Le Flacon)*.

In *Parfum Exotique*, scent does not restore old images, but creates new ones. In inhaling the perfume of his loved one, the poet is guided upon a voyage to a tropical port where he can see the masts and sails of the ships, hear the sea-songs of the sailors, and smell the tamarind trees in the heat.

Odor has become the force which has cast off the anchor from the world as it has always been and set it to travel in a new world of imaginative possibilities.

An admirer of Baudelaire's poetry, Joris Karl Huysmans (1848–1907) left another use of scent in his novel *A Rebours*. The highly sensitive hero, Des Essentes, became

> skilled in the science of scent. He was convinced that the olfactory sense was able to furnish joys equal to those of ear and eye, each sense being able to perceive new impressions, by both its natural disposition and by training, and to disengage one from another, coordinate them and to compose what would amount to a work of art. There was nothing, indeed, abnormal that an art should exist in detaching fluid odorants than in other people taking sound waves to make them hit the ear in tones of varied colorations.[9]

Thus with these aromatic stanzas, he was able to make an "escape to an immense terrain."

Marcel Proust also paid much attention to aromatic perceptions. In his famous *Remembrance of Things Past*, he describes an emotion stirred from his depths by the simple perception of the aroma of a madeleine pastry. This percept, falling on a sensibility able to open to it

> made the vicissitudes of life of no importance to me, its disasters harmless, its shortness illusory, just as love fills me with a precious essence, or indeed, an essence was not *in* me, but *was* me. I had ceased seeming to be mediocre, vulnerable, and mortal. Where could this powerful joy have come from? I sensed that it was linked to the perception of the tea and cake, but that it exceeded it and could not have come from the same nature. Where had it come from? What did it mean? How could I keep it?[10]

Proust tried to recapture this mystical experience, with diminishing success, by again and again drinking the tea and tasting the madeleine, urging the stimulus to release strengths that, until the stimulus, had remained locked in his mind.

François Mauriac wrote an autobiographical novel in 1925, *La Robe Prétexte*, using many scent-based memories to recreate the life of a youth between fourteen and sixteen. An odor will revive the past, but also, because it is a conditioned reflex, the past with all its attendant circumstances. Thus, for Mauriac, the smell of stone in the first hot days of summer revived with it the memories of writing long final exams in June, and sitting afterwards through the solemn distribution of scholastic prizes.

The poet Czeslaw Milosz described the experience of opening the door of a linen closet as "filled with the mute tumult of memories." For the modern poetess Colette Wartz, this same, very olfactory experience meant:

Odonnance. Harmonie.	Order and harmony.
Piles de draps de l'armoire.	Sheets piled in the closet;
Lavande dans le linge.	Lavender in the linens.[11]

Although far more subtle than the drugs taken for "trips," odors can be invitations to voyages to those realms of imagination, which, as Baudelaire said, are "most truly real." This has been the witness of the great writers of France.

THE HISTORY
OF AROMATICS

3

The Near East

The Fertile Crescent

The story of perfumes opens with the birth of urban life in the ancient Near East over four thousand years ago. The first "perfumes" were the aromatics kindled as incense to the gods. Although small in size, they exuded an aura perceptible throughout the entire temple, and their emanations were believed to attract good influences and repel baleful spirits.

The most prized of all incenses to the Mesopotamians was the fragrant cedar of Lebanon *(Cedrus Libani)*. This had to be imported from the "luxuriant forests of Marduk" in Lebanon and brought to the city-states of the Tigris and Euphrates Valley. Indeed "Lebanon" comes from the Akkadian word *lubbunu*, "incense."

The uncoiling smoke, like a gaseous ziggurat spiralling upwards, would attract heavenly beings "like flies" around the sacrificer. Those who had died and were beyond the reach of their survivors, in the shadowy afterlife, could, nonetheless, live upon the smoke burned by their children for them. Incense was employed in exorcisms, in healing the sick, and used ritually after sexual intercourse.

In addition to the cedarwood imported from Lebanon to the west, the Babylonians made use of pine, cypress, and fir resins, and myrtle (even today a favorite aromatic in Middle Eastern gardens), known as *asu*. Myrtle was especially sacred to Shamash, god of the sun. The three conifers, of course, possess the cool odor of the evergreens. Myrtle, too, although not a conifer, has a piney smell that is attractive and refreshing. Juniper berries, familiar to us as the source of the odor and flavor of gin, were also used, as well as gum galbanum, a powerfully green odorant, still very much a part of "green" perfumes such as Vent Vert. All parts of the sweet flag *(Acorus calamus)*, with its crisp cinnamic scent, were used.

There has been a great deal of controversy over whether or not the list of aromatics could include the queen of flowers, the rose. Assyrian medical tablets employ the word *kasi sar*, and the Assyriologist and botanist R. C. Thompson believed this referred to the ancestor of our modern rose. Others felt that it was *Sinapsis nigra*, a mustard, but the text described thorns, not an attribute of any of the mustards. One would think that frankincense and myrrh would have been used, but these civilizations were so ancient that these resins had not yet been exported from their distant homeland, modern Yemen. By the time of the Persians, however, the eight-hundred-mile trek had been made, and both aromatics appeared in Persian cities. As we shall see, they were absorbed, along with so much of Persian life, by Alexander the Great.

Similarly, we know that in the sixth century sandalwood was being imported from India into the Fertile Crescent, rather a late date for Mesopotamia. It is to the Mesopotamians that credit must go for the great Jewish incense cult, which was established after the return of the Jews from the Babylonian captivity instigated by Nabuchodonosor (604–562 B.C.). While the biblical books ascribe elaborate incensings to Moses, most biblical scholars are convinced that this represents a practice prevalent at the time the books were written but not true of the Hebrew cult at the time of Moses himself (approximately 1250 B.C.).

Even the royal architecture in this region was aromatic. Sargon II (722–705 B.C.) used cedarwood for his palace at Khorsabad, and this

Olfactory architecture: The Nanmu Hall at the Imperial Summer Palace of the Manchu emperors at Ch'eng-te (Jehol). The fragrant wood of the nanmu (Machilus nanmu) used in the construction of the beams and panelling of this hall were left free of lacquer or paint so that the cedar-like redolence of the wood could be appreciated. The hall was one of the most stately apartments of the vast complex built in southern Manchuria by the Emperor K'ang-hsi in 1703. Aromatic woods had been used in architecture at Babylon, the construction of the temple of Solomon, and in Buddhist temples in India.

material was used again by Sennacherib (705–681 B.C.) so that the doors of his palace would release "an agreeable odor when opened or shut." The ultimate in fragrant architecture was the palace of Nabuchodonosor with its Hanging Gardens, one of the wonders of the world. This king, mentioned in connection with the Exile, built a series of stone terraces, waterproofed with bitumen, for his wife Amytes, who longed for the lilies and other fragrant plants of her native Media high in the hills, so unlike the flatness of Babylon.

Glass has always been the most important material for containing perfumes and it was the Fertile Crescent that was the home of glass technology, not Egypt as is often thought. Aromatics were used in unguents for anointing the body as salves and as cosmetics, and the recipes that go as far back as Ur in the third century B.C. indicate that the herbalists measured their medical resins by weight and their unguents by volume. Measurement, again, is often associated only with the Egyptians, but here it is the Near East that holds pride of precedence.

Less certain is the claim that distillation goes back to Akkadian times. Cuneiform tablets—dating from the thirteenth through the twelfth centuries—dealing with perfume manufacture discuss vessels with rings, or shelves, about the center. These shelves may have served to collect a distillate that condensed on the top of the egg-shaped vessel, much like the shelved aludel (*itrīz*) of later Arabic alchemy. As the distillate condensed, the gutter around the middle of the vessel would be wiped and the residue wrung into a container. We are not certain, however, if this is the correct interpretation of the texts and artifacts that remain. The process does not seem to have become enough of a practice to warrant replication except perhaps locally, and the classical world of Greece and Rome seems to have been completely unaware of distillation. It was only in late antiquity that the principle was finally apprehended and described by the Alexandrian alchemists. When this principle was carried over to Asia Minor, it is possible that enclaves of technologists conserved implements like these stills, which could be traced directly back to the mysterious egg-shaped cookers of the unguent makers.

Egypt

The city-states that rose from the sea of neolithic villages throughout the length and breadth of the Fertile Crescent were constantly raiding each other. In addition, the wild and wooly inhabitants from the surrounding uplands might often swoop down upon the cities of the plain. But Egypt was protected from this warfare because the entrance to the Nile valley could easily be defended and the inhospitable desert to the east and west ruled out competitors. Thus it is not surprising that life (*ankh*) was the leitmotiv of that culture and that its history has an

Marble statue of Queen Hatshepsut taken from a chapel of her shrine at Deir al-Bahri, at Thebes. This woman-pharao dispatched an expedition to Somalia (the biblical land of Punt) to bring back incense resins for use in worship, and small trees to grow before her massive temples at Thebes. The holes for the root balls of those plants have been discovered by archaeologists although the incense trees themselves had disappeared. Courtesy of The Metropolitan Museum of Art

elegance and lightness that is missing from that of Mesopotamia.

In Egypt we find an interest in incense almost as early as that of Sumer's. In 2800 B.C., King Isesi sent an expedition to the land of Pwenet (the Punt of the Bible, modern Eritrea) for gum resins. Other expeditions were sent in 2100 B.C. and in 2000 B.C., but the word for incense, *'ntyw*, appears in texts even earlier. However, it was the female pharaoh, Queen Hatshepsut of the New Kingdom (1558–1085 B.C.), who put incense on the cultural map. Her expedition for that precious commodity was recorded for all time in elegant bas-reliefs on the walls of her temple at Deir al-Bahari, near Thebes. This forceful ruler, who had herself represented with the headdress of a king and the mane of a lion, had a botanical garden created along the great ramps leading to the temple. Her plants were also from Pwenet. "I have led them on water and on land to explore the waters of inaccessible channels, and I have reached the incense terraces," she boasted of her expedition.[1] Great quantities of trees and incense were brought back to exude their balm in the garden of Amen-Ra, patron of the nation. (Even today the image of one of these incense trees, its roots bound for transport, adorns the Frank Meyer Medal for Botanical Exploration, the Nobel prize of plant explorers.)

What was the true nature of the plants imported in that famous argosy? We know that they represent the East African species of two genera of the balsam family *(Burseraceae): Boswellia papyrifera* and *Commiphora erythraea*. This was not the frankincense or myrrh presented to the Christ child and burned in great quantities by Romans. That was from a species found on the other side of the Straits of Aden in Arabia but not yet known to the Egyptians of the New Kingdom of Egypt, who were afraid to sail across the Gulf of Aden. Likewise, their incense was not as fine as the Arabian myrrh of later antiquity. These plants still thrive in the parched air of Eritrea, eastern Ethiopia, and Somalia.

The resins of these two balsams are created by nature to protect the sap of the trees, or bushes, from drying out in the harsh climate. The resin oozes over any cuts made by an insect or animal, or by the incense gatherers, and is initially thick but viscous. Later it hardens to a candylike substance that can be scraped off and transported over great distances.

In their elaborate religious cults, the Egyptians consumed great quantities of these resins from East Africa. Long thurifers (censers) extended the fragrant smoke for the gods to inhale. Incense was always burned before the opening of the shrine, at the coronation of the pharaoh, and for national celebrations. The souls of the dead were thought to ascend above as a cloud of smoke, and incense was burned to avert baneful spirits from the bodies of the deceased.

This type of myrrh could also be prepared with a fatty oil such as olive or *Balanites aegyptica* (oil of balanos) for use as an unguent. Priests anointed the statues of the gods and goddesses every morning with this myrrh compound *(molt)* to ritually reawaken them and fortify them for another day of suppliants. The aromatic ceremony was known as the "opening of the mouth and of the eyes," the morning coffee of the Egyptian deities.

Aromatics figured prominently in the preoccupation with the survival of life in the next world: beautiful alabaster jars and coffers of ebony (from the Egyptian word *hebon*) contained these unguents that would render supple once again the skin of the deceased after his or her regeneration in the next world. The embalming process involved eviscerating the dead body, which was then washed with natron (sodium salts from the Wadi el Natrum, fifty miles northwest of Cairo), and stuffing the cavities with myrrh and oakmoss. The type of oakmoss that was used *(Pseudevernia furfuracea)* is not native to Egypt but, like incense, is an import, in this case from the Greek islands. Oakmoss (both *Pseudevernia furfuracea* and the more common *Evernia prunastri*) is much used in modern perfumery. It has an exquisite soft and sweet odor of great tenacity. It contains usnic acid, an antibiotic that served admirably in the mummifying process. Pine resin, another essential-oil substance with antimicrobial properties, was also part of this elaborate packaging of the corpse for delivery into eternity. The entire process took about thirty days.

By the time of Egypt's New Kingdom, the essences that had been exploited in the service of the gods and the deceased began to be applied to the art of mortals as well.

During Egypt's Golden Age, the human body became an object of esteem to be anointed with perfumed oils, and the great gods did not seem to become jealous. Initially many of these cosmetics were of a magical character, meant to avert the hexes that leaked out from the stars, the moon, or inauspicious localities; they were also medicinal, such as the mascara used to shade the eyes from the glare of the African sun. But although magic and medicine continue to be allied with the cosmetic arts even today, beauty lotions soon were enjoyed for their own sake. One recipe promised to "turn an old man into a youth," another to "expel wrinkles"—promises that remain to this day embedded in cosmetic advertising—while others, more modest, promised to soften the skin or to color the hair.

Most cosmetics bore a fragrance: African frankincense and myrrh, lilies, pine, cedar of Lebanon, gum mastic (from *Pictacia lentiscus*), bitter almond, terebinth from Israel, mints, and other herbs. These gave scent to a base of vegetable oils: olive, safflower, linseed, castor, almond, radish seed, lettuce seed, and balanos (balanos came from a tree said to bear the names of priests and pharaohs on its leaves, as inscribed by Thoth, god of wisdom). Balanos oil, the "balm" of Gilead mentioned in Jeremiah 8:22, was made by pounding its fruits, which were then boiled and filtered to produce an oil thought to have healing properties. Some aromatics were cooked into such fatty oils, but the Egyptians also knew the propensity of animal fats to absorb odors from aromatics placed upon them. Thus enfleurage was discovered by the early priest-technologists of Egypt. The fragrance cones *(bit)* made of such scented

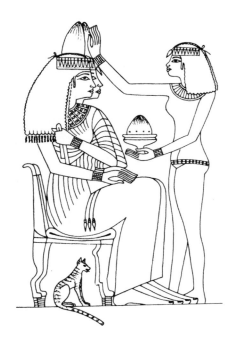

The maidservant adds a few dabs of the scented fat to the perfumed cones of aristocratic Egyptian women. Theban wall painting.

fats adorned the coiffures of both men and women and may be seen in countless paintings from the time of the New Kingdom on.

Both lard and tallow were used for enfleurage and for maceration. They will liquify if saturated with scent over heat, but they congeal again at room temperature and undergo molding. As the heat of the day increased along the Nile, such scented fat products would begin to melt and coat the body with an emollient cream, releasing perfume at the same time. The Egyptians enjoyed these scents for their own sakes; they were not used to mask body odors, for bathing was a great feature of life for the Egyptians. The priests washed as often as three times a day. Among them hairiness was considered unclean and uncouth, so in addition to removing dirt, they regularly shaved the face, chest, armpits, and pubic regions. Since soap had not yet been invented, unguents were utilized to smooth the shaving process.

This great variety of oils for the bath, shaving oils, skin emollients, hair dyes, depilatories, mascara, and perfume unguents were contained in exquisitely turned containers of alabaster, glass, earthenware, and faience. The Egyptian *garniture de toilette* is irresistible. Each piece is so sensitively rendered that one longs to hold it, caress and use it. Alabaster was the most commonly employed material; glass was discovered in western Asia but was introduced by the Eighteenth Dynasty

An exquisite garniture de toilette *from the Twelfth Dynasty in Egypt made of gold rims on obsidian. This close-grained dark stone was not found in Egypt, but was imported, possibly from as far away as Afghanistan. The Egyptian culture was certainly religious—incense and unguents were applied to the statues of the entire pantheon—but the ancient Egyptians did not hesitate to deflect these attentions to the adornment and enjoyment of human life as well. Courtesy of The Metropolitan Museum of Art*

(1558 B.C.). At first glass was more precious than jewels; very likely Syrian prisoners of war had brought the glassmaking process back to Chem, the Black Land of the Nile. Craftsmen in Egypt learned to form a core of dung and clay and pull the molten glass across it like taffy. Once the form was covered, the sides were worked smooth and the container was heated again for toughening in an annealing oven. The core was then scraped out, cleaned, and sent to the "labs" in the temples, where perfumed oils were manufactured.

The Egyptians also knew how to create the beautiful *millefiori* glass by pulling various colored strands of molten glass and working them into a cable. This cable was then cut up and each piece put together against the walls of the mold, producing the effect of a thousand co-ruscating flowers. This technique was used again centuries later by the Venetian glassmakers of Murano, and it was likewise used for flacons. Although glassmaking seems to have deteriorated after the Twentieth Dynasty (1200–1085 B.C.), it flared to unexcelled brilliance after the

Egyptian cosmetic vase of opaque yellow glass in the form of a pomegranate, Twentieth Dynasty. However, the form is almost indistinguishable from the shape of the opium poppy capsule, and it is known that Cyprus exported to Egypt many flacons of this type, which contained gum opium, but were later used as perfume vases when their original contents were emptied. Opium was used in Cyprus in connection with the rites of the goddess of fertility, and opiated products widely distributed throughout the eastern Mediterranean. Courtesy of The Metropolitan Museum of Art

founding of Alexandria in 332 B.C. The Romans, Arabs, and eventually the Italians were to benefit from this tradition.

Another receptacle for the scented unguents unique to the Egyptians was the perfume spoon. This was a cross between a spatula and a spoon, deep enough to contain some scented unguent but wide enough to allow one to handle it like a palette. Elegance and imagination marked the design of the perfume spoons; water-lily buds, shells, leaves, fish and ducks, garden pools bordered with flowers, and of course the ubiquitous *ankh*, symbol of life. These artifacts are judged to rank among the finest achievements of the decorative arts in Egypt. Each object would engender pleasant daydreams in the mind of the belle who sat adorning herself.

The Egyptians loved gardens, and the chief flower in them was the fragrant *Nymphaea coerulea (sarpat)*, the blue water lily. This is often called, incorrectly, the "lotus." The lotus is an entirely different species, *Nelumbo nucifera*, an East Asian flower associated with Indian religion. The true lotus was introduced into Egypt at a late date by the Persians and was known as *neheb*, but it was the blue water lily that captivated the hearts of the Egyptians with its intensely sweet perfume and its associations with Ra, the sun god. The ovary, with its rayed stigma of bright yellow set against the blue floral corolla, was like Ra, shining in the blue heavens. The blue water lily bloomed from December to March, rising slightly above the waters to open at dawn and then closing its petals at midday without descending again beneath the water. In later Egyptian mysticism it came to signify the resurrection of Osiris under the ministrations of Isis.

The flower figured prominently in the long, rectangular garden pools. The blossoms were picked from the pools of noble residences and inhaled as nosegays during banquets and celebrations. We now know that the narcotic and hallucinogenic substances nupharine, nupharidine,

The Egyptian "lotus" was actually a water-lily (Nymphaea coerulea *or* Nymphaea lotus) *but like the true East Asian sacred lotus* (Nelumbo nucifera) *was a highly aromatic water plant with a great overlay of symbolic connotations. The gold disk in the blue corolla symbolized Ra in the vault of heaven. The flower was planted in every garden, and individual blooms would be held in the hand at a banquet.*

and nuciferine are part of the chemistry of this plant[2] and that if simple inhalation was insufficient for mystical transports, a water-lily potion was prepared by steeping the flower heads in wine, the Egyptians' favorite drink. Here we discover the first instance of the association of inhalation of perfumes with inhalation of hallucinogens. Marijuana (*Cannabis sativa*) may have first been an incense in the ancient Near East, and most probably tobacco leaves (which also often contain hallucinogenic substances) were kindled by the Amerindians as a ritual incense.

Egyptian love for other perfumed plants extended to the white water lily *(sushin), Nymphaea lotus.* This flower blooms during the night and gives out a piquant scent that is less intoxicating than its blue counterpart. Lilies (*Lilium candidum* and *spp.*) were also used. The Egyptians used the leaves of henna (*Lawsonia inermis*) as a hair dye and as a stain for the soles of the feet, and the fragrant flowers for perfume oils. The Hebrew Song of Solomon echoed the Egyptian love of henna:

> *A bundle of myrrh is my beloved unto me;*
> *he shall lay all night between my breasts.*
> *My beloved is unto me as a cluster of camphire*
> *[flowers of henna] in the vineyards of Engedi.*
> (JERUSALEM BIBLE 1. 13, 14)

The rock rose (*Cistus ladaniferus, C. creticus*) was imported into Egypt from Crete. The leaves exude a resin that has a gratifying, honeyed aroma—an ancient article of commerce that is still used extensively in modern perfumery for its softness and great tenacity. These wonderful ingredients were used singly and also blended into compositions with their own names. Pliny (23–79 A.D.) recorded the names of two perfumes, one called "Mendes" after a town famous for fragrances, and the other called "Kyphi," the scent "welcome to the gods," compounded from cypress (*Cyperus longus*), juniper, incense resins, henna flowers, mint, sweet flag, and aromatic grasses imported from India. The compounder extends the scent with honey; it was indeed a heady brew.

Greeks and Romans, like Dioscorides and Pliny, retained an enormous respect for the Egyptians' pharmaceutical and perfumery skill. Unlike the later Greeks and Romans in Egypt, the intellectual class—made up chiefly of priests—did not have an aversion to dabbling in

The Egyptian lily (Nymphaea coerulea) *was the garden flower of Egypt, much as the rose gives color and perfume to our gardens today. Steeped in wine, the flower could also confer some mildly mind-altering alkaloids. A perfume flask with the water lily design motif. Courtesy of The Metropolitan Museum of Art*

pots of animal fats, herbs, dye vats, and chemicals. Greek and Roman thinkers preferred to leave such messy putterings to women and slaves. The Egyptians, however, preserved their findings in temple libraries so that by Hellenistic times, the body of research was considerable. Egypt maintained its lead in chemistry well into the Islamic period.

The trade in commodities that had begun even before Hatshepsut's time remained constant. When Alexandria was founded in 332 B.C., goods from Africa, southern Arabia, and India were unloaded for local consumption and for reshipment to Crete, Greece, Italy, and Asia Minor. Some distinctions should be pointed out: the "cinnamon" (from the Hebrew *kinamon̂*) often referred to in Egyptian books was not our familiar cinnamon. Pliny places its origin in the land of the Ethiopians;[3] it was probably an aromatic bark of African origin (possibly *Amyris kataf*) that was replaced by the finer Ceylonese cinnamon only in late antiquity, when many Indian products were becoming common in Alexandria.

"Cassia" is another anachronism; most books speak of the "cassia" employed in Egyptian unguents. This, as with cinnamon, and with African frankincense and myrrh, was probably a case of one product being eclipsed by another, yet retaining an old name. Today "cassia" refers exclusively to the Chinese *kuei pi (Cinnamomum cassia)*, a Chinese variant of Ceylon cinnamon, much used today in flavoring cola beverages. Cassia grows only in China and Indochina, and we cannot assume any evidence for navigation around the tip of Indochina westward before the second century B.C., and even that date is early. Cassia (Hebrew *ketziah*) is also mentioned in the Bible in association with cinnamon. It was probably costus root *(Saussurea lappa)*, a strong herb from India.

Other imports that were unloaded at Alexandria were spikenard *(Nardostachys jatamansi)*, fragrant grasses of the *Andropogon* and *Cymbopogon* genera, ginger, pepper, and sandalwood. The reason there were so many Indian aromatics is that traders from Egypt had discovered the secret of the monsoons, which would waft them toward India in warm weather and away in cool almost as though on a conveyor belt. Another factor was the domestication of the camel. By the fifth century B.C., this animal had begun replacing donkeys as the pack animal of Arabia, making the two-thousand-mile trek to Alexandria possible. Because of the notorious windlessness of the Red Sea, land transport was important if the "spices of Araby" were to reach market. Alexandria was built on a stretch of land between Lake Mareotis and the Mediterranean, with the lighthouse island of Pharos over against it; this natural anchorage made it a center for the trade in aromatics from its inception until 1600 A.D., when the Red Sea and the Arabian overland routes were definitively replaced by the oceanic routes around the Cape.

Today Egypt is one of the greatest producers of essential-oil plants for the world perfume trade. Abundant labor, beneficent climate, and agricultural expertise contribute to this, but if tradition could play a part, one could think of no better home for the perfume crops than the Black Land of the Nile.

Israel and the Perfumes of the Bible

The Bible records those times when thought and civilization were being forged in the Near East. Although few of us regularly read the Egyptian Book of the Dead or the early medical papyri, we are familiar with Moses, Solomon, Judith, and Christ. Among the sacred scriptures, none is so saturated with scent images as the Song of Songs, the Song of Solomon. Every other stanza alludes to a scent with an olfactory opulence unmatched in literature until Baudelaire and the Symbolists.

Who is this that cometh up from the desert like a
    column of smoke,
breathing of myrrh and frankincense,
and of every perfume the merchant knows.[4]

How delicious is your love, more delicious than wine!
How fragrant your perfumes,
more fragrant than all other spices!
The rarest essences are yours:
nard and saffron,
calamus and cinnamon,
with all the incense-bearing trees;
myrrh and aloes,
with the subtlest odors.
Fountain that makes the gardens fertile,
well of living water,
streams flowing down from Lebanon.
Awake, north wind,
come, wind of the south!
Breathe over my garden,
to spread its sweet smell around.[5]

Jewish betrothal ring, hinged for the insertion of leaves of myrtle, from Venice, sixteenth century. Myrtle (the Hebrew hadas) *was associated with Queen Esther (*Hadassah *in Hebrew) and has always been esteemed in the Near East for its fragrant, shiny green foliage. Rings with compartments for a few grains of musk, ambergris, or a spice, have long been used in the Near East and in India. Courtesy of The Metropolitan Museum of Art*

This book was probably written in the 400s or 300s before our era, so the ascription to Solomon is purely symbolic. The brief but intense poem is a dialogue, back and forth, between two lovers intoxicated by the scent of each other's bodies, by their perfumes, and by the setting of a garden abloom with lilies and hyacinths, fanned by the cedars of Lebanon. It is also a complicated allegory between the soul and the Divine, Israel and Yahweh. Perfume is used throughout the poem as an invisible but inexorable attractant.

Once we realize its late date, we can identify precisely the aromatics described so rhapsodically. By the 300s B.C., true frankincense and myrrh were reaching the Mediterranean cultures. The lilies described were probably the same lilies as our Madonna lily, or a closely related species. The *Hyacinthus orientalis*, our familiar garden hyacinth, was subsumed under the same Hebrew word *(shoshanah)* and represents the Biblical "lily of the valley." The flower was not our familiar lily of the valley *(Lilium convallarium)*. Saffron, although today no longer used as a perfume, was our *Crocus sativus* (Hebrew *karkom* and Greek *krokos*). The Arabic word is *kurkum*. "Saffron" is from the Arabic *zafran*, meaning "yellow"; the stigmata of this flower were used not only for aroma, but for color. Today the crocus is used only for flavor. "Aloes" were probably aloewood *(Aquillaria agallocha)*, an Indian product that was exported to western Asia at that time, although some authorities believe that it was the more common sandalwood. Aloewood is still distilled to extract its wonderfully soft and sweet essence, which is much prized in East Asia but has only limited use in Western perfumery. The "aloes" of the Song of Songs is not the *Aloes vera*, used as a skin salve; the confusion is due to the similarly bitter taste of the two botanicals, each bearing the name "aloes."

The "nard," or "spikenard," in the poem was another Indian product, exported westward in Hellenistic times. *Nardostachys jatamansi*, a member of the valerian family, is related to the familiar *Valeriana officinalis*, which is often taken as a sleep-inducing agent. Spikenard, however, has a more pungent and more agreeable smell than Valeriana. Today Indian women continue to use *Nardostachys* to perfume their hair. "Very costly" spikenard was chosen by Mary Magdalene to perfume the feet of Jesus for which she was rebuked by those around her, but not by Christ.

Many people believe that King Solomon fell in love with the queen of Sheba, a kingdom in southern Arabia that produced the frankincense and myrrh of Hellenistic times. This is not the case, however; the trade in these incenses had not developed during Solomon's time (from 970 to about 931 B.C.). Sheba was probably the queen of a northern Arabian tribe, the Sabaeans, who were engaged in trade east and west across the northern neck of the Arabian peninsula. The trade routes from the south had not yet been established. She might have traded in one of the "balms," or "balsams," mentioned in the Bible, that were found in that region, such as *Pistacia lentiscus* or the related *Pistacia terebinthus, var. palaestina*, the biblical "terebinth." The resin of both trees is pungent and aromatic.

Solomon did use the cedars of Lebanon, however, to construct the temple. Trees were felled in Lebanon, brought by sea to Jaffa, and then up to Jerusalem. Phoenician craftsmen were engaged to construct the temple because they were familiar with the wood. After the destruction of Solomon's temple and the deportation to Babylon in 586 B.C., a new temple was begun in 535 B.C. with help from the Persians. Again the fragrant cedar of Lebanon was the material of choice, as it was in the restoration of 20 B.C., the temple in which Christ taught.

By the time of Christ, the incense burned in the temple was made of the true frankincense and myrrh from Arabia, galbanum and "onycha." The latter refers to gum labdanum, which was a soft, warm, honeylike, rich, musky scent, soothing and balsamic to inhale. The gum is exuded from the leaves of the rockrose, *Cistus creticus, C. ladaniferus*, and other species of *cistus*. The flower looks like a briar rose and may well be the "rose of Sharon" of Song 2:1.

A host of other scent terms appear in the Sacred Scriptures: "bdellim"

Labdanum is a sticky resin exuded from the leaves of the Cistus ladaniferus, *a plant native to the Middle East. The resin has a soft honey-like scent and has been popular since classical antiquity. It is probable that this plant represents the true "Rose of Sharon" of the Bible.*

is simply a type of myrrh; the "hyssop" of the Bible refers to *Marjorana syriaca*, even today a source of *Za'atar*, a popular condiment in the Middle East. Myrtle was used to make booths at the original Feast of Tabernacles, and olive branches and pine boughs (Nehemiah 8:15) were used in the festivals observed after the return of the exiles from Babylon. One of the promises to Israel was that "instead of the brier shall come up the myrtle tree" (Isaiah 55:13, KJV). As anyone would know who has stood in the Court of the Myrtles at the Alhambra or in any Arabic garden where these beautiful evergreens grow, this was indeed consolation. Myrtles have a piney, crisp, almost eau-de-cologne scent when the leaves are rubbed; this odor will diffuse out in the heat and permeate a garden. The Hebrew word for myrtle was *hadas*, and much play was made on the similarity of that word to Hadassah, the name of Queen Esther.

Myrtle flowers, fruits, bark, and roots all contain glands that produce essential oil. Until recently they were sold as sachet material in the bazaars of Jerusalem and Damascus. The Turks used myrtle to impart an odor to leather in the tanning process. Modern perfumery stills use a steam-distilled myrtle oil.

In the Bible, too, we find the first reference to perfume's use as a weapon in the story of Judith who

> removed the sackcloth she was wearing and, taking off her widow's dress, washed all over, anointed herself with costly perfumes, dressed her hair, wrapped a turban around it and put on the dress she used to wear on joyful occasions when her husband Manasseh was alive. She put sandals on her feet, put on her necklaces, bracelets, rings, earrings and all her jewelry.[6]

Thus fortified, she gained access to the tent of Holofernes, where she seduced and slew him.

Perfume had been used as a deadly weapon?

4

The Classical World and Its Heritage

Greece

By comparison with the cultures discussed above, Greek culture was young. But the link between Greece and these earlier cultures is to be found on the islands of Crete and Cyprus. Crete, in particular, had an elegant culture that lasted from 2600 to 1250 B.C., when it was besieged by invading tribes. Phoenician ships from Tyre and Sidon brought Cretan rhyton vessels to Egypt and Egyptian luxury items to Crete and Cyprus. Some of these rhyta contained aromatic oils that were used to anoint Crete's legendary athletes, who leaped over the horns of the sacred bull. Other containers held opium—the sole painkiller known at the time—which was grown in the two islands and exported throughout the eastern Mediterranean. It is hard to determine whether a rhyton was used for perfumes, for opium, or for both.

The flowers that this pre-Greek culture preferred included, above all, the lily. A stele dating to 2000 B.C. reads;

The lily carved here is the scented symbol
of Seka, who in life emanated only perfume.[1]

We also find definite evidence that the Cretans used the rose: In a fresco from Knossos there appears a natural hybrid of *Rosa phoenicia* and *Rosa gallica* that dates from around 1719 B.C., at the Palace of Minos.

After the flowering of Minoan civilization, there was a hiatus before Greek culture developed on the mainland. The Doric tribes that had invaded cared little for the amenities of civilized life. However, by the seventh century B.C. Athens and Corinth enjoyed a brisk business in the production of fragranced oils contained in elegant ceramic vessels of great artistry. Olive oil, almond oil, castor oil, sesame oil, and linseed oil were used as the vehicles for perfumes compounded of lilies, marjoram, thyme, sage, roses, anise, and iris root. Some perfume containers were round, others shaped like wine-vessels, others flat and round like a modern powder box, but all were decorated with imagination—elegant women in draped robes, birds, proud lions, or satyrs with enormous phalli. Scents were widely used by both men and women, despite the ban by the lawgiver Solon in the sixth century. For him, such unguents were associated with the luxurious life-style of Persia, the traditional enemy of Greece.

By the sixth century incense became common on municipal altars throughout Greece; prior to that, the burning of animal sacrifices had been offered to the gods.

After the "orientalization" of Greek life under Alexander the Great, the use of both unguents for personal comfort and the use of incense in civic piety became much more widespread. The young conqueror himself sent seeds and cuttings of Persian plants to his classmate Theophrastus of Athens who created the first botanical garden. In order to ascertain the origins of Arabian incense, Alexander sent his deputy Anaxicrates on an exploratory mission to what is now modern-day Yemen and Oman. His account has been preserved in the writings of Theophrastus:

> The trees of frankincense and myrrh grow partly in the mountains, partly on private estates at the foot of the mountains; wherefore some are under cultivation, others not; the mountains, they say, are lofty, forest-covered and subject to snow, and rivers from them flow down into the plain. The frankincense tree, it is said, is not

tall, about five cubits hight and is much branched; . . . The myrrh tree is said to be still much smaller in stature and more bushy.[2]

Anaxicrates correctly described *Boswellia carteri*, used today to produce the olibanum of modern perfumery so important in oriental blends. *Commiphora myrrha*, the principal source of the finest myrrh, was also truly portrayed.

The first treatise on scent per se was the study "Concerning Odors" by Theophrastus. Not only did he take elaborate inventory of all the Greek and imported aromatics, but he discussed ways in which they could be most artfully blended by the perfumer. He considered the properties of the various oils used as carriers of scent, scents in wine, the use of dried flowers and herbs, the shelf-life of scented products, and the suitability of various perfumes for states of mind and of health for men and for women. Theophrastus also explored the process by which we are able to perceive smells and noted the similarity between odor and flavor perception.

Alexander the Great used aromatics freely toward the end of his career, and at his death was cremated on an emormous pyre of costly resins. His successors used incense to awe their subjects. In 278 B.C., Ptolemy II organized a pomp at Alexandria in which women dressed as Victories bore censers nine foot high, followed by youths in Tyrian purple bearing trays of incense and saffron.

Cleopatra (69–30 B.C.) was the last and the most beautiful representative of the dynasties established by Alexander in the East. She was the descendant of the Ptolemies and heir to both the Egyptian and the Greek traditions of beauty. The ship upon which she received Antony had sails which had been perfumed, incense burners surrounded her throne, and her body was clothed in the most diaphanous of garments but scented with the finest of perfumes. Her dream and that of her Roman lover was to unite the Orient to the rising power of Rome. This dream was not to be realized, but Cleopatra herself, who portrayed herself as a living Venus, became the symbol of beauty in the classical world.

Rome

Although the Romans took over the eastern Mediterranean, Greek customs continued and influenced Rome. Early Roman culture was

Roman perfume flask of the first century of our era. This elegant onyx glass bottle would be held on a metal tripod, or could be inserted into a shelf with cylindrical holes in the perfumer's workshop. After the Republican period, the Romans became avid users of scents, even to the point of creating balance of payment problems due to their great consumption of frankincense and myrrh. The Roman urguenta exotica *were aromatics in an olive oil base, and were applied in conjunction with the bath ritual. Courtesy of The Metropolitan Museum of Art, gift of J. Pierpont Morgan, 1917*

rough but the Etruscans (eighth to second century B.C.) brought a civilizing influence to early Latin society. The Etruscans made use of the myrtle, Spanish broom (*Cistus junceus*), labdanum, and pine in addition to imported incense resins. They stored their essences in fine perfume-holding brooches and hollowed-out jewels. As Roman contacts with the Etruscans increased as well as contacts with the Phoenicians and the Greeks, the use of perfumes increased. By the second century B.C., Plautus mentions importing incense from Arabia for use in temples. During Republican times, the use of fragrances was restrained and balanced, but later, during the Imperial period, a certain abuse marked their consumption. After the death of Alexander, the Hellenistic world had made great use of scent, but Roman use exceeded all known limits.

Men and women literally bathed in perfume; slaves called *cosmetae* prepared scents for Roman matrons, who used pigeon dung to render their locks blonde and white lead to lighten their complexions. Silks were carried overland from distant China for consumers who would pay any price for self-adornment, and we can estimate with near certainty that in the first century A.D., Rome absorbed between twenty-five hundred and three thousand tons of frankincense and from four hundred and fifty to six hundred tons of myrrh from southern Arabia.[3] The taste and discretion so evident in Theophrastus was absent from Imperial Rome. Pliny decried the abuse of perfumes by his contemporaries: At one of Nero's feasts a guest was asphyxiated by showers of roses.

A number of components went into Roman perfumery: roses, sweet flag, iris (the rhizomes of the *Iris germanica, var. pallida*, with their violet scent, are still in use today), narcissus (a plant originally from Anatolia and Persia), saffron, mastic, oakmoss—each from Italy or the eastern Mediterranean. From their extensive trade networks, pepper, East Indian cinnamon, cardamon, nutmeg and ginger, costus, spikenard, aloewood, and fragrant grasses were imported from India. Arabian gum resins completed the perfumer's arsenal, as described in Book XII of Pliny's *Natural History*.

Of all flowers, the Romans loved the rose the most. They adorned themselves with it at banquets, decorated their villas with it, and on the occasion of a victory, they strew roses through the streets. Nero consumed four million sesterces worth of roses (about $100,000) at one celebration, and the feast of Rosalia was created to honor this flower. The Latins had extensive rose plantations on the Campanian plains, but rose consumption was so great that flowers were grown in Egypt as well.

The perfume makers, *aromatarii*, sold tenacious unguents in red clay *buccheri* and scented wines in *amphorae*. The famous Roman baths were one of the chief places where these products were used. The Romans were extremely clean and used scent for its own sake rather than to mask infrequent bathing. The Roman custom of bathing for socializa-

Illustrator George Barbier's re-creation of the soins de beauté *in ancient Rome. Bathing was a daily practice, and anointing with scented cosmetics always followed the bath.*

Frankincense, the most sought after of all the gum resins, is exuded from the trunk of Boswellia carteri, *and related species. The land that produced this plant was known to the Romans as* Arabia Felix, *"Arabia the Blessed," modern Oman and Yemen.*

tion and relaxation was continued by the Arabs, who were their heirs in Syria, Egypt, and Mesopotamia.

For all the abuses to which perfumes were subjected during the late Imperial age, the Romans can be credited with real achievements: The great consumption of perfume stimulated the creation of difficult trade routes to Arabia, India, and even to China; the need for perfume containers gave glassmaking an unprecedented boost; and interest in the senses found intelligent expression in writings by Pliny and the great physicians Galen and Celsus.

While Christianity later did much to divert the Roman mind from sensory stimulation, it was the political and economic collapse of the empire that brought to an abrupt halt the most lavish consumption of aromatics history had seen.

Before leaving the Roman period completely, however, we must discuss an "underground" movement that went on outside of official life and concerned two of the most important aspects of perfume history: the rise of alchemy and the use of the still. By the second century A.D., Alexandria was the meeting-ground of all the great cultures of antiquity: Egyptians, Romans, Greeks, Jews, Syrians, and Persians.

Among this diverse group a great intellectual ferment was underway. The Romans had lost faith in the traditional gods, whose foibles had become the butt of satirists, and the state cult was formal and empty. From the first century A.D. through the fourth, we find a religious revival, deeply concerned with *soteria*, personal salvation. Christianity, Gnosticism, the mystery religions, and Stoicism endeavored to find a release from the limitations of the world as defined by the classical world, and alchemy was the fruit of this ferment.

The philosophy of the alchemists expressed the conviction that the spark of divinity could be discovered in matter. By submitting botanical and mineral substances to heating in water baths and stills, the alchemists hoped to extract a divine, eternal spirit *(pneuma)*. The essential oil extracted from a mixture of water and the botanicals was an example of such a spirit. Essential oils, which seemed to the alchemists like deathless essences, and alcohol were products of the still, their contribution to chemistry. The records of the alchemists indicate that the first true still was the invention of one Maria the Jewess (Maria Prophetissima)—almost nothing is known about her.

The Rosa gallica *was known to the Roman naturalist Pliny, who described it as "the rose of a hundred petals"—a highly doubled form. The Persians called it* gul sad berk, *a literal translation, and in Islamic times it became hybridized to form the damask rose* (Rosa damascena), *a rose plant widely and eventually brought by the Turks to Bulgaria. From George Nicholson,* The Illustrated Dictionary of Gardening, *London, 1888.*

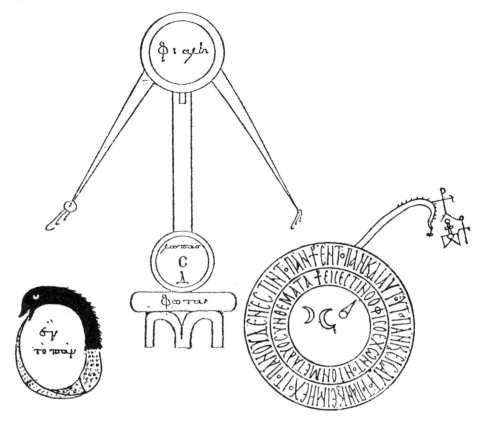

The first representation of a still, from The Gold-Making of Cleopatra, *an Alexandrian text of the first or second century of our era. The text credits the invention of this, the perfumer's tool* par excellence, *to one Maria Prophetissima, or Maria the Jewess. Although unusual in having two lead-off ducts instead of the one conventional goose-neck, we are in the unmistakable presence of a true still, with the heat source below, the flask for the matrix, the glass condensing head (called the* phiale, *in Greek) and the two tubes with the condensate coming out. Underneath, the cosmic serpent grasps his tail with the alchemical creed "All is one," inscribed within; the circle on the left announces that "It is towards oneness that all phenomena tend."*

Alchemy had deep roots in the craft tradition of Egypt. The concept of a "tincture" came from the dyer's art; the furnace was the *phournos* of the baker; and metallurgy, jewelrymaking, glassworks, and ceramic art entered into the tools and processes of these chemists. In the second-century alchemical text, "The Gold-Making of Cleopatra" (author un-known), we have an incontrovertible diagram of a still, and numerous references indicate that the general principles of distillation were understood.

The dictum of the alchemists was "To sublimate that which was bodily, and to embody that which was spirit."[5] In the still, vapors from the mixture of plant material and water would rise and condense upon the inner surface of the still cap. Then they would slowly trickle down the lead-off spout and collect in a flask. The oils in the plant material ("bodily") had been sublimed, and then condensed ("embodied") and collected.

At first, perfume oils were almost exclusively the result of the distillation of plant material, but eventually alcohol would be extracted from the still, once the condenser had been more efficiently designed (in the medieval period). In Alexandria, a long line of alchemists continued to explore the utilizations of the technique of distillation throughout the late Roman, Christian, and Byzantine periods. Among them we find Hermes Trimegistos (whence the term a "hermetic" seal), Ostanes the Persian, Cleopatra (not the queen), Isis, Zosimus and his consort Theosebeia, Christianus and Theodorus, author of the *Corpus Hermeticum*, the repository of the writings of these inspired chemists. This work was prepared after Alexandria had passed to the Arabs in the seventh century, for Islam did not extinguish the scientific spirit which it encountered.

The Arab World

Westerners are so accustomed to the idea of the Dark Ages that is hard to appreciate that many of the supposedly "lost" arts and sciences were never lost in the East. Byzantium retained the language, culture, and institutions of Constantine the Great until 1453 A.D. But the real "missing link" that connects antiquity and the modern world is Islam, which drew in the learning and technology of the Greco-Roman world and diffused it across vast areas of Asia, northern Africa, and southern Europe. Islam's role is often minimized by our frequent assumption that if Europe went through a Dark Age, the rest of the world must have done so as well, and also as a result of our disdain for Arabic culture, which persists as a relic of the Crusading times. Students of perfumery and pharmacy cannot afford to neglect Islamic culture. They must remember that Renaissance technologists did not simply exhume

Roman materials and methods but drew from the contributions made by the Muslim world during the intervening millennium.

What is most startling about the history of Islam is the speed with which it spread across the eastern and southern Mediterranean. By 732, a century after Muhammed's death, societies from Morocco to Turkestan were linked in a common religion, language, and trade network. Islam taught the brotherhood of man, which greatly facilitated the give and take of commerce; it also indulged the needs of traders, for the Prophet himself had come from a mercantile background, and Mecca was one of the most important stops on the caravan route from the incense lands of southern Arabia. The lot of the farmer was not always given its due praise, but the lot of the merchant always was.

Unlike Christianity, Islam was relatively relaxed as far as the comforts of life were concerned. Muhammed himself is said to have loved women, children, and perfumes above all else.

Alexandria was the greatest city of Egypt, with a cultural heritage that was both Egyptian and Hellenistic. It guarded the way to North Africa, and from its port came countless luxury items and the grain that helped to feed the new Rome at Byzantium. For these reasons, Umar, one of the first caliphs, instructed Amir ibn-al-As to capture this great city. Leaving the Jordan River, Amir traveled west and attacked Alexandria with a force of twenty thousand troops. By November 8, 641, he had taken it over and had negotiated a peace with the Coptic bishop to spare the lives of the inhabitants. There was no wholesale burning of libraries as is often alleged; Christians and Jews were not forced to convert but only made to pay a poll tax. Amir laid the groundwork for the growth of trade by dredging the old canal of the pharaohs that connected the Nile valley and the Red Sea, a task neglected since the time of the Emperor Trajan. Ostensibly this was done to facilitate the *hadj*, the pilgrimage to Mecca, but it served commerce as well.

Arab forces also took over Damascus in Syria. Shortly afterwards, Nestorian Christians began the work of translating the works of classical Greece and Rome into Arabic. Many of the amenities of Roman civilization were simply incorporated into Muslim life, particularly the bath, the *thermae*, which became the *hamman*. By 750, a new, planned city, Baghdad, "City of Gardens," became the center of Islamic culture. This center of the urbane Abbasid dynasty was situated between the "sea of the West," the Mediterranean, and the "sea of the East," the Indian Ocean, a magnet for trade goods from Morocco and the Far East.

ARAB ACCOMPLISHMENTS

The writings of Dioscorides, Galen, Pliny, and Zosimus were translated for the burgeoning Arabic world at Edessa in Syria and Misibis in Iraq. Once these medical, botanical, and alchemical classics were available it was not long before they fueled the birth of a purely Islamic body of knowledge. Ar-Razi (ca.850–ca.924), an herbalist and physician of Baghdad, was one of the greatest alchemists of the Arab world. Another was Jabir ibn Hayyan, known to the West as Geber, who left an encyclopedia of all knowledge, the *Summa Perfectionis*, of which several chapters treat on the subject of distillation. The Jabiran writings discuss both distillation with water and dry distillation. It is not known for sure whether the name Jabir represents one man or, more likely, a coterie of alchemists and scientists working in Baghdad.

Yakub al-Kindi (fl. 803–870) left a work entitled *The Book of Perfume Chemistry and Distillations (Kitab Kimiya' al-'Itr wa'l-Tas'idat)*, in which he discussed the distillation of musk and the balsams; he also described the manufacture of attar of rose.

Ibn-Sina (980–1037) was a philosopher whose experimental works merited him the name "Prince of Pharmacists." Attar of rose was his cure for ailments of the digestive tract. This scholar, known to the West as Avicenna, urged a rational approach to the transformations of alchemy: "As to the claims of the alchemists, it must be clearly understood that it was not in their power to bring about any true change of species. The essential nature remains unchanged."[6] The oil that had been in the plant appeared in the condenser; the heat had not created a new entity as some believed.

A Spaniard, ibn-al-'Awwam of Seville, left a *Treatise on Agriculture (al-Filahah)* in the twelfth century that discussed the requirements of over five hundred species of plants and included sections on grafting and fertilizing. He studied the cultural practices of the rose and noted that the white varieties in Spain had from forty to fifty petals and the red one hundred, indicating the ancestors of the *Rosa alba* and the *Rosa damascena*. Another Spaniard, 'Abdullah ibn-al-Baytar (d. 1248) traveled widely throughout the Muslim world and left a *materia medica* that included fourteen hundred entries, presenting an inventory of the useful properties of the plant wealth that had become available to the trade network that spanned three continents.

In addition to the establishment of a body of literature, Arab technologists made practical improvements in the techniques of distillation.

The "Moor's Head" cooler for the still resembled a turban and rested on top of the still. It was filled with cold water and represented the first attempt to replace air cooling with water cooling. It is likely that this practice actually originated in China, but it was through the Arab world that the West learned of it. Measurement became important, and pharmacy became known as the art of the "mizan," the scales. The Arabs introduced filtration in laboratory operations, derived from the felt *(feltre)* of the Central Asians who gradually entered the Islamic orbit. Experiments were made with inorganic compounds in distillation such as cinnabar (mercury sulfide), realgar (arsenic sulfides), naphtha, and other fractions of petroleum. Glassware was perfected, including the manufacture of pieces that could withstand the heat of distilling. Another achievement of great importance was the invention of true soapmaking. By the eighth century in Syria, the Arabs had learned to put water through a mixture of wood ash and quicklime, solving the problem of causticizing soda for the manufacture of solid soap.

One industrial process of great importance that seems to have eluded these technologists was the extraction of ethyl alcohol from wine. The Jabiran corpus noted that the vapors of wine would catch fire, but the Arab world was apparently unable to extract the ethyl alcohol consistently. The essential oils have boiling points much higher than that of water, and cooling the vapors is not as critical as it is for alcohol vapors. The proto-chemists of Islam made many steps toward this critical stage, but they were never quite able to extract significant quantities of alcohol for want of an effective cooling device.

The forging of trade links over thousands of miles was another practical achievement of the Arab world. Producing areas, such as India, that had been in slight contact with the old Greco-Roman world entered into steady trade with the Mediterranean. Other areas such as the islands of what is now known as Indonesia, and the eastern coast of China, which had never before been in contact with the Mediterranean, were soon connected by this merchant civilization. Ancillary benefits of this new commerce were the adoption of the Hindu numeral system, including its use of the cipher—so superior to the cumbrous Roman system—the use of paper and of paper money, and the compass, another Chinese innovation that the Arabs used themselves and passed on to other cultures.

Arab traders reached India by 700 and established trading colonies in the major cities along the western coast. Soon they expanded into the Malay Archipelago to where nutmeg, mace, and cloves were produced. By 800 traders from Persia had reached Canton, and in the succeeding years they were so numerous that mosques were founded to serve them. On land, the Silk Route linked Persia to Ch'ang-an, the modern city of Sian, and Chinese musk and silk went west.

To the north, Arab trade reached into the steppe; and to the west, Sicily, Spain, and the Maghreb (northern Africa) were connected. To the south, caravans went far along the eastern coast of Africa in search of slaves, ebony, and ambergris. Whether by camel or by oceangoing vessels, products from the Atlantic to the Pacific played a part in an enormous trade system.

Naturally the system was not always harmonious, for in 1055 the Seljuk Turks occupied Baghdad, disrupting overland trade routes. The Mongols so thoroughly destroyed the region that by the thirteenth century, this once important cosmopolitan center was reduced to insignificance, and Cairo and Alexandria became the most important *entrepôts*. Goods from the Spice Islands and India could bypass the Mongols and approach Egypt by means of the Indian Ocean and the Red Sea. The enormous trade with China was arbitrarily terminated by the isolationist policies of the Ming dynasty in the late fifteenth century. In that century Europe would end its own long isolation and enter the spice trade.

What were the aromatics that were traded during the heyday of Islamic commerce? The word "spices" connoted anything that had little bulk but high value; true spices were among the most important components of this category, but drugs were also called "spices." A document by Amr ibn-Bahr (al-Jahiz, d. 864 or 869) of Basra lists incense from Yemen, balsam from Egypt, saffron and flavored syrups from Isfahan, cumin from Kirman, jasmine ointment from Fars, sandalwood from India, and cassia from China. In addition, scented gloves were an important article of commerce, and sugar was sold as a precious commodity by itself and in syrups flavored with roses and violets.

Gum mastic was imported from Chios in the Aegean Islands, ambergris and civet from Ethiopia, agarwood from India and Burma, and cinnamon, pepper, ginger, cloves, and nutmegs from the East Indies. Camphor came from Szechwan in western China or from the coastal cities of Hangchou, Chüan-chou (the Zayton of Marco Polo), and Canton. Musk came from either Szechwan or Tibet.

The ninth-century work, *The Beauties of Commerce*, gives the Arab trader the following counsel:

> The spice merchant must know the different drugs, remedies, potions and perfumes, their good and bad sorts as well as the counterfeits. He must know what commodities are subject to rapid change and spoil and which ones are not, and what means ought to be used to preserve and to restore them, and lastly he must understand the blends of electuaries and potions, of powders and drugs. . . . This type of merchant above all needs early information on the relative situation of wares in the places of origin and native lands, whether the quantity on hand is great or small, cheap or dear, whether business has prospered abundantly and is in a good state or whether it has turned out poorly and has deteriorated, whether the import routes are cut off or are safe. He must try to obtain the knowledge of all this through inquiries and precise questioning of the caravans.[7]

THE FRAGRANCES OF ARABIA

Of all the aromatics in the Arabic treasury, pride of place must be given to musk and attar of rose. Travelers described the mixing of musk with the mortar of mosques so that when the rays of the sun struck the buildings, the soft scent would be exuded. Firdausi, a great poet of Persia, declared that musk was the perfume of the houris of paradise.

But the Persian poets, especially Hafiz and Sa'adi, waxed even more eloquent in praise of the rose—*the* flower of Islamic culture. Sa'adi's greatest poem is the *Gulistan*, "Garden of Roses"; the Sufis encouraged the practice of meditation in a rose garden, and the figure of such gardens is one of the most common themes in Persian carpets and miniatures.

Placing this flower in a still produced the attar of rose, attar derived from the Farsi *aettr*, "fat," hence "oil." The rose is unique in being able to withstand the considerable heat of distillation; most flowers, such as the jasmine, honeysuckle, violet, and hyacinth, would yield no essence if distilled. It is also unique in having a high degree of solubility in water. Most oils will not mix with water, but enough of the rose oil remains in the waters of distillation to give it a distinctly rosy scent and flavor. Today "attar of rose" means the oil as separated from the rosewater, but until the seventeenth century, Arab perfumers spoke of both rosewater and pure rose oil as "attar of rose."

The heady perfume of the hyacinth (Hy-
acinthus orientalis) *is often referred to in*
Persian poetry. The plant became common
in western Europe with the bulb craze of
the seventeenth century; it was the favorite
of Madame de Pompadour. The absolute of
hyacinth possesses the sweetness of the
flower, together with a sharp green note.
From George Nicholson, Illustrated
Dictionary of Gardening,
London, *1888.*

According to Ibn Khaldun, Farsistan in southern Iran was one of the principal centers of attar production, charged with providing the caliph at Baghdad with thirty thousand bottles annually. Al-Dimashqi described another center in Syria, a thirteenth-century Grasse known as *al-Munazzah* ("the Incomparable") for the clearness of the air, its many flowers and fruits, and above all, for the industry of making rose per-

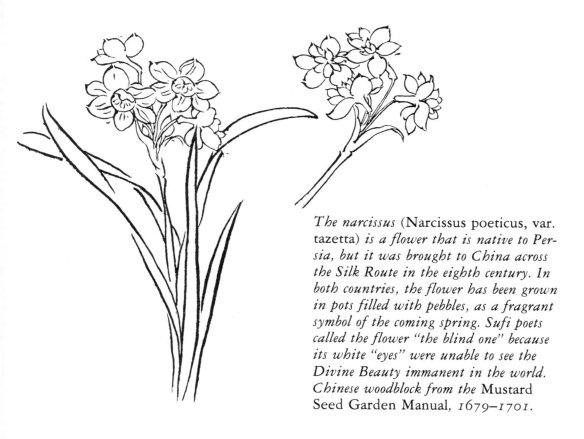

The narcissus (Narcissus poeticus, var. tazetta) is a flower that is native to Persia, but it was brought to China across the Silk Route in the eighth century. In both countries, the flower has been grown in pots filled with pebbles, as a fragrant symbol of the coming spring. Sufi poets called the flower "the blind one" because its white "eyes" were unable to see the Divine Beauty immanent in the world. Chinese woodblock from the Mustard Seed Garden Manual, *1679–1701.*

fume. Complex multiple stills produced the fragrance that was then exported to India, the Maghreb, and China.

Islamic courtesy decreed the sprinkling of a guest with rosewater from a long flask known as a *gulabdan*. It was also used in flavoring sherbets (from the Persian *sharbat*) and pastries such as the *lockoum*, which we know as Turkish Delight.

Rose attar was employed in the scenting of gloves, one of the oriental luxuries that the Crusaders sought to take back to Europe with them, just as American doughboys essayed to return home in 1918 with French perfumes. The great Saladin employed rosewater when he wished to purify the Mosque of Omar at Jerusalem, which he retook from the Christians in 1187. Mohamet II had the Church of Sancta Sophia similarly dedicated as a mosque after his capture of Constantinople in 1453.

It was a Turkish merchant who introduced the culture of the rose into the Ottoman province of Eastern Roumelia (modern Bulgaria), thus initiating what was to become the world's largest rose plantation. Muslim influence has long since left that country, but one of its finer mementos remains. Today the valley of Kazanluk blooms with the red damask rose *(Rosa damascena)*, hedged around by plantings of the hardier white *Rosa alba*. Even the name *damascena* evokes the memory of the first Ummayed capital. The Spanish word for the same flower calls to mind another great Islamic center, *la rosa de Alejandria*.

In no other culture were flowers made to bloom in the world of feeling as in Islam. Because of their beauty and fragrance, they became symbols of the highest spiritual attainments of the Sufis. The rose, for example, was supposed to expire "Allah, Allah!" by means of its fra-

Persian rose-water sprinkler of blue glass, seventeenth century. The rose was the first flower to be distilled, and the beautiful attar that was produced became an important part of Islamic civilization; in Persia, guests would be sprinkled with drops of this scent from a tapering gulabdan such as this. Most oils separate from the waters of distillation quite readily, but the essence of rose remains perceptible in the condensing water as well, thus attar (or otto) of rose is used in Islamic literature to mean both the pure oil or the rose-scented distilled water. Courtesy of The Metropolitan Museum of Art, Gift of J. Pierpont Morgan, 1917

grance according to Yunus Emre, a great mystic of Anatolia. The Persian Kamal Khojandi wrote a poem placed on the lips of the rose wherein the flower declares: "My whole body is soul/I am completely spirit, like Jesus."[8] Other poets compared the rose to Solomon reigning from his throne of emerald. And still another tradition credits the existence of the rose to a drop of sweat from Muhammed as he rose to heaven on al-Burak, his part-human, part-animal beast of burden. One of the more recent poets of Islam, Muhammed Iqbal, has echoed an ancient concept of his tradition:

> In the state of union the single beings of the world are one,
> All the petals of the rose are together one.[9]

The narcissus, with its white "eye," was a lesson to not be blind to the divine glory present in the world, and the violet taught adoration, bowing down like the faithful at prayer in the courtyard of the mosque. Hafiz is said to have been ready to bypass the bread stalls in the bazaar and spend his last cent to buy a hyacinth "to feed his soul."

The Arab world could also put aromatics to more pedestrian uses than for fueling flights of fancy. When, in the desert, a guest entered one's tent, a few grains of incense would be sprinkled over the brazier to permeate the robes with its clean, resinous scent. In cities like Baghdad, Damascus, or Isfahan, long-handled braziers made of finely wrought brass would serve the same function. Incensing was also observed at births and weddings.

Arab women were fond of cosmetics and especially of perfume, which they wore after bathing. Kohl is the best-known of Muslim adornments, a mascara made of antimony sulfide ground to an extremely fine powder and applied with a thin applicator to the eyes. Kohl eventually took on a generalized meaning in Arabian science, denoting "a fine essence." At a time when Arabian influence was still very great in European practice, this word was chosen to express the ethanol that Italian alchemists were increasingly able to extract from wine. It was called *alcohol vini*, "essence of wine," our "alcohol."

Aromatics were also crushed in a mortar and pestle and made into a paste with gum arabic. Then the mixture was shaped into balls and allowed to dry. The beads were threaded, and as they were worn in the heat of the day, they would exude the scent of sandalwood, frankincense, mastic, saffron, and musk. Sometimes these fragrant pieces of jewelry were worn in alternation with coral or pearls, and there was also jewelry that was made with special cavities for fragrance.

Incense-burner in the shape of a partridge, Persian, twelfth century. The technologies and amenities of civilized life that prevailed in Greek and Roman times were not lost in the East after the fall of the Empire as they were in western Europe. Byzantium imported incense gums from Arabia for religious ceremonies, and from Muslim urban centers such as Cairo and Baghdad for use in social life. Courtesy of The Metropolitan Museum of Art, Rogers Fund, 1949

Islam has had an important role in the story of perfumes. It conserved the achievements of antiquity and also advanced the level of chemical and pharmaceutical technology by contributions of its own. It made a panoply of goods available through a vast trade network, and explored the ways in which to use this wealth. And Islamic poetry has raised the plants of perfume to a level of analogy for the world of spirit.

5

The Aromatic East

Part of the great importance of the role of Islam was that it placed the West into contact with two extremely rich cultural areas—India and China. Indeed, the cultural and technical sophistication of these two areas helped to create modern Europe. The Arab trade network made the goods of these two civilizations accessible beyond their borders, but what was each one like in itself?

India

No other region on earth possesses such a wealth of aromatic plants. The Indian peninsula extends from the highest mountains on earth, the Himalayas, into the warm waters of the Indian Ocean, thus producing plants of every climatic zone. The customs of both the Dravidian and

Aryan populations that inhabited India freely encouraged lavish use of this natural endowment. The religions of the Jains, the Buddhists, and the brahmins all encouraged frequent bathings and ritual washings, and fragrant oils, powders, and pastes were added to the body after these cleansings.

One Sanscrit author (Someshvara, ca. 1130) described the pleasure (*bhoga*) to which the ritual necessity of the daily bath could give to the ruler. In his *Manasollasa*, even the decor of the royal bath is described— the pillars of the apartment must be artfully painted. Beautiful attendants should pour warm water on the king's body, and his hair and scalp should be washed with the perfumed pulp of the fragrant *amalaka* (*Emblic myrobalan*) and then rinsed off. After drying, athletes should massage the entire body, and a fragrant oil should be applied by female attendants. The oil was very complex: Basically it was a base of sesame oil perfumed with jasmine, coriander, cardamon, holy basil (*tulasi, Ocimum sanctum*), costus, pandanus, agarwood, pine, saffron, champac, and clove. Once this rubdown was finished, the king would be dressed in a clean cotton garment and, fully refreshed, emerge to face the day.

The *Kama Sutra* (ca. 400 A.D.) described the life of the typical high-caste Hindu male in similar terms:

> He must get up early in the morning, answer the calls of nature, wash his teeth, smear his body with just a little fragrant paste, inhale fragrant smoke, wear some flower, just give the lips a rub with wax and red juice, look at his face in the mirror, chew betel leaves along with some mouth deodorants, and then attend to his work.[1]

The *Ritusanhara*, a classic poem of India, is no less detailed about the effects of such ministrations on women:

> With their soft hips covered with beautiful fabrics and wrappings, their breasts perfumed with sandalwood, covered with necklaces and jewels, and with hair perfumed from the bath, the beautiful women coax their lovers to burning desire.[2]

Indian women were not required to veil their faces as were Muslim women. Indeed, judging from the frescos and statues that remain of the classical Gupta period (ca. 300–540 A.D.), there was very little that covered the body except jewels, cosmetics, and perfumes.

Another utilization of aromatics was the making of *khuschiks*, screens of vetiver rootlets that were woven, placed over the openings of a verandah, and dampened with water. As the breeze entered the interior of the palace or temple, it would be perfume-laden and cooled. Similar mats, *khus tattis*, were woven to incorporate the scent of vetiver (known in India as *khus khus* or *khas*) in the room. Like Sargon and Sennacherib in the ancient Fertile Crescent, India knew the use of fragrance in architecture. Sandalwood was eminently suited for important entry-ways, not only for its scent but for its resistance to termites. Temples were termed "houses of fragrance" *(gandhakuti)*.

Cremation was the customary means of treating the body of the deceased since the high water table of the Gangetic plain made inter-ment in the soil hazardous; sandalwood, spices, and other aromatics were used to cover the odor of the cremation. Benares (Varanasi) was the most sacred site for such observances, so it is not surprising to find the capital of Indian perfumery, Ghazipur, located nearby, a little down-river and on the opposite side of the Ganges. Buddhists described the transit to the afterlife as the passage to the "fragrant mountain" *(gan-dhamadana)*.

A less solemn occasion in Indian life was the spring festival of Holi, when the normal rules of propriety were bent, and colored and scented waters were squirted through long tube syringes on all and sundry. This saturnalia is often depicted in all its color in the Indian miniatures.

The vendor of the materials used at either occasion, solemn or merry, was the *gandhika*, the "perfume dealer." Treatises dating to between 500 and 1000 A.D. could furnish him with concepts about the nature of odor and with more practical advice on the choice of materials. Gangadhara, author of one such early text, the *Gandhasara*, spoke of the trade in the following terms:

> This science of cosmetics and perfumery is helpful in the worship of gods; which requires the use of auspicious perfumes and in-cense; it contributes to the pleasures of men; it leads to the at-tainment of the three ends of human life (viz, religious merit, worldly prosperity and sensual enjoyment); it removes one's own poverty; it contributes to the pleasures of kings and it gives the highest delight to the minds of accomplished ladies.[3]

The *gandhika* plied his trade amid colorful and fragrant heaps of spices, gleaming fragments of gum benzoin, chips of sandalwood and agarwood, vetiver roots, and dried leaves of patchouli. They would be ground into powders, fashioned into pastes for joss sticks or macerated into vegetable oils for cosmetics. The Indian perfumer employed a kind of enfleurage by placing jasmine flowers amongst warm, hulled sesame seeds. Like the lard used in the West, the sesame seeds eventually acquired the odor of the flowers. Then the flowers were sifted out and the oil pressed. Sesame oil contains an "anti-rancidification factor," the full secrets of which have not yet been ascertained; it will last longer at room temperature than any other fixed oil. The most important use of this *Chameli ka tel*, jasmine oil, was to dress the hair, which has always been considered one of the finest ornaments of Indian women. Hair, like leather and other animal protein, has a great ability to retain scent, so tresses groomed with this jasmine oil would exude the scent for some time afterward. And since the hair was frequently washed, the oil prevented dryness and gave gloss.

Eyes were enhanced by mascara, and the dot placed between them (*ushnisha*) was made with sandalwood paste, which symbolized the gaze within.

Many scented flowers were made into garlands (*rasamala*) to be placed around the neck of the king, a deity, the bride and groom at a wedding, or an honored guest. The Indians, like the Hawaiians, made these garlands an inseparable part of their ceremonial life.

One use of aromatics, however, remains unique to India, namely, that of the *abhyanga*, or perfumed rubdown, given to the female elephant after her bath. This was confidently expected to inflame the bull elephant to passion and thus assure future generations of this great animal.

Just as Greece had a zone of influence beyond her true borders, known as *Magna Graecia*, the term "Greater India" refers to those countries to the south and east—Ceylon, Thailand, Cambodia, Burma, Sumatra, Java, and the "red lands" (Malaya)—that absorbed Indian culture and religion. Indian culture percolated down to these areas through the numerous traders who came from India in search of materials not found at home. The great temple of Borobadur at Java and the beauties of the dance at Bali testify to the Indianized cultures that grew up in Southeast Asia. Many native elites grew rich on the sale of cloves, gum benzoin, ginger, nutmeg, and patchouli. What was not available in India was therefore made available by trade, giving Hindu culture the world's fullest deck of aromatic substances with which to play.

* * *

THE AROMATICS OF INDIA

What were the aromatics of Indian culture? Pride of place must certainly go to a word derived from sandalwood (*chandana*), the Sanscrit word for the wood whose soft scent was said to induce the calm sought by all the spiritualities of India. It is only by coincidence that "sandalwood" resembles the English word "sandal," but the "wood" part is true enough, for the finely grained heartwood is the source of the essential oil. Sandalwood was one of India's earliest export commodities, valued equally in the Near and Far East.

Chandana is mentioned in the early epic poems, the *Mahabharata* and the *Ramayana* (the subject of the Balinese dances), and in the *Arthashastra* and the Buddhist *Dhammapada*—all dating before the Christian era. The source for *chandana* is *Santalum album*, a species found only in India and on the Indonesian island of Timor. Mysore State is the principal source of this fragrance plant, although the genus *Santalum* originally extended widely across the Indonesian islands, through Australia, and out into the Pacific atolls. However, the very aromaticity of these various sandalwoods proved their undoing, and today the cultivated plantations of Mysore are the world's greatest source of sandalwood.

The true sandalwood has one of the most unusual natural histories of any plant, as exotic as India itself. It is a hemiparasite, which means that although it is capable of photosynthesis, it must parasitize the roots of neighboring trees and plants for certain other nutrients. Nitrogen and phosphorus are ingested into the plant by means of octopus-like suckers called haustoria. Eventually this bleeding of the host results in its death, but it is a slow death. Over thirty species—among them teak, clove, bamboo, and the tropical guava tree—can nourish this vampire tree that yields such an exquisite perfume.

The growing of this crop is no easy matter for the essential oil appears only in a tree over twenty-five years old; a tree will be harvested only between the ages of thirty years and sixty years. One cannot say that such a tree will be simply "felled." A further process is used because the oil is in the roots as well as in the trunk and major branches. Indian loggers have learned to make an ally of the terrible white ant, the tropical termite. Since the heartwood is impervious to the ants' attack, the carcass that has been unearthed will be left to these insect hordes. They make quick work of the nonodorous sapwood and the bark and leave the valuable heartwood for man.

An ancient craft still practiced is the carving of statuettes and fine caskets from sandalwood. It is close-grained and works well without splitting, and the artifacts retain the scent indefinitely. The sawdust from these carvings is always collected to be used in powders and incense.

Sandalwood oil, which can be extracted from the wood by distillation, is India's great gift to modern perfumery. It has a soft, smooth fragrance with almost a hint of rosiness, and it is remarkably tenacious.

Another well-known Indian aromatic is vetiver, which in Sanscrit literature was called *reshira* or *sugandhimula*. The later name, *khus khus* or *khas*, is more familiar (though it has nothing to do with the homonym *couscous*, however, a cereal dish of North Africa). Vetiver is a member of the grass family, *Vetiveria zizanoides*, of a genus found only in the Old World. It grows mainly in the south of India in cultivated form, although wild plants are to be found right up to the Himalayan uplands. Unlike the somewhat neurotic growth habits of sandalwood, vetiver has no unusual tastes and has been successfully transplanted to many places in the tropics in recent centuries. But Southeast Asia, especially Java, remains one of the principal suppliers even today. There plants derive ultimately from stock introduced by Indian traders who reached Java as early as the fifth century A.D. The name for vetiver in Java is *akar wangi*, "fragrant root." Local rulers were fond of being cooled by large ceremonial fans of woven vetiver. The roots of vetiver, which are the source of its fragrance, are fine and wirelike, easily manipulated.

To create a quality fragrance, vetiver requires two years of growing time. Harvesting is done by raising the entire plant by pitchfork and vigorously shaking the dirt and stones from the roots. The roots are a light yellow, sometimes a reddish brown. Vetiver's scent is unique and is anything but "perfumey." It is pungent, green, reminiscent of roots, soil, and wood. Its greenness suggests coolness, which is probably why it was used in the screens that cooled windows and archways. Chemically, the essential oil that can be distilled from the roots is one of the most complex. In its pure state it is also one of the most viscous.

The French *Compagnie des Indes Orientales* in the eighteenth century brought vetiver to the colonies of Haiti and Louisiana. Creole belles adopted the custom of the ancient Indians, the vetiver fan.

Patchouli is another Indian aromatic that was long used in the culture of the region that produced it and has also become one of the key items in modern international perfumery. It is a tropical member of the mint family and it grows to about one meter high. Like vetiver, it too is grown throughout the tropics today. The name of this plant *(Pogostemon cablin, P. heyneanus)* is from the language of southern India, Tamil, *paccilai,* "green leaf."

The first European to encounter patchouli in the East Indies gave it the name *Melissa lotoria,* "balm of the bath." It was also used to ward off moths from carpets and fine woven goods as shawls and jackets. The leaves and stems, which turn quite brown upon drying, were chopped up and sprinkled among the fabrics. They could also be pulverized for incorporation into incense blends. Fine patchouli has a winelike, ethereal quality, deep and woody, spicy, almost dry and earthy. It is a haunting scent but, like vetiver, not a "pretty" one.

The screw pine, *Pandanus fascicularis,* or *P. odoratissimus,* produces a "flower" (actually the male spadix) that has a sweet, heavy fragrance. While this *kewda* was processed by enfleurage in sesame seeds, in recent times it has been successfully hydrodistilled. A mature plant produces fifteen to twenty flowers and is harvested during the warm summer months. The screw pine does well along the coast, and the eastern province of Orissa has been known for its production.

Costus is the modern trade name for the Sanscrit *kushta,* a root of *Saussurea lappa* in the daisy and chrysanthemum family. It is a tall plant, growing up to four meters and chiefly found in the higher regions of the country such as Kashmir and Uttar Pradesh, where it grows scattered among birches and willows. Like so many other aromatics, the root was valued as a drug as well as a fragrance, and it was exported to Iran and China, where it was believed to increase sexual activity. As they did with patchouli, Kashmiri shawl makers also used bits of the root as a deterrent for moths. Costus oil, when extracted, is extremely viscous; its odor is violetlike, cool and green, with some animal undertones. In modern perfumery the slightest amount of costus can lend a fascinating note to a composition. Traditionally costus was ground for use as incense. The odor is reminiscent of another root, orris.

The lower hills of the Himalayas, in both India and Nepal, produce the *Hedychium* genus, with thirty-eight species, *Hedychium spicatum* the one principally used in Indian perfumery. The root of this plant is dried and is known as *kapur-kachri,* an incense ingredient with a violet note. Visitors to Hawaii are familiar with the *Hedychium coronarium,* which has been introduced there and used as material for the making of leis— the fragrant "white ginger." The roots of a closely related species, *Alpinia officinarum*—with a spicy, ginger note—have been used for both fragrance and flavor. The oil is known as galangal. True ginger (*Zingiber officinale*) has a fragrance and a flavor that need no explanation. This spice was exported from India in Roman times; it is still as a flavor that it is known today. Nevertheless, traces of the oil from this root give interesting green-leaf nuances to oriental perfumes and to spice-type after-shave lotions.

Another aromatic not used at all in modern perfumery but famous to Westerners is spikenard, *Nardostachys jatamansi*, a member of the valerian family. The fragrance is slightly musky, with notes of patchouli and valerian. Spikenard was exported to the West in Roman times, and it was with a pound of this precious ointment that Mary Magdalene anointed the feet of Jesus. In local markets, spikenard is still sold in alabaster jars like the ancient one mentioned in John 12:3. The Magdalene thus won her role as patron saint of French perfumery—from medieval times onward, she was the patroness of the perfumery guild. Dioscorides called spikenard *gangitis*, "product of the Ganges." It had a reputation for combatting epilepsy, hysteria, and other convulsions, as well as for restoring hue to graying hair. Spikenard, like costus, is a product of the Himalayan foothills.

Gum benzoin was a balsam grown in the forests of Greater India—in Java, Sumatra, Cambodia, and Thailand; it is an exudation of two species of *Styrax, S. benzoin* and *S. tonkinense*. Both have a pleasant vanillalike note, but the latter variety is finer and sweeter. The resin is collected by wounding the bark of the trees and scraping the "almonds" that form with a scalpel made of sharpened bamboo. Amarasimha, the Indian lexicographer of the sixth century A.D., mentioned benzoin along with cloves; this was the first appearance of benzoin in world literature.

The Western names for this resin—gum benzoin and gum benjamin—come from a corruption of the Arabic word for the material, *luban jawi*, "incense of Java". Actually *luban* was frequently used for the most important incense, frankincense. Arab traders felt at home with this Eastern frankincense and conducted a brisk trade in it, purchasing supplies from the Hinduized monarchs of Southeast Asia and conveying the resin to the vast Chinese spice markets. Europeans who worked with Arab traders heard *luban jawi* and rendered it *banjawi, benji, benzoi, benzoin*, and *benjamin*. It had nothing to do with the biblical Benjamin; an unfamiliar expression was simply cast in terms of a more familiar one.

The East Indians used benzoin medicinally as well as for incense.

Even today doctors use tincture of benzoin in an inhalant to enable a patient to relieve and expectorate a "dry" cough. When diluted in alcohol, it fortifies the skin with a kind of glaze and so is used as a preparation for bandages with sticky adhesives that might otherwise tear the skin when removed.

Among the Malays, benzoin was used as a "holy smoke" to ward off devils, and it was burned at the rice-reaping ceremony. In India benzoin was burned before the Trimurti, the dramatic image made by combining the faces of Brahma, Creator of the world, Shiva, Destroyer of illusion, and Vishnu, Regenerator of the world.

Agarwood, derived from the Sanscrit *aguru*, has a long history that requires much untangling. It is often called "aloeswood," "lignaloes," or even "aloes," in addition to "agar." And so people confuse it with the familiar *Aloes vera*, grown as a common houseplant and used as a salve for burns, a plant with wonderful qualities but a distinctly rank odor. Agarwood is also confused with the *Aloes socotrana* and *Aloes perryi* (of Socotra Island off the Arabian coast), themselves ancient commodity items, valued as cathartics. Nor does agarwood have anything in common with "agar-agar," the seaweed used as a gel in laboratory experiments.

The agarwood mentioned in the sacred scriptures is a product of a tall evergreen tree, *Aquilaria agallocha*, found native to India, Burma, Southeast Asia, and the Philippines. Like sandalwood, it has an exotic twist, for only the diseased wood is fragrant. Normal agarwood is odorless until a fungus of the group *Imperfecti* attacks it, leaving dark, irregular patches charged with oleoresin. And normal agarwood is light in weight, but when it is affected by this pathogen, it becomes so heavy that it sinks in water. The Chinese name for the material is *ch'en hsiang*, "sinking fragrance," the Japanese *jinko*. This fungus infection is sometimes found in young trees under twenty years old, but it is more common in trees a half-century old or more. From time to time a botanical gold mine is found where the tissue under the bark has been entirely transformed into the precious agarwood. *Aquilaria* trees grow to a height of twenty-one meters. In the past, maharajas paid enormous prices for a section of this hard, rich-brown agarwood, the minutest sliver of which releases a pervasive perfume on an incense brazier. Today industrialists in Japan will pay comparable prices; the Japanese are great connoisseurs of incense, and *jinko* is the best. Agarwood has been used as a tonic and a carminative. It has the bitter taste of the

Socotra aloes; perhaps it was this common element that led to the confusion of names. In India the wood is also pulverized for use as a dusting powder in keeping insects away from the body and clothing.

The list of Indian aromatics is dizzying. Some are used only locally, but many of them have entered the international perfume and flavor markets. Cardamon (*Elettaria cardamomum*) takes its botanical name from the Sanscrit *ela* and was mentioned in the *Ayurvedic* (medical vedas) texts of the fourth century B.C. It was an export from as early as Hellenistic times. Up until recently, wild plants were sufficient to meet India's needs and for export, but the demand today has led to cultivated plantations. In India cardamon was much appreciated as a masticatory for consumption after a feast, and it enjoyed the reputation of being an aphrodisiac. It is said that the average Arab would rather forego rice than cardamon, which is used to flavor Turkish coffee. Cardamon has become one of the principal seasonings of Scandinavia. After saffron, cardamon holds the honor of being the world's most expensive spice.

Another Indian aromatic, not as renowned outside the subcontinent, is Indian basil, *tulsi (Ocimum sanctum)*, the herb sacred to Krishna, the pied piper of the soul. Although Krishna's shrine is at Vrindaban, homes all over the country maintain a plant of basil in his honor. *Davana* is *Artemisia pallens*, which has a strong penetrating oil. This is an export product, but the aromatic grass oils are far more important in terms of quantity: *Cymbopogon citratus*, lemongrass, *Cymbopogon martini*, palmarosa, and *Cymbopogon nardus*, citronella oil. An inferior form of *Cymbopogon martini* yields ginger-grass oil. These oils have been used for centuries in India, but their latest incarnation is as material for the modern soap industry. Ivory soap carries the scent of oil of citronella, a natural germicide, but it is only one of the better-known products to employ a grass oil. Citronella oil is also known for its ability to repel insects.

Musk has been known in India, although China has always been the principal supplier, for the musk deer inhabits the cool foothills of the Himalayas, in Indian as well as Chinese territory.

As well as fragrant woods, resins, grasses, and spices, flowers have long adorned Indic culture. Forty-three species of jasmine are found in India. This flower, the Hindi *chameli*, has been celebrated in Hindu verse; today it is celebrated in perfumery as "the king of the flowers," the rose, of course, being the queen. The perfume of this plant is inimitable, and a drop of true jasmine is usually added to soften a synthetic jasmine (which can now be made quite easily). Kashmir, at the border of India and Iran, is the original habitat of the jasmine. The Chinese words for the two types of jasmine indicate which came from which side of the border: *Jasminum officinale* was known as *ye-hsi-ming*, from the Arabic *yasmin*, from Persia. But the *Jasminum sambac* was *mo-li*, from the Sanscrit *mallika*. Both types are used in modern perfumery, but the former, in the *grandiflorum* variety, is more common in Europe, while the latter, with its pearl-like flowers, is used as the scent of jasmine tea in China. In India, Ghazipur has been famous for the cultivation of this flower. In France, the jasmine was first cultivated in Provence in 1548—a gift of the Arab trade network.

Another perfume flower of India is the *champaka (Michelia champaca)*, a close relative of our garden magnolias, which it closely resembles, but possessed of a strong, languorous, fruity-floral scent somewhat like the more well-known tropical perfume oil, ylang-ylang. The earliest mention of the champac is in the work of the grammarian Patanjali (ca. 150 A.D.). The flower was used in the making of leis, garlands for king, god, and goddess, and treated like jasmine in the enfleurage in sesame oil. The flower is cream-colored, but a blue champac is said to bloom in the empyrean before Brahma. Buddhist monks from India took the champac to China in the T'ang dynasty (618–905), and it became as popular there as in India. The flower has become a part of Chinese horticulture, and Chinese gourmets have long used it in tea, like jasmine.

The lotus *(Nelumbo nucifera)* is almost the symbol of India. The scent is sweet and fruity, with a suggestion of anise; both pink and white varieties have the perfume. Buddhism adopted the flower as a symbol of its *dharma* because although its roots are in the mire, it blooms pure and clear above the waters. Monks have carried this plant to every corner of Asia; its image has become a dominant one in Southeast Asian, Chinese, Korean, and Japanese art. The flower was used in *puja*, the offering of the devotee to a shrine, but it is too delicate and its blooming life is too short to permit its adoption for use in commercial extractive processes.

THE MUSLIM INFLUENCE

The Muslim presence in northern India had been constant since shortly after the death of Muhammed, first as merely a trading presence but after the year 1000 as a cultural presence. The greatest Muslim regime was that of the Mughuls, who set up their empire following the descent of Babur (Zahif ud-Din Babur, 1483–1530) into the plain of the Ganges in 1525. Babur claimed descent from the Mongols (hence the name "Mughul"). His homeland was in the region of Samarkand and Bukhara, and his reign saw a great fusion of Central Asian, Persian, and Arabic influences with the native Hindu culture.

Babur himself was a great lover of gardens—several famous gardens in Kabul and northern India owe their existence to him—and of the great floristic wealth of India. He was convinced that "from the exellencies of its sweet-scented flowers, one may prefer the fragrances of India to those of the flowers of the whole world. It has so many that nothing in the universe can be compared to them."[4]

The Great Mughuls disregarded the Muslim ban on representations of living things and adorned the marble of their buildings with bas-reliefs of lotuses, narcissi, roses, and countless other garden flowers. Mughul miniatures depicted scenes from Sa'adi's *Gulistan*, and the rose was introduced in every important center of the dynasty. Since Mughul times, rose attar has become an important scent among all Indians. An apocryphal account of the origins of this perfume is recorded in the *History of the Great Mughuls* by Muhammed Hakim and indicates the fondness of the rulers of India for the scent:

> The emperor's favorite sultana, called "Light of the World," resting languidly on his arm, was strolling through their garden perfumed with rose water, which ran along a small canal bordered by flowers, when she noticed that on that running water lay a light, semi-solid foam, which when it had been gathered and separated, was recognized as *attar*, that is to say, as essence of rose, which, in its maximum state of concentration produced the sweetest and most penetrating perfume ever known until that time.[5]

"Light of the World" was the capable empress, Nur Jehan Begum, strolling through the garden with Shah Jehangir. However, the extraction-of-rose oil well antedated this incident recounted of 1612. The Mughuls were extremely partial to this fragrance; the centers of production even now are in the cities of Delhi, Agra, and Aligarh, important foci of Mughul culture. Attar of rose was copiously employed in the imperial *hammans*, or baths.

Nur Jehan Begum also had a role in the creation of the famous garden of Shalimar in Kashmir. The site had long predated the Mughuls, for

King Pravarasena II had laid out the garden in the sixth century A.D., but it had since fallen into neglect. Nur Jehan Begum and Jehangir reworked and adorned the site and created Shalimar ("Abode of Love") as it is today. They introduced carnations, flowering orange trees, oleanders, almonds, peaches, narcissi, and roses as well as long pools, fountains, and pavilions. The Mughuls called Shalimar *Farah-Baksh*, "Bestower of Joy," and originated the famous saying in Persian: "If indeed there be a paradise upon earth, it is here, it is here, it is here!"

Eventually the tolerant and liberal interpretation of Islam, generously larded with borrowings from Hindu philosophy, was overthrown by the fanatic emperor Aurangzeb (1658–1707). He extirpated all Hindus from the Mughul civil service and declared war on all nonbelievers. With India in a civil war of Hindu against Muslim, the way was paved for the takeover of the subcontinent by the British East India Company. The Emperor Akbar (1560–1605) had had himself weighed at the public receptions called durbars in both gold and perfumes for distribution to his followers. For nearly a century and a half, this great wealth would be diverted away from India to the enrichment of England.

Shortly after independence from England in 1947, a series of eleven large volumes began to appear, entitled *The Wealth of India*.[6] The "wealth" consisted of those botanical and mineral riches that are unique to India and so important to world perfumery. Today, it is not uncommon to find modern stills and solvent extraction apparatus preparing high-tech extracts for the international industry within sight of the stalls of the ancient gandhikas making redolent attars, *agarbattis*, cosmetics, spices, and fragrant oils for the hair in ways that have remained unchanged for centuries.

China

Compared with the riot of materials found in India and Greater India, China's contribution to fragrance is modest. This does not mean to say that this huge area, dominating all of East Asia, had no native aromatics. It did. Its camphor, cassia, almost all of the citruses, the peach, and the apricot have played an important part in the story of perfumery. But the most important contribution to this story from China was the great fillip this populous market gave to the trade from the eighth through the fifteenth centuries. Not only was there an enormous and prosperous populace, but the culture stressed pleasant odors, creating avid consumers of whatever fragrances could be brought to their doors.

In addition, the sophistication of Chinese culture during the T'ang (618–905), Sung (960–1276), Yüan (Mongol) (1276–1368), and Ming (1368–1644) dynasties provided mankind in general with a number of technical advances that helped prepare for the emergence of the modern era. Paper, porcelain, printing, and alcohol are all used daily in the contemporary perfume industry, and all owe a considerable part of their development to work done in China during those four dynasties.

Let us begin this section by examining the aromatics that were native to China. Musk was widely distributed throughout the Chinese cultural area, principally in Szechwan near the Tibetan massif, and it showed up in other mountainous provinces in central and northern China as well. Musk is a product of the diminutive deer, *Moschus moschiferus*, which at one time ranged as far north as Lake Baikal. However, the animal was easy to stalk.

The camphor tree reaches a height of fifty feet at maturity (forty years), with a girth of twenty feet. Since it will not grow in northern China, the earliest Chinese dynasties did not know its use, but in the third century A.D., as emigration accelerated from the Yellow River to the Yangtze River valley, camphor became a part of Chinese civilization, with building, medical, and perfumery applications.

The camphor tree is extremely handsome, and there are several centuries-old trees standing in the famous gardens of Hangchow, Suchou, and in temple courts throughout Szechwan and the Yangtze valley. Hangchow boasts trees dating to the Sung dynasty, which predate Marco Polo's visit to that city (he called it Quinsai). The camphor leaves are lustrous and bright green, and the general habit of the tree is attractive. The leaves emit a camphor scent when crushed, and the seeds have a cardamon odor.

When people think of "camphor," moth-balls usually come to mind. The moth-ball odor is harsh, whereas natural camphor is fresh and almost tonic; it is also optically active—it will turn a plane of polarized light to the right—whereas synthetic camphor is not. Synthetic camphor can be obtained by the fractional distillation of petroleum and is about five hundred percent cheaper than the botanical.

Like oil of rose, camphor is slightly water soluble, more so than most essential oils. Thus it has been used in China as a gastric stimulant and a carminative in herbal tea form. It has also been added to wine and used in cooking. Camphor chicken is prepared by steeping the poultry in tea and then steaming it over camphor leaves. The Chinese also use it as an ingredient in firecracker manufacture.

Because camphorwood withstands the attacks of termites as does sandalwood, it was used in building elegant boiseries in palaces and lattice filigrees in temples, where elegance and durability were required. The rosaries of Buddhist monks and nuns were always fashioned out of this fine-grained, fragrant wood, which became more lustrous by repeated use. Sutra chests are often made of camphor as it deters insects from the books and scrolls, and clothes' cabinets are made of it for much the same reason. However, the Chinese believe that the fragrance has a deleterious effect on the strength of silks and will store only cottons in camphorwood chests.

The literati chose camphorwood for the rafters of the long arcades that allowed meditative rambles outside in all weather. The arcade (lang) at the Chinese Garden Court at the Metropolitan Museum of Art in New York City uses these camphor rafters. Camphorwood was also the chosen material for the enormous effigies of Buddha, such as the one at the Spiritual Grove Temple (Ling-yin ssu) at Hangchow, over fifty feet high and made of twenty-four blocks of camphor, and that at the Temple of Universal Peace at Ch'eng-te (Jehol), over sixty feet high and weighing a hundred and twenty-one tons.

Camphor has the special quality of forming a crystalline solid upon distillation; it is one of the few essential oils to become a solid at room temperature. Mint oil will do the same, forming menthol crystals above the fractions that remain liquid, and so will thyme. Orris oil will also form a solid. All of these solid oils were called "camphors" after the most common example of the type. We are uncertain as to the exact date of the Chinese distillation of camphor, but it was early. The ninth-century text of al-Kindi describes camphor distillation in the Arabic world, and it is likely that the Chinese who supplied the camphor were distilling it as well. An independent tradition of distillation grew up among the Chinese alchemists, coming slightly later than the distillation apparatus was developed among the Alexandrian alchemists. A "rainbow still" (kung teng) was an apparatus found from the Han dynasty (206 B.C. to 221 A.D.); it had an arc that may have served as a gooseneck for distilling camphor. It is possible that wet cloths were wrapped about the metal "rainbow" to cool and precipitate the vapors of camphor.

Almost any part of the camphor tree could be put into the still—

leaves, twigs, wood, or roots. The entire tree is made up of 1.2 percent essential oil. Pure camphor will form on the top of the condensing flask, but other fractions that remain liquid leak over and have a less ethereal, more medicinal odor. Normally cultivators simply top the tree for leaves and branches; felling the tree is done only for construction or massive carving projects.

Machilus nanmu is another fragrant Chinese wood. The Chinese word *nan-mu* means "southern wood," as the tree grows only in warm areas, principally in Szechwan. This wood has an odor reminiscent of cedar. Elegant paneling was made for the apartments of the Garden to Linger In (Liu Yüan) in Suchou and for the great audience hall at the Manchu "Palace for the Fleeing of the Heat" at Ch'eng-te. Mount O-mei, the sacred Buddhist mountain of the west, boasts many of these great trees, preserved for centuries by the monks.

The modern fragrance and flavor industry would be unthinkable without the next Chinese aromatic, the citruses. Walter T. Swingle, a United States Department of Agriculture botanist who did pioneer work in this genus, estimates that China has over five hundred, and possibly one thousand, species of citrus plants. Only the true citron (*Citrus medica*) is not of East Asian origin.

The *Citrus aurantium* of China gave us the Seville orange, which first reached the Mediterranean world in the tenth century (through the Arabs). The *Citrus sinensis* gave us the sweet valencia type (and from that, the naval orange). Tangerines, with their inimitable fragrance, are from the *Citrus nobilis* and *Citrus deliciosa*, also Chinese, and the kumquat is from a species of *Fortunella*. Lemons (*Citrus limonia*) probably originated in southern China or in Southeast Asia. It is hard to realize that all of these common fruits were completely unknown to the Greeks and Romans; there are no references to them in classical literature.

Citrus medica, var. foshan, is a peculiar-looking citron with elongated folds at the blossom end of the fruit that resemble fingers. The Chinese call it "Buddha's Hand" and are fond of this fruit, which they frequently set in a porcelain bowl to scent a room.

The earliest mention of citruses in world literature occurs in the *Nan-fang ts'ao mu (Trees and Plants of the South)* written around 300 A.D. by

Chi Han. He observed that citruses that had ants were good and those that lacked them were not. Over a millennium afterward, Swingle discovered that this was not a flight of fancy; the farmers of Canton used the ant *Oecophylla smaragdina*, which builds its nest in the trees, to feed off of various pests that attack the crop. The first known monograph devoted exclusively to the citrus fruits appeared in 1178, the *Citrus Chronicle (Chü lu)* written by the mandarin Han Yen-chih. Several others followed.

Also in the twelfth century, Chang Shih-nan described the placing of orange flowers in a burner and heating them until "drops of liquid collect like sweat." The distillate was then poured over agarwood and kept in a sealed porcelain jar to produce a fragrance "of extraordinary elegance." This was technically realistic, for orange blossoms, unlike most flowers except the rose, can withstand the heat of distillation. Orange-blossom oil has a delicacy and freshness that is far more flowered than the simple citrus note of the peel. In the trade today the generic name for this orange blossom oil is neroli. The sweet orange produces neroli Portugal, and the bitter orange of Seville produces neroli Bigarade, which is considered finer. The Arabs, and later the Italians, loved to use distilled orange blossoms in confectionary, and centuries later the same oil would be utilized in various eaux de cologne.

Cassia is another aromatic that has been taken up by international trade, but far more as a flavor than as a fragrance. Cassia oil is important for soft drinks of the cola variety. A drop of cassia oil in a mixture of lemon and limeade produces a taste resembling Coca-Cola. The tree that produces the bark, and hence the oil of cassia, is *Cinnamomum cassia*, a close relative of cinnamon. The taste of the two barks is very similar, and both are sold in quills. Cassia is much cheaper, however, and therefore suitable for mass-marketed products, but it grows only in China and contiguous parts of Vietnam.

Traditionally, cassia bark was ground into incense blends to be taken internally as a carminative, or it was used as a culinary seasoning. Modern perfumery uses cassia oil only as a blender in heavier perfumes, but it has been used in the famous Brown Windsor Soaps made by Yardley's of London.

Star anise *(Illicium verum)* is a Chinese spice derived from a stately evergreen that develops slowly but can reach a height of sixty feet. The

Osmanthus is a Chinese shrub which bears very small flowers with an intense and sweet odor. The plant was used for its fragrance by garden designers in China, and is today used for a costly floral absolute.

yellow flowers resemble a narcissus, but when the fruit ripens, it opens into an eight-pointed star, hence the name. A related species, *Illicium religiosum*, is so called because the tree is often planted in Buddhist groves. The leaves have a marked odor, and the fruits contain a toxin, hananomin, that discourages browsing animals from the sacred precincts. *Illicium verum* has a pleasant anise odor and is used in medicine and food. In perfumery it is used as a source of anethole, an important material in its own right.

The peach *(Prunus persica)* and apricot *(Prunus armeniaca)* both come from China. Their Latin names reveal the places where they were received by Western traders at the termini of the Silk Route from Cathay. Extracts of these fruits are used in flavor work, but their odors are referred to as "fruity," like the perfume Mitsouko by Guerlain. These peach and apricot notes are obtained by synthetics based on the structure of aldehydes found in the fruits.

A gardenia scent is commonly used to describe a perfume—full, floral, and heady—and yet this flower refuses to yield its perfume to any extractive process known. Modern gardenia scents are blends of many synthetic and natural materials. The sole method used for extracting fragrance from *Gardenia florida* is the ancient Chinese one of steeping it in tea leaves, which releases the scent in making the brew. Champac is also used in this way, and the petals of chrysanthemums (*Chrysanthemum hortorum*) are used as a tea in themselves.

To complete the list of Chinese products, we must mention an unusual animal source that gave the ancient Chinese a "shell aromatic." This was from a gastropod, *Eburna japonica*, whose opercula were extracted, ground, and dried. Another species, *Potamides micropterus*, was also used in making incense.

CHINA'S PART IN THE SPICE TRADE

Since China's cornucopia of scent materials was not as rich as that of India and the Indic lands—one T'ang dynasty writer said that China's aromatics were only "beggar's incense" by comparison—fragrances had to be imported. From the late 700s on, China had the wealth to buy and the superstructure to disseminate all the spices of the Indies. Arab traders were the first purveyors to the Chinese market and long remained so, but by the Sung dynasty, oceangoing junks were being built that placed some of this lucrative trade in Chinese hands.

Imported aromatics—from India, the South Seas, or Arabia—included sandalwood, agarwood, ambergris, nutmeg, clove, cardamon, gum benzoin, Borneos camphor (*Dryobalanops camphora*, from the archipelago but with an odor like camphor), patchouli, frankincense, and civet. Persian rosewater was a processed botanical that was popular among the Chinese elite, and so was the Indian jasmine oil that was processed with oil of sesame.

How did trade articles reach Cathay? The earliest artery was the Silk Route, which had been established during the Han dynasty so that silk could be transported to wealthy Romans. No one trader made the entire route; products were passed from post to post in relays. The Silk Route languished when the Han dynasty fell, not to mention the decline of the western empire at Rome, but it was revived during the T'ang dynasty in cooperation with Arab and Persian merchants. Ch'ang-an, the eastern terminus (modern Sian), was probably the most populous city on earth for the time; it had two million persons. Incense gums, jasmines, and attar of rose went to the court there, and musk and camphor were shipped west along with bolts of silk. The route skirted the Gobi and the Taklamakan deserts and then crossed the Pamirs, the "roof of the world."

Arab ships also left Basra, filled their holds with spices and sandal-wood in India and the Malayan archipelago, and skirted Vietnam to reach Canton, Chüan-chow, and Hangchow, the great ports of the East China Sea. The first such trip was accomplished as early as the rule of the second Abbassid caliph, al-Mansur. By the middle of the eighth century several embassies had been exchanged between the Chinese and the Abbassids. The contacts resulted in the Chinese assimilation of the Hindu zero system of counting and the Arabic adoption of the compass and the balanced stern rudder. By the eleventh century the Arab ships generally used the compass.

When the Chinese government finally decided to corner some of the lucrative spice trade for itself, its moves were dramatic. From 1130 to 1237 the navy grew from eleven squadrons with three thousand sailors to twenty squadrons with fifty thousand men. One contemporary wrote:

> The ships which sail the Southern Sea and south of it are like houses. When their sails are spread, they are like great clouds in the sky. Their rudders are several tens of feet long. A single ship carries several hundred men. It has stored on board a year's supply of grain.[7]

Some of these oceangoing junks had six masts and four decks; they often towed two or three large boats and could carry six thousand baskets of spices.

The imperial government attempted to create an official monopoly on all business with Southeast Asia and penalized officials who made deals with independent traders. By 1189 this policy had yielded rev-enues of sixty-five million strings of cash. Nevertheless, the Chinese "love of oddities," as one writer put it, was so great that the country suffered from a "cash famine." The government responded by printing special paper money, made with silk floss and even perfumed, but during the Sung dynasty imperial treasuries continued to decline. By 1279 the dynasty was taken by the victorious Mongols.

During the Yüan, or Mongol, dynasty, we find a revival of the Silk

Route and parallel paths to the West. Marco Polo was the most famous vistor to China during Mongol times; he reached the court of the Great Khan by one of the overland routes and returned to Venice through the myriad isles of the Malay archipelago. He saw for himself the spice-producing "7,448 islands" of the *Nan-hai*, putting to an end all European ambiguity about the sources of these wonderful products.

During the brief period when the Mongols controlled nearly the whole of Eurasia, the Republic of Genoa began negotiations with them in hopes of outflanking the Arab-Venetian monopoly on the spice trade. However, this great hope was dashed by the breakup of the *khanates* (jurisdiction of the khans) and the conversion of the Persian Ilkhanate to Islam. But, abortive as it was, the attempt had given Europe a glimpse of what it would be like to trade directly with the Far East, and that idea was never lost sight of.

When the native Chinese finally overthrew the Mongol domination and created the Ming (1368–1644) dynasty, they resuscitated the Sung effort to create a Chinese maritime empire. The second Ming ruler, Yung-lo, sent Cheng Ho (himself a Muslim) on a long voyage with a fleet of sixty-three ships through modern Indonesia, India, Persia, Arabia, and as far as Somalia in East Africa. Cheng Ho set up trade agreements with the rulers he encountered and made numerous observations about sea lanes and navigation. Unfortunately, however, Chinese trade was to come to an end shortly after this very successful expedition in the first years of the 1400s. The attacks from above the Great Wall led succeeding emperors to withdraw from trade abroad. Chinese were forbidden to leave home or even to communicate with foreigners. As a result, the Japanese began to harry the entire coast with piracy and the nation was isolated at a time when Europe was beginning to break out of its own isolation and enter the Asian trade. The export porcelains of the late Ming period were carried abroad by Arab and European vessels, not by Chinese.

SCENT AND CHINESE CULTURE

During these four dynasties the scholarly caste put the various aromatics to many uses:

> There was little clear-cut distinction among drugs, spices, perfumes and incenses—that is, among substances which nourish the body and those which nourish the spirit. . . . A man or woman of

the upper classes lived in clouds of incense and mists of perfume. The body was perfumed, the bath was scented, the costume was hung with sachets. The home was sweet-smelling, the office was fragrant, the temple was redolent of a thousand sweet-smelling balms and essences.[8]

However, Professor Kentaro Yamada, an author of several studies in Japanese on perfumery in East Asia, has emphasized that the Chinese and Japanese have always tended to perfume the environment more than the body itself. He believes there is a physiological basis for this marked difference to the development of perfumery in Europe, where scenting the body was so important. This seems to be confirmed by contemporary research in olfaction. The apocrine glands responsible for bodily odor are strikingly absent from the Chinese, somewhat more present among the Japanese, and almost completely lacking among the Koreans. Among Europeans, however, the apocrine glands under the arm are so dense that they almost form a round object. These glands feed directly into the shaft of the hair follicles. Also, bathing was common in East Asia whereas it was tabooed in the West for many centuries. The need for reodorizing the body itself was therefore greater in the West than in the East, explaining why, in addition to cultural preferences, the cultures of China, Japan, and Korea had a greater choice as to whether to perfume the person or to perfume the environment, and more frequently they chose the latter.

Incense in Chinese culture was primarily used as a part of religious ceremonies. Much of this was ascribable to Buddhism, which had come to China over the Silk Route and, to a lesser degree, by the sea routes. The central act of worship for the average temple-goer, then as now, was to light three sticks of incense, hold them in the hands, blow three times, place them in the incense burner before the image of Buddha or one of his bodhisattvas, and bow again, palms pressed together.

The Taoists, who believe that a great current, or stream of life (the Tao), pervades the world, were the products of a Chinese philosophy of life first formulated by Lao Tze and Chuang Tze in the fourth century B.C. They made great use of the native tradition of burning incense, which can be dated to the Shang dynasty in the Bronze Age (1766–1123 B.C.), and imitated and even surpassed the Buddhists in their enthusiasm for the newer uses of incense. The incense burner became the most important focus of the Taoist temples, greater than any image or placard:

Every liturgy starts with the lighting of the incense-burner (*fa lu*) and every liturgy ends with a return to it (*fu lu*). As the liturgical texts repeatedly say: "Whether within or beyond the Three Worlds, the Tao alone is worthy of worship; among the ten thousand rites, the burning of incense has the primacy.[9]

Memorials were then dispatched to the Court of Heaven. A mock near-tragedy was staged wherein the devils made a vain attempt to filch the hand-held incense burner (*shou lu*). However, the temple orchestra, to the accompaniment of firecrackers, stopped the theft with a great burst of noise, the officiants grabbed back the incense burner, and the disturbing demons were put in jail. Following this colorful to-do, the prayer at the final incensing begged the blessed ones to make appear that divine mushroom (*ling chih*), which brought with it heavenly qualities and the ability to live to an advanced age.

Taoism was fascinated by the process of transformation, and the changes of the seasons were a great source of wonder. Taoist alchemy sought transformation from man's mortal state to a kind of physical immortality, just as the fire transmuted the solid incense stick into the fragrance that rose from it.

Incense burners in China were usually tripod vessels made of bronze and filled with cinders that supported the sticks placed within. Another variety was the "hill censer," which had a round bottom burner but a perforated conical cap created to look like a mountain peak, with folds and gullies. When the incense was burned within, the smoke coiled around the "peaks," like mist rising from the mountain.

Massive incense stoves that looked like our potbellied coal stoves were also used in Chinese temples and palaces, and the type was introduced by the Chinese missionary monks to Japan. These blended both forms: They were often tripodal but had a perforated lid on top. Unlike potbellied stoves, the burners were cast in bronze, some of them superlative examples of the foundryman's art. Hand-held censers were also used, as noted above, and they closely resembled those held before the gods in ancient Egypt.

Taoist practitioners were aware of the hallucinogenic properties of marijuana (*Cannabis sativa, C. indica*). One herbal states that if one takes the drug over a long period of time, "one can communicate with the spirits and one's body becomes light," (a sign of increasing immortality).[10] It seems that in addition to aromatic botanicals, psychoac-

Bronze incense-burner at the Lama Temple, Peking. Buddhists usually employed fragrant pine woods, sandalwood, camphor, and imported spices in such burners. The more unorthodox Taoists, however, were known to add the flowering tops of marijuana as well.

tive botanicals were tossed into the incense burner as well. The smoke induced reveries, no doubt, and helped the adepts in their transformations: "For those who begin practising the Tao it is not necessary to go into the mountains. . . . Some with purifying incense and sprinkling and sweeping are also able to call down the Perfected Immortals."[11] One liturgical text repeated the injunction, "Don't look away!"—very likely to make the most of the hallucinogenic emanations.

MAKING AND USING INCENSE

The process of blending the less exotic, day-to-day incense blends was more complex than simply strewing grains of incense resin on hot coals, as was done in western Asia. The first step in the East Asian method was to collect the various scented woods, gum resins, spices, and dried leaves and pulverize them in a mortar and pestle. When the work was done on a larger scale, a foot-operated mill was employed. In addition to the above materials, gum arabic, pine resin, the inner bark of the elm (*Ulmus campestris*), and the leaves of *Perilla frutescens*, sawdust from cedars and other conifers, and sometimes saltpeter were also ground with the mixture to aid in the burning or in the making of a paste. Saltpeter (potassium nitrate) acted as an efflorescence on decaying organic wastes and produced an even burn. It was also an ingredient in firecrackers and gunpowder. The dried powder of all ingredients was then sifted through a silk screen to ensure uniform particle size, and water, wine, or alcohol was added to make a paste of workable consistency. Sometimes the paste was simply worked into small cones that burned from the tip down; monks were branded as followers of Buddha by letting a cone burn down to the shaven forehead of the candidate for ordination. This ceremony was called "receiving the fire," and if the monk proved unworthy of his vows, he would have to undergo the ceremony once again.

But the most common form of making incense in East Asia was to extrude the paste through holes in a drawplate under pressure. This was the same technology the Chinese used in making noodles. The strands thus produced could be left straight or formed into a spiral while still moist. The straight sticks were the "joss sticks" held by the devout in worshiping the image of Buddha; the spirals were left to hang in the air like mobiles, turning in the slightest breeze. Incense was also cast in the shape of a certain character from the Chinese alphabet, especially *shou*, "long life," or *fu*, "happiness." Or else the paste would be pressed into a shallow mold that was carved in an elaborate abstract maze. Such "incense seals," as they were called, would burn if lit and placed on a bed of ashes. Sometimes a segment of such a maze would indicate that an hour had passed, and notches were set into joss sticks for the same time-keeping purpose. These "incense clocks" were fairly reliable if kept away from drafts because so much care was given to ensuring uniform particle size. Incense clocks served miners, monks engaged in evening meditations, and those who sought to keep track of night watches on board ship. Joss sticks were also placed in a horizontal trough of metal and a thread placed at the appropriate notch. Two balls were connected to the thread, and would clang down into a metal dish when the fuse burned its way to the desired hour. This was one of the world's first alarm clocks. Pere Magalhaens (1611-1677) noted these horological uses of incense sticks and called them "an invention worthy of the marvelous industry of this nation" and said that "this method of measuring time is so accurate and certain that no one has ever noted a considerable error."[12]

Another practical use of incensing was to incorporate rue *(Ruta graveolens)*, pyrethrum, and the *Illicium religiosum* mentioned above into the smoke as a fumigant to destroy bookworms and other insect pests in libraries and rooms.

The Chinese used incense for purely aesthetic reasons too. Clothes were perfumed by means of special braziers, and camphor and juniper-seed oil were used in making inks so that when the ink stick was wetted for use, the scent would be released. Even paper was sometimes fragranced. The Chinese scholar enjoyed those correspondences between scent, form, texture, and color in the materials that surrounded him at his study. On a larger scale, the arrangement of the garden was designed so that pavilions would be situated at particularly redolent microenvironments, such as downwind from a lotus pond or in a grove of pines.

Women used many cosmetic oils that had been scented; the bases were sesame, rapeseed, or tea oils (from the *Camellia oleifera*). Sachets were worn in the folds of garments, and in the T'ang dynasty a dance was performed that included the pelting of the spectators with perfumed sachets.

When the folding fan was introduced into China from Japan in the Ming dynasty, the custom developed of making the ribs of the fan from the fragrant sandalwood. The close grain of this wood permitted intricate cutout work, resembling the craft of the Chinese ivory workers.

Chinese extruded incense coil burning before a female deity in the Tibetan tantric style. Such sculptural, hanging incense pieces are common in Chinese temples—this one is cast as an abstraction of a fish, which is a symbol of enlightenment since its eyes never close. Pans below catch the ashes, which are then collected to anchor upright incense (joss) sticks.

Aromatics formed a separate category in the monumental compendiums of Chinese medicine, the *Great Herbal* of Li Shih-chen and the *Pen Ts'au Kang Mu* of 1578. Over thirty aromatics were import goods. The carminative powers of the essential-oil plants were recognized, and the aromatherapeutic effects of these plants were also appreciated.

The Chinese scented alcoholic beverages with cassia, citrus peel, herbs, and the petals of the Chinese *Rosa banksia*. From the T'ang dynasty on, the cuisine was also improved by incorporating many spices and flavorings. The monk I Ching, who traveled throughout India and Greater India in search of Buddhist scriptures, complained that "in China people of the present time eat fish and vegetables mostly uncooked; no Indians do this. All vegetables are to be well cooked and to be eaten after mixing with the asafoetida, clarified butter, oil, or any spice."[13] Needless to say, his complaints fell upon ready ears, for the raw fish and vegetables have now been changed into the countless sauces and seasonings of Chinese haute cuisine.

TRADE, TECHNOLOGY, AND THE SCENT MARKET

Progress in perfumery went hand in hand with technological progress. Paper was invented around 100 A.D., and its importance to perfumery can hardly be overstated. Since the times of the great dynasties, paper has been used as a vehicle of fragrance; the use of paper specie has greatly lightened world commerce, paper artwork has advertised perfumes, and paper labels have identified them. *Cartonnage*, the art of boxing perfume products, is another corollary of this invention. The ancient papyrus of the Egyptian was obtained by simply pressing the pith of the papyrus sedge *(Cyperus papyrus)*, a process that basically made a kind of pressed felt out of the vegetable fiber. But in papermaking the fibers of bamboo and mulberry bark were broken and separated by pounding and then allowed to meld freely in a vat of cellulose "soup." After this, a fine silk mesh was drawn up through the mixture, and the fibers and the glues and sizings that had been added were pressed dry and the screen removed. The fibers were then rearranged, and the membrane thus formed was bound together by a myriad of combinations. Chinese and later Japanese craftsmen worked out a variety of materials that could be made into paper, giving nuances of color and texture that are studied even today by Western package designers.

The first paper mill outside China was set up in Samarkand in 751, on the border of the Persian and Chinese cultural areas. Eventually paper wholly replaced the use of parchment in Persia, and by 1190 a paper mill was opened in Herault, France.

Printing was another breakthrough that accelerated the exchange of trade and ideas. Block printing dates from the ninth century in China, movable type from the next century, and the first movable metal type appeared in Korea in 1403. The entire Taoist canon was set into print in 1019 during the Sung dynasty, at a time when printing had become the rule rather than the exception for official documents in China.

Porcelain was another Chinese discovery brought to perfection in the Sung dynasty. Porcelain made wonderful containers for aromatic products because it is as nonreactive as glass.

The Chinese also made a great improvement in distillation technique by isolating the step that extracted the ethyl alcohol from wine. This was the cooling of the condenser by means of cold water. Taoist alchemists had perfected stills for the sublimation of cinnabar by the time of Sun Ssu-miao (581–ca. 673), and it was probably soon after that that a water cooler was attached to the still head to improve upon merely atmospheric cooling of the vapors. It is uncertain as to whether or not the Chinese regularly used this technique before the time of the Mongols, but it seems likely that alcoholic solutions of at least forty percent ethanol were being extracted. But the lead even this level of sophistication gave the European alchemists was invaluable. The cooler was known to them as a "Moor's Head" condenser, probably indicating both the turban shape of the condenser and the cultural route of transmission. The condenser improved their experiments with water cooling, which culminated, as we shall see, in the regular production of alcohol of high proof.

Another Chinese contribution to science was the publication of a series of monographs, or treatises, called *p'u*. These elegant but accurate studies of various plants, products, and processes began to appear during the Sung dynasty. The *Chih p'u*, for example, was a study of paper and paper manufacture; the earliest known *p'u*, however, was that of Su I-chien at the end of the tenth century. We have already mentioned the *Citrus Chronicle*, the world's first monograph on that genus; there were serveral *Hsiang P'u*, treatises on incense making; the earliest of these studies we have in its entirety is that of Hung Chu, about 1115. Many others followed in the next dynasties, culminating in the lengthy *Records of Incense* by Chou Chia-chou of the Ming dynasty, written between 1618 and 1641.

Related studies done around the same time included Ch'en Ching-i's encyclopedia of botany, done in the thirteenth century, and Chao Ju-kua's *Notes on the Various Countries Overseas (Chu-fan-chih)*, an important work on the various products (mostly aromatic) imported from the South Seas, with observations about the country of origin of each. As a result of all this writing, botanical illustration was advanced; Swingle considered the woodcuts done for an herbal of 1159 to be "far better than most European herbals of the fifteenth and sixteenth centuries."[14]

In the thirteenth, fourteenth, and early fifteenth centuries China ranged out into the sea lanes. Somalia, the source of ambergris for Chinese temples and the court, was known to Chao Ju-kua. But there were movements toward the East from Europe as well. Andrew, the Christian "Bishop of Zayton," wrote his compatriots in Europe that this distant civilization surpassed credibility:

As to wealth and splendor of this Court and its Emperor, the size of his dominions, the multitude of his subjects, the number of his cities, the peace and order of his realm, I will attempt no description, for it would seem incredible.[15]

Marco Polo described Hangchow as "the greatest city which may be found in the world, where so many pleasures may be found that one fancies himself to be in Paradise."[16] Not one, but ten markets supplied this city, while at the southern ports along the coast, Odoric of Pordenone declared, "It is something hard to believe when you hear of, or even see, the vast scale of the shipping in these parts."[17]

These descriptions gave Europe a vision of other ways of living, of a highly urbane civilization, and an awareness of an enormously rich market beyond the Arab world. It was not too long before the geographical and political barriers that separated the antipodes were to be overcome.

Japan

The refinements of Chinese culture were carried across the East China Sea to the Land of the Rising Sun by numerous Ch'an (Zen) monks and trade delegations. China made contact with Japan at intervals from as early as the Han dynasty, but the real Chinese influence on Japanese culture began in the T'ang dynasty and continued through the Sung dynasties. However, the Japanese were not simply containers into which another culture was poured. Everything they imported—the style of writing, art, papermaking, horticulture, and architecture—they adapted and created anew, placing their own stamp upon it.

Thus many of the Japanese fragrances will be familiar, although transformed: We find the burning of incense before the great temples, and within, each image is wreathed in the smoke of the joss sticks burned before it. We also find scented powders, the use of cosmetic oils, and perfumed sachets hidden among the kimono folds. Camphor trees, as in China, were cultivated and venerated; indeed, one camphor at the Hachiman Shrine in Kagoshim Prefecture is over twelve hundred years old.

But more uniquely Japanese are such things as the *inros*. These were diminutive lacquer cases, often with tiers attached one to another by a silken cord, that were hung on a clasp in the kimono. In them one might find perfumes, medicines, aromatics for inhaling, or whatever was small but possessed a distinct effect. These cases were exquisitely designed, their very delicacy forcing a dramatic compression of design element. The modern perfume Opium was packaged in a container modeled on one of these *inros*. The *fusego* was a special rack created to hold the kimono while it was steeped in fragrant smoke, and the *kohmakura* was a headrest from which fragrance emanated to perfume the hair of a court lady.

Japanese craftspeople have created dramatic expressions in lacquer, porcelain, and other materials for the storing of scents, medicines, and cosmetics. The inro *was such a box hung within the kimono by silk cords; its design has been the inspiration for the Opium package and of several other perfume containers. This cosmetic box* (te-bako) *was designed by Mizuuchi Kyohei (1910–). From the collection of Elaine Ehrenkranz. Illustrated in* A Sprinkling of Gold, *by Barbra Teri Okada.*

Japanese designers fashioned scent and cosmetic boxes with dramatic artistry. Highly stylized representations of plants were used in gold, as accents to the black lacquer body of the individual pieces. Shown here are the peony (Peonia suffroticosa), *pine needles* (Pinus species), *the Chinese plum blossom* (Prunus mume), *the chrysanthemum* (Chyrsanthemum x morifolium) *and the wisteria* (Wisteria japonica, *and* W. sinensis).

The Japanese also adopted the incense clock; in one clever variation they put the taper horizontally in a wooden box with chimneys set at regular intervals so that one could tell the time by a glance at which chimney the smoke was issuing from. It is believed that the Japanese even made tapers with different blends along an hour's interval so that simply sniffing the air would inform them of the approximate time. Geishas were paid by the number of incense sticks that had to be lit by the proprietor during a girl's engagement with a client. By the nineteenth century, however, less poetic methods of reckoning were adopted. Our familiar timepieces were introduced by the Portuguese missionary, Francis Xavier, but especially in geisha houses, incense clocks remained in use until 1854.

Lady Murasaki (whose name means "wisteria") left later generations a shimmering vision of the elegant life of Kyoto in her *World of the Shining Prince*, the *Tale of Genji*, written sometime between 967 and

1068. In Volume 4 of the Waley translation we read about "incense parties" typical of the Heian Period, where two players "listened" to different types of fragrances and discussed the qualities and characteristics of each. This evolved into the *kumikoh*, or "grouping" of incense, where a literary scene was conjured up by experiencing two or more incense types and olfaction slid into revelry and fantasy. In the Muromachi period of the seventeenth and eighteenth centuries, schools of incense culture *(koh-do)* developed to give instructions on the personal and group use of incense to cultivate discipline and values. The Oiye-ryu school was founded by the courtiers of the imperial family, and the Shino-ryu by the samurai.

"Incense games" were another highly disciplined use of aromatics wherein participants would try to correctly identify different materials on a tally sheet. The tally sheets were made of beautifully designed papers, and the boxes that kept them and the other appurtenances of the game were also attractive in themselves. Porcelain containers held the slivers of the materials to be guessed. The aromatics were either of native pine and cedar or of the precious exotics, such as sandalwood and agarwood from the South Seas. The former were called *wagikoh*, the latter the *kohboku*.

Adepts of incense culture claimed that its virtues included communication with the transcendent, purification of body and mind, peace in turmoil, companionship, and alertness. Today a Japanese cosmetic company, Shiseido, has given a perfume form to all these virtues, subsumed under the name Zen (1965).

6

Europe:
The Rise of Perfumery
in the Late Middle Ages,
the Sixteenth and
Seventeenth Centuries

We shall now look at the unfolding of perfumery in the West as it began at the close of the Dark Ages in Europe and continued into the industry we know today. What were some of the landmarks in that development? The earliest was the final solution of the secret of alcohol by the technologists of southern Europe around 1200. The basis for this critical breakthrough was the ancient still of the Alexandrian alchemists, which had been perfected by succeeding generations of Arab and Chinese technologists.

A second landmark was the galaxy of technical studies that appeared during the early Renaissance on all subjects related to our theme—distillation, botany, chemistry, and glassmaking. And the advances made by one were soon the advances made by all because printing had recently come into its own in Europe. Northern and western Europe became as fully erudite in technical arts as only southern Europe had previously been.

The third development was the quickening of the pulse of trade; this began as a result of bypassing the old Arab network and discovering a truly European road to the riches of the Indies: the southern route around Africa. Marco Polo's description of the rich Chinese market and the identity of the spice-producing islands of the Malayan archipelago whetted Europe's appetite, which was only made keener by the innumerable delays created by man or nature. When the path was finally forged, Dutch, British, French, and Scandinavian traders soon followed the route of the pioneering Portuguese.

The fourth factor in the growth of perfume's popularity in the West was the new humanism ushered in by the Renaissance. Adorning the body and celebrating the glory of man were no longer unusual concepts. The nobility of the human condition, which had been preached by the Neoplatonists of the Academy of the Medici at Florence, was taken up by thinkers throughout Italy and then absorbed by the French, who followed François I on his sojourn in Italy. The rest of Europe was not slow to fall in step. The growing capitalism of the Renaissance also assured the ability to buy whatever could be had from the rich sources of supplies made available by the new ocean lanes. The New World provided many such products, but far more came from the wealth of India and greater India. Even so, New World gold, which had given capitalism such a boost, certainly helped to purchase these aromatics.

By the end of the seventeenth century, Western alcoholic perfumery, the form that is most characteristic of the industry today, was well on its way. The eighteenth and nineteenth centuries saw only further expansion and ramification, and the twentieth century has witnessed a veritable explosion of products, processes, materials, packages, forms, and vehicles of scent.

Having outlined the scope of this development in broad strokes, let us return to its origins and carefully retrace the story of the birth of Western perfumery.

We left the story of Western perfumery with the world of the Romans. When that world tottered and fell in the fifth century A.D., precious little of the civilized arts remained. What was left was certainly not perfumery directly, but the vestiges of medicine and pharmacy retained by the monks in cloistered gardens during the sixth through the eleventh centuries. These exquisite spaces, borrowed from the *atrium,* or enclosed court, of the ancient Roman villas, were oases of peace and order in an otherwise violent and chaotic world. Monks and nuns tended classical herbs such as bay laurel, basil, sage and the sclary sage *(Salvia sclarea)* that is so important today in perfumes, lavender, dill, thyme, rosemary, valerian, chamomile, pennyroyal *(Mentha pulegium),* spearmint, and peppermint. Most of these herbs were reserved for healing, for not only was perfumery not practised but even ornamental horticulture was of the most rudimentary kind. Sclary sage, for example, received its name for its supposed ability to clarify sight, from the Latin *clarus,* "clear." Two early treatments of these herbs were the work of Odo, Abbot of Beauprai, *De Viribus Herbarum* ("On the Powers of Herbs"), and the *Causae et Curae* ("Causes [of Illness] and Cures") of Saint Hildegarde, Abbesse of Bingen (1098–1179). Her highest praise went to lavender, that most European of all perfumery plants. The modern European love affair with this plant—with its tonic lifting, herbal-floral scent—truly began at the very dawn of modern times.

But the difficult Dark Ages of the post-classical era were to end; a series of events known as the Crusades focused Europe's attention on the more technically advanced East. The wars of religion that followed the First Crusade in 1096 did not convert anyone, but by serendipity Europe received an invaluable schooling in medicine, pharmacy, chemistry, commerce, and perfumery. The Crusades were a dramatic cross-cultural contact between Europe and the Arab world, although the percolation northward and westward had begun even earlier. Spain was divided for centuries, and the marauding knights became enamored of the fine gloves scented with citrus, rose, and musk that the Moors made so well. *(Peau d'Espagne* is still a fragrance note of perfumes based on this accord.) Sicily and southern Italy were other places of sporadic Arab settlement and trade.

In Salerno, a Benedictine monastery was transformed into a university, founded, according to tradition, by Salernus, an Italian, Pontus, a Greek, Adale, an Arab, and Elinus, a Jew. Whether or not these men actually founded the University of Salerno, the story is an accurate portrayal of the cultural melding in the region at the time of its founding (1090). The school soon received a guest teacher, Constantinus Africanus, an Arab of Baghdad, who had sojourned in northern Africa and eventually in Italy. He began lecturing in pharmacy and medicine, and the important herbal, *Circa Instans,* is believed to represent his notes as collected and developed by Matthaeus Platearius. The *Antidotarium Magnum,* another early manual of plants with active elements, also drew

upon the teaching of Constantinus. At the end of his life he became a
Benedictine monk and died at the ancient abbey of Monte Cassino.

The Europeans proved to be ready learners. Platearius is known to
have made translations of Arab pharmacological works around 1150,
and Gerard of Cremona translated ar-Razi. At the end of the twelfth
century, Alfred of Sarshel translated ibn-Sina, the pharmacist known
to the Europeans as Avicenna.

The Breakthrough in Distillation

When was alcohol first extracted by these students of Arab science? It
is not mentioned in the *Circa Instans*, but it is mentioned in the work
of the Magister Salernus, who flourished at the University of Salerno
between 1130 and 1160. Albert the Great, a scholar and saint who
lived between 1193 and 1280, gave instructions for the making of this
new substance, which he described by a reference to a very old one.
"When wine is sublimed like rose water, a light, inflammable liquid is
obtained."

Imagine seeing alcohol for the first time! What could one call it? The
closest thing it resembled was water since it was colorless, of a similar
viscosity and weight, and could be taken internally. And yet since it
was obviously different, a number of qualifiers were added to this
"water" by the dazzled technologists who had succeeded in obtaining
it: alcohol was the "admirable" water, "burning" water, water "of wine,"
water "of life." It was also the "quintessence," that fifth essence that
complemented water, air, fire, and earth, the "prime essence," "subtle
spirit," "spirit of the wine," "vegetal quicksilver," and "soul of heaven."
Many of these terms derived from the great Spaniard, Raimundo Lull
(1235–1315), who studied Arabic for nine years and was convinced
that the newly acquired substance was a veritable panacea. Another
Catalan, John of Rupecissa (mid-fourteenth century), is credited with
the word "quintessentia." Albert the Great had even used the term "oil
of wine" to indicate that it would burn, as would the fatty oils. The
word we use most commonly is "alcohol," although "water" has per-
sisted in perfumery, surviving in *eau de cologne* and in toilet "water."
The earliest use of the word "alcohol"; (in the writings of the great
Salernitan, Arnold of Villanova) was in conjunction with *vini; alcohol
vini* was the "finest essence of the wine" retrieved by distillation.

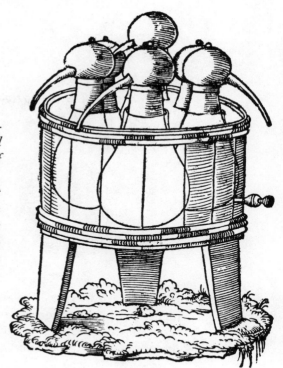

The Renaissance witnessed an explosion of interest in technical processes; distillation was one of the most primary of these concerns. Here a water-bath is used to heat six stills. From Adam Lonitzer's Herbal *of 1577, published at Frankfort. Courtesy of the Rare Book Collection, The New York Botanical Garden*

The trick, of course, was the efficient water-cooling device. The Chinese suggestion of the "Moor's Head" cooling cap for the still had been changed into a bucket filled with constantly running cold water into which the leadoff tube of the still had been fitted by coiling it. The first mention of this "serpentine" (or "worm" or "coil") occurred in the writings of Michael Savonarola (1384–1464), grandfather of the reformer, but the device was known considerably earlier. He also wrote about the need to insulate the process well, known as "luting" from the Latin *luteum*, meaning "mud." Savonarola described multiple distillations ("cohobation") as well.

These pioneers would usually distill the wine once, which would yield a solution of sixty percent alcohol, and then redistill it, producing alcohol that was ninety-five percent pure. One hundred percent alcohol was impossible at that time as ethanol is hydroscopic and would absorb about five percent water from the atmosphere itself.

This "admirable water" was a success from the very start. Cardinal Vitalis de Furno declared it to be a "panacea" for all ills, and every

A woodcut of a Renaissance galley-oven, where one heat source fires many small stills—a technique practiced extensively among the Islamic producers of rose water and transmitted to the Italians who were the carriers of Arabic science to Europe.

pharmaceutical school began busily distilling this cure. All the ancient medicinal herbs inherited from the classical world and preserved by the abbeys and convents could be steeped in this solution to produce the numerous liqueurs and cordials of the monks and nuns. Initally, of course, they were for medicinal purposes only, but it was not long before Italian merchants began the manufacture of a *rosoglio*, a liqueur flavored with oil of rose and sweetened with that Arabian import, sugar. The Black Death created a great surge of interest in alcohol because it was recognized that although water might become tainted, alcohol was germicidal and would not. It was not long before the labors of apothecaries were replaced by professional suppliers of alcohol. The earliest such industry was at Modena in 1320, and Venice followed shortly thereafter.

Improvements in distillation, which made the vehicle of perfume possible, also helped in the extraction of the essential oils, the source of perfume. Large plantations of lavender, roses, and sage were set up in Burgundy in the fourteenth century, and by 1370 perfume in the modern sense appeared. This combination of essential oils and alcohol, known as "Hungary Water," was named after Queen Elizabeth of Hungary. It was based upon oil of rosemary but was later reinforced and sweetened by the addition of oil of lavender. The legend that went along with the first perfume will probably accompany the last: The hermit who presented the fragrance to the queen assured her that it would preserve her great beauty unimpaired until her death. Perhaps it was true, for at the age of seventy-two, Queen Elizabeth was asked in marriage by the king of Poland.

A second early perfume was the eau de Carmes, compounded in 1379 by the nuns of the Abbaye St. Juste for Charles V of France. *Melissa officinalis* ("balm"), angelica, and other herbal oils went into this Carmelite Water. Lavender Water was a third such perfume, potable, and almost indistinguishable from a liqueur. Early perfumes freshened the outside of the body (greatly needed in Europe, where bathing was viewed as dangerous to body and soul) and the inside as well.

Salerno's greatest "daughter" university was that of Montpellier in southern France, which soon became Europe's second center of pharmacy. At the end of the Middle Ages, so many learned Spaniards, Christians and Jews came to this mecca of learning that it was called

Lavender has always been one of the most popular of the European herbs. Its name derives from the Latin lavare, *"to wash." It was associated with Roman baths and, later, with storage of freshly washed linens. Large stills, such as this one from the* Book of Perfumery, *by Septimus Piesse (1891) are necessary for the great amounts of oil extracted from the true lavender and the lavandin hybrids.*

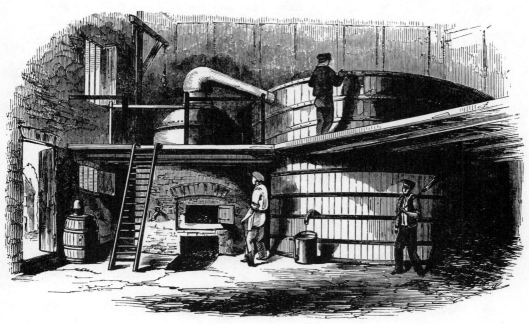

the Mozarabic university. The gentle climate of Languedoc permitted the cultivation of the full repertory of Mediterranean herbs, and their strong and bracing odors filled the atmosphere around the town. Grasse, farther to the east, was later to become the definitive capital of perfumery, but during the late Middle Ages and until the eighteenth century, aromatics and "scents from Montpellier" *(senteurs en odeur de Montpellier)* were synonymous.

Distillation was still unperfected, however, and in the late fourteenth or early fifteenth century the *Libellus de Distillatione Philosophica (Book on Intelligent Distilling)* noted that tinctures of herbs in alcohol are impervious to decay, and it gave the advice (not always followed) that herbs should not be distilled in vessels of lead. The "hermetic" sealing of the apparatus should be observed so that the precious essences would not volatilize in the process.

An early distilled oil was the herb of grace, rue *(Ruta graveolens),* with its pungent cat-spray odor. Soon cinnamon was also placed in stills. By the sixteenth century, pine, frankincense, gum mastic, costus, cedarwood, benzoin, and sweet flag *(Acorus calamus)* had all been put in the still. Between 1500 and 1540 the list increased to include agarwood, anise, cardamon, fennel, nutmeg, mace, pepper, sandalwood, and juniper. And during the seventeenth century the list was rounded out with ambergris, thyme, asafoetida, coriander, dill, labdanum, marjoram, mint, carrot seed, cloves, orris, ginger, saffron, and wormwood *(Artemisia absinthum).*

In the Renaissance, distilling was furthered by the publication of Hieronymus Brunschwig's magisterial *Liber de arte Distillandi de Simplicibus,* his handbook for the distiller, which described the tools of the trade and the wealth of plant materials that might be placed in the still. The final section detailed which ailment could be cured by which distillate. Although Brunschwig lived between 1450 and 1534, the ancient *Emerald Tablet* guided his work. In the old English of its first translation (1527): "Dystyllyng is none other thynge, but onely a puryfyeng of the grosse from the subtyll, and the subtyll from the grosse."[1] Encouraged by the reception of his first work, Brunschwig brought out a second, his *Liber de Arte Distillandi de Compositis,* with even more illustrations of laboratory equipment and herbs. Distillers differentiated between his two publications as the "Big Book" and the earlier "Small Book." The "Big Book" went through six hundred and eight editions appearing in every European language and spreading the news of how

Brueghel-like scene of the herb garden in Hieronymus Brunschwigk's Liber de Arte Distillandi, *published at Strassburg in* 1500. *To distillers, this important work was simply* "The Small Book of Distillation," *but was so successful that it was followed in* 1519 *by* "The Big Book of Distillation."

to distill lavender, rosemary, pine, and Brunschwigk's own special combination of clove, cinnamon, gum mastic, and frankincense.

Western science was next enlightened by the fiery Theophrastus Bambastus von Hehnheim, called Paracelsus (1493–1541), who revolutionized both medicine and alchemy by diverting the latter away from its lingering interest in changing lead into gold and opening up the former to the materials and tools used by the alchemists. Paracelsus was the Martin Luther of medicine, castigating in rude and unflattering language those in the medical profession who merely followed the texts of the ancient Greek and Roman herbalists and would not test their materials and processes by experience. "Let him not belong to another who may be his own," was his motto.[2]

Philip Ulstad and Walter Reiff continued to study distillation. Reiff noted that lavender oil was imported into Germany from France "in small bottles and sold at a high price."[3] Valerius Cordus (1515–1544) noted the distinction between fixed and essential oils (*oleum terrestre* and *oleum aereum*, "earthly" and "heavenly" oils). He noted that oil of clove will sink below the water distilled with it, unlike most oils, which would swim on top. Both oils were distilled in a Florentine flask, a device that had a leadoff spout for the oil that separated from the water.

Two Italian names are of great importance in this period of intellectual awakening. Piero Andrea Mattioli (1500–1572) left a most accurate *Commentary* on the ancient herbalist Dioscorides in which he surveyed the medicinal, fragrance, and cosmetic potentials of countless herbs and imported spices; an appendix contained a special section on distilling. Giovanni Battista della Porta (1537–1615) was a follower of both Brunschwigk and Paracelsus. His wonderful *Magia Naturalis* (*Natural Magic*) appeared in two installments, one in 1558 and one in 1569. His work included a section on distilling and one on perfume-making. Della Porta was the first to measure the yield of essential oil from a particular plant; he was aware of the contamination of oils by improper equipment and advocated the use of glassware because it was nonreactive.

The Rise of Glassmaking

In the sixteenth and seventeenth centuries, Italy was the acknowledged leader in glass technology. Georg Bauer (1490–1555), who wrote under the Latin name of Agricola, included sections on glassmaking in his

Distillation of the essential oils, and their packaging were dependent on the development of the glass-maker's craft. In the Renaissance, the most advanced lab-ware was to be found in Italy, where the Venetians had something of a monopoly on the trade. However, as individual craftsmen escaped their virtual prison on the island of Murano, advanced techniques appeared in Bohemia, France, and England. A glass still from Poncelet's Chymie du Goût et de l'Odorat, *1766. From the Collection of Florence Wall*

authoritative study of metals, *De Re Metallica*; his glass oven could be recognized by a glassmaker of today. But the first study devoted entirely to this art was *L'Arte Vetraria* (ca. 1612) by the Florentine, Antonio Neri. Venice was the glassmaking center. Her commerce with the East had introduced her to the glassblowing techniques developed in Syria and Egypt. The fact that the local industry that arose was centered on the island of Murano had two advantages: The flames of the furnaces

Italian pharmacy jar (albarello) *of the sixteenth century, for* syroppo violatto, *the syrup of violets. The turbaned head indicates the role of such Italian city-states as Venice and Genoa as middle-men between the Islamic East and northern Europe. At the time of the Renaissance, Italy possessed both the largest supply of aromatics in Europe and the most advanced means of processing them. Such* albarelli *were flared at top and bottom to prevent being dropped when taken from or replaced on the pharmacists' shelves. The form was borrowed from the Arabic world. Courtesy of The Metropolitan Museum of Art, Gift of William B. Osgood Field, 1902*

could be kept safely away from the main part of the city and the craftsmen could be kept practically under house arrest, thereby preventing the tricks of the trade from leaking out to the competition. Glassmaking materials could be found nearby: the silica came from crushed quartz pebbles of the River Ticino, and the flux came from the saltwort *(Salsola soda)* that grew around the Adriatic beaches. The Venetians employed a two-to-one ratio of the crushed pebbles (or white sand) and the glass salt obtained by burning the soda plants. The result was an extremely transparent and easily shaped substance—the fine *cristallo* of Murano. Since Roman times, glass had been blown through an iron tube, but the Venetian craftsmen brought it to heights it had not yet reached. Glass was available for perfumes, for the Paracelsan herbal extracts, and for Porta's labware.

Despite heavy penalties, Venetian glassmakers did escape from Murano, and their style (*façon de Venise*) was taken to France, Germany, and Bohemia. Because northern glassmakers did not have access to the Adriatic and Mediterranean plants, they used ashes of the beech tree or the bracken fern to flux the molten sand. As a result, northern glass tended to have a more gemlike, less fluid look than the Venetian glass.

By the end of the seventeenth century, English technologists perfected lead, or "flint," glass, brought about in part by the need to switch from wood to coal (because of deforestation). Coal allowed a higher heat, and the glass produced in this way had a high index of refraction and could be wheel cut or deeply engraved without breaking. Flint glass also shipped well and with less breakage than the more fragile *cristallo*.

The Romance and Intrigue of the Spice Trade

At this point let us consider the relation of European trade to the sources of supplies that lay outside its region, far to the east in India and the East Indies. And let us look also at the story of the ever-quickening commerce between the two areas.

During the late medieval period, Italy monopolized the trade that had developed with the Eastern world as a consequence of the Crusades. Amalfi, Pisa, Genoa, and Venice all competed for control of this lucrative trade. After the battle at Chioggia (1380), Venice had bested Genoa and emerged as undisputed Queen of the Sea.

Venetian trade was not always pretty. Frequently deals were made with local potentates that undermined the battles of their fellow Christian Crusaders; adulteration of goods was far from unknown; and the Venetians played a great part in the slave trade whereby Circassian boys were shipped to Egypt to become cadets in the army of the Mamluks. Since new recruits, not heirs, were critical, the Venetian trade to southern Russia was always assured.

But it was the spice trade that was the real source of revenue for the Venetians. What were "spices"? This was a catchall term for any ware that was sold in small quantities at high prices, not simply the culinary "spices" of today. Aromatics and medicines were important among these "minute spices," as they were called, but the term embraced even such unlikely "spices" as cotton, tin, ivory, and silk. The *Practica della*

Fourteenth-century bowl bearing the inscription, "Of what was made by order of the Imam, the High, the Mamluk, the Amir the Great, the Wise, the Leonine, Sayf ad-din, the Eternal, the Victorious King." Such bowls served for storage of spices or for lustrations with rose water. The Mamluks in Egypt controlled the flow of Indian and East Indian aromatics westward, often charging mark-ups of as much as 300%. Their trade partners were the Venetians, who united with them in all attempts to block efforts by other European powers to break their joint monopoly on the spice trade. Courtesy of The Metropolitan Museum of Art, Bequest of Edward C. Moore, 1891

Mercatura (Practice of Business) of Francesco Pegolotti, written between 1310 and 1340, lists the following "spices":

anise	fennel
ambergris	ginger
rosewater	spikenard
balsam	frankincense
cinnamon	agarwood
cassia	musk
cardamons	mastic
cumin	nutmegs
camphor	olive oil
paper	pepper
sweet flag	pine resin
costus	sandalwood
citrons	sugar fragranced with rose and
cloves	violets[4]

Once the Venetian galleys had met the caravans at Aleppo or Alexandria, they would transport their wares back to Europe, where an ever-widening network of commerce was ready to receive them. Several guilds handled the aromatics thus brought into Europe: the Pepperers, a guild chartered as early as the eleventh century; the Grocers (so called from the Italian *peso grosso*, the standard weight of commerce); the Spicers; the Apothecaries; the Perfumers (chartered in 1190); and the Glovers. The latter, recognized as a *corporation* at Paris in 1268, were concerned with fragrance materials because the tanning process made use of nitrogenous wastes, which were so malodorous they made reodorizing the gloves and leather goods a necessity.

In the eleventh century Pope Sylvester II had introduced the Indo-Arabic system of numeral notation, and in the thirteenth century the Tuscans developed double-entry bookkeeping. Paper letters of credit became common, another factor in speeding the rate of trade.

The flood of rural workers into the growing cities of Venice, Florence, Genoa, Paris, Cologne, and London created vast problems of contam-

The wealth of India, so highly coveted by the various European East India companies. From left to right: *clove buds, cinnamon quills, chips of sandalwood, nutmegs, and vetiver root.*

ination, and the Plague created an even greater demand for Arab spices. One of the standard means of purifying a city was the burning of spices in a public square to "disinfect" the city. Although essential oils are powerful germicides and the principle was not that farfetched, diffusing of minute quantities of essential oils over the filth of a late medieval city was to no avail. Nonetheless, Venetians rushed to fill orders for these cleansing aromatics; their Flanders Fleet rounded Gibraltar in the 1300s to bring spices to Sandwich, London, Southampton, Sluys, and Antwerp. The merchandise was transported by galleys, each with two hundred oarsmen protected by a large company of archers.

But although demand for those goods had never been higher and the trading system never better, supplies suddenly dried up. The problem was the Mongol juggernaut; it wreaked havoc with the Muslim trade routes that in turn emptied into the Venetian routes. The two Polos set out to Cathay to encounter the source of this great change in trade. They thought that perhaps they could avoid the Muslim middleman: even the Venetians knew that the Mamluks often placed a three-hundred percent markup on goods sold to Europeans.

The Genoese, who hated the Venetian-Mamluk alliance, openly courted the khan in Persia for a Genoese-Mongol connection. Neither trading partner was Muslim—might they not have something in common? Genoese hopes, however, were soon dashed by the conversion of the Persian Ilkhanate to Islam. But both their envoys and the Polos had learned a great deal more about the source of the precious imports in the lands beyond the Arabs. And although Europe now knew more than ever about where spices came from, its merchants still could not lay hands on them.

PORTUGAL'S NEW ROUTE

The end of this East-West trading impasse came from a particularly unlikely quarter, Portugal. Prince Henry the Navigator, son of a Portuguese father and an English mother (Philippa of Lancaster), set up a shipyard and a school for navigation on the Bay of Lagos in southwestern Portugal. He studied the writings of Marco Polo and the Italian *portolani*, the trade maps made by the merchant republics "in order to find a new way to India," since it seemed to him that if he or some other lord did not gain that knowledge, no mariners or merchants would ever dare to attempt it, "for it is clear that such would never trouble to sail

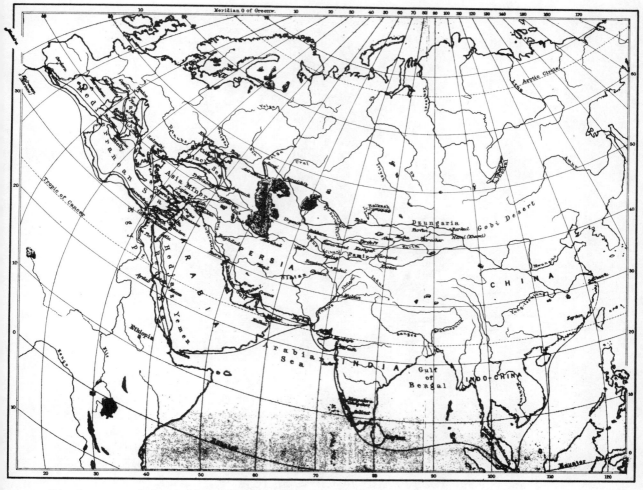

Trade routes of the medieval and early Renaissance spice routes to the East. From Hoffman, F. and Gildemeister, E., The Volatile Oils

to a place where there is not a sure and certain hope of profit. And seeing that no other prince took any pains in the matter, he sent his own ships to those parts."[5]

Farther and farther around the bulge of West Africa went the Portuguese caravels. Prince Henry died before the decisive rounding of the cape of Storms (renamed by the king the Cape of Good Hope) by Bartolomeo Diaz. Finally, in 1497, Vasco da Gama set sail for India, bringing a definitive climax to Portugal's long effort to connect the

The East India companies of Portugal, Holland, France, and Great Britain sought spices, tea, silks, and porcelain from the Orient. Seventeenth- and eighteenth-century ships were broad-beamed in order to carry great loads and to sustain the recoil from their cannon. In the nineteenth century, the armaments were reduced, allowing the design of the streamlined clipper ships. Shown here is a British vessel, c. 1775. From Edwin Tunis, Oars, Sails and Steam, *World Publishing, Cleveland, 1952*

Atlantic with the sources of supply in the Indian Ocean. Da Gama used a heavier ship than the first exploratory caravels, and he had taken aboard an Indian pilot at Malindi who taught him how to harness the monsoon winds for a swift and easy passage. He reached Calicut, the most important trading city on the western coast, on May 20, 1498, to the cheering cry of his sailors, *"Christos e espiciarias!"* "For Christ and spices!" The ship stayed three months in India, loading up with cloves, cinnamon, ginger, pepper, benzoin, and an abundance of gems. He returned to Lisbon with a king's ransom. The news hit Venice like a bombshell. Its stock market fell, and envoys were immediately sent to Egypt to plot with their allies the destruction of their new rival.

In 1508, Khansu al-Ghawri, a former slave, took Venice's suggestion and sent his fleets to do battle with the interloper in the Indian Ocean. The great sea battle at Chaul, off the northwestern coast, resulted in an overwhelming victory for Portugal, whose fleet was commanded by Dom Francisco de Almeida. When the last Flander's Fleet reached England in 1509, it was ridiculed for its paltriness of supplies; Venice had practically nothing to sell, whereas, in Lisbon, nutmegs were said to roll in the streets. The center of trade had made a decisive shift—from the Mediterranean, where it had rested for centuries, to the Atlantic, where it still remains.

Almeida's successor as viceroy of the Indies was Affonso d'Albuquerque; he pushed opportunity still farther. The port of Goa was taken in 1510, then Ceylon with its cinnamon forests, and in 1511, Malacca, key entry to the innumerable islands of the East Indies. Commercial treaties were negotiated with Bengal, Burma, Siam, and finally with China, who had withdrawn from its former activity in the South Seas. Only the Arabs remained to compete for the spice trade, and although these ancient traders remained as a local force, their ancient grip on commerce at the heart of Eurasia was broken.

The New World was never as important as an acquisition for European spice traders as were the East Indies. The Portuguese King Affonso V had briefly considered a plan by the Italian geographer

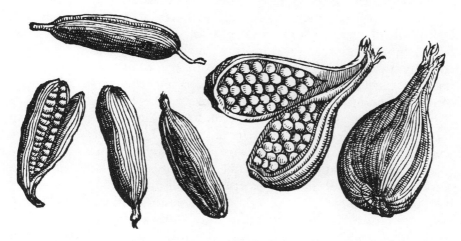

Cardamon, as depicted in the herbal of the Venetian, Andrea Matthioli. Cardamon is a spice native to India, where the grains are chewed as an aromatic breath-freshener. From the Commentary on Dioscorides, *1568. Courtesy of The Rare Book Collection, The New York Botanical Garden*

Toscanelli, who offered him "a shorter way of going by sea to the land of spices than that which you are now making by Guinea."[6] As we know, the Portuguese rejected this idea, and it was later taken up by Christopher Columbus and offered to the Spanish.

Columbus hoped to reach the islands that Marco Polo said supplied the vast market of China. The Indies he found, however, were the West, not the East Indies; they were rich in food plants but somewhat poor in aromatics. Vanilla, the tuberose, balsam of tolu, balsam of Peru, bay oil (used in bay rum), amyris (called West Indian sandalwood), copal, which had been burned by the Mayans as incense, and allspice were some of the major aromatics of the New World. They were not as important as the corn, beans, potato, and tomato that so changed the European diet. Tobacco was another New World botanical that was touted in Europe as a fumigant against plague; even children were encouraged to inhale it in times of pestilence. The plant riches of the New World have not been fully explored, however. It might well be that the huge Amazonian flora contains valuable aromatics.

But it is the East that remains the center of the spice trade drama. The Portuguese king had appropriated the grandiloquent title of "Lord of the Conquest, Navigation and Commerce of India, Ethiopia, Arabia, and Persia," and clearly the Portuguese trade was important business. It is estimated that by the end of the sixteenth century three million pounds of pepper alone had been imported into Europe. Such doubling and trebling of the amounts of available spices made experimentation by the distillers and apothecaries possible, and although prices went down, more uses for spices were being found. Spices were critical commodities, for although Indian cottons and gems were traded, silk manufacture had already been introduced into the West, and spices remained the most common form of currency.

However, the skill that the Portuguese had shown in exploring and capturing new lands was soon to fail them. In the last half of the sixteenth century, many areas were very badly administered. There were outbreaks against Portuguese cruelty in Ceylon, Malacca, and in the Spice Islands. Rumors of Portuguese mismanagement and awareness of the high stakes involved brought another Atlantic power into the ring, Holland. The Portuguese were suspicious of their northern rivals and guarded trade secrets jealously, but an unsuspected loophole gave the Dutch the secrets they needed to enter the competition. It happened that a young Dutch boy had a hankering for distant places, and at the age of seventeen, Jan Huyghen van Linschoten left home to find work in Portugal in a trading firm. In 1583 he obtained an appointment as a clerk to a prelate who was leaving for the Indies to become Archbishop of Goa. For four years Linschoten observed everything he could—the rich life of Goa, where all religions were allowed and Portuguese women were carried through the streets like maharanis; the sources of the spices that poured into the city; and the paths of the sea lanes that brought them to Lisbon—and on his return, he collected and published his impressions in his *Itinerary*. The Portuguese, despite their cruelty and carelessness elsewhere, had achieved certain things in Goa, nearly the size of London. Intermarriage was practiced between Indian and Portuguese; the Crown supported a hospital; the Jesuits had established a university, but coercion was not used to win converts.

The first European inventory of India's plant wealth was taken in Goa in 1563: Garcia da Orta's *Colloquies on the Simples and Drugs of India*, which put to rest any lingering European doubts about the origin of any aromatic. But what really caught the attention of the Dutch was Linschoten's verification of the enormous wealth to be made in East Indian spices.

THE DUTCH MONOPOLY ON THE SPICE TRADE

Wealthy capitalists in Amsterdam organized the Company of the Far Countries *(Compagnie van Veer)*, which sent four ships to Java. The venture was not a financial success, but the second attempt, in 1598, was. The Dutch government intervened to grant a monopoly to the newly organized East India Company in 1602 so that individual merchants would not undercut one another and the Dutch attack on the Portuguese monopoly could be mounted by a united front of merchants from Amsterdam, Delft, Rotterdam, and Zeeland. The strategy was to gradually oust the Portuguese from as many trading posts as possible and to oblige all local Indonesian rulers to grant the Dutch exclusive trading rights to their spices. Force would back up this policy wherever needed.

In March of 1609 a powerful fleet arrived at the island of Neira in the nutmeg-producing Banda Islands and demanded the right to construct a fort to command the harbor. When the Indonesians refused, preferring to maintain their independence as they had with Chinese, Arab, and even Portuguese buyers, the Dutch landed an army of twelve hundred men and built the fort by force. The same tactics were followed from Achin on the tip of Sumatra to Ternate and Tidore in the Moluccas.

Britain, next, entered the fray. Lured by accounts of the spice riches of the Indonesian islands, several ships of London's East India Company entered waters which the Dutch now considered theirs. Like the Portuguese, they would pay the price asked by the islanders (whereas the Dutch would only pay half). Hostilities broke out and the Indonesians sided with the British. But the Governor General Jan Pieters-zoon Coen vowed to end British interference in the growing Dutch monopoly and break native resistance. The two East India companies engaged in a series of naval confrontations; English traders were tortured at Amboina in 1623, and by 1681 the entire Indonesian archipelago was under Dutch control. The remaining Portuguese outposts had been taken, one by one—Malacca in 1651, the Celebes in 1660, and even Ceylon in 1658. East Indians who dared trade with Portuguese, British, Arab, or Chinese merchants were beaten and tortured. Even nature was controlled, by the forcible uprooting of all nutmegs except for those allowed to grow on Banda and all clove trees except for those at Amboina. This ensured the Dutch monopoly and allowed the manipulation of prices.

The Dutch monopoly of the spice plants continued until the French adventurer Pierre Poivre (1719–1786) was able to spirit plants away at great risk and transport them to French colonies in the Indian Ocean and the West Indies. The Dutch political rule had none of the *laisser-vivre* of the Portuguese in Goa; their strict control of the islanders ensured Dutch rule until the Japanese invasion of Southeast Asia in World War II. By that time great fortunes had been made for Dutch investors: even within the first six years of the East India Company's founding in 1602, investors were receiving from twenty-five to thirty percent annual return.

Dutch superiority was not simply the result of derring-do. The East Indiamen were the most technically advanced carriers of the seventeenth century. Dutch shipwrights used windmills to power saws that turned out uniform planks and spars, cut to precise specifications. Every fitting was tested to bear the stresses of the long ocean voyage from Holland to South Africa and out to the distant Indies. This expertise made Dutch shipbuilding faster and more accurate than the hit-or-miss manufacture prevalent in England, France, and elsewhere.

A Dutch ship, its many flags flying high, was indeed a masterpiece of workmanship and a joy to behold. However, on board all was not romance. Sailors relieved themselves in any corner of the vessel. The crew was compressed between decks into tight quarters that were unventilated when the hatches had to be closed in rough weather. At times there was so little oxygen in their quarters that a candle refused to burn. The Company had to rely on *zielverkoopers* ("sellers of souls") in order to sign or lure ignorant peasants or urban derelicts into the spice trade; it was extremely grudging on the amount of food permitted the crews; and keelhauling, lashing, and other severe punishments were permitted. One Dutch veteran of the spice trade declared that transporting the aromatics of the East was truly work "suitable for convicts."

The Dutch rout of the British in the East Indies was so successful that John Company knew it would have to find greener pastures elsewhere. The target was not long in presenting itself in India; although the country was rich and powerful, it had real internal weaknesses that could be exploited. The fanatical hunting of Hindus and nonorthodox Muslims set the stage for the British takeover of this wealthy empire. By patience, bribes, force, and skillfully pitting one faction against another, the British succeeded in winning an enormous spice empire for itself by the eighteenth century.

FRENCH INVOLVEMENT

Would France, which had an important Atlantic coastland, remain out of this lucrative race for the wealth of the East? Conflicts at home had precluded the French entry into the competition until the time of Louis XIV, and yet there was great reason for France to enter the arena: The French courtly style of life had made France Europe's greatest consumer of spices and aromatics. When Jean-Baptiste Colbert pointed out this incongruity to the young monarch, the twenty-six-year-old king gave him leave in 1664 to charter the *Compagnie des Indes Orientales*. Colbert set up a port for the oriental trade on the Bay of Biscay, which he called Lorient; he bamboozled funds from reluctant financiers; and he proceeded to raid the Dutch East India Company for pilots and sailors. Because he offered the men better pay and better working conditions than they were getting, he soon had all the crew he needed. The venture was a success. By the second quarter of the eighteenth century, nineteen ships a year went East and France was second only to England in Indian trading. Great plantings of aromatics were established on the Île-de-France and the island of Bourbon in the Indian

Ocean. The former is now the British Mauritius, and the revolutionaries of 1789 renamed the latter Réunion. But the perfume trade still retains the old names in the shipments of patchouli "Bourbon," oil of vetiver "Bourbon," and vanilla "Bourbon." Poivre's raid on the Dutch plantations had much enriched the offerings of these islands.

Colbert was an indulgent godfather to the French perfume industry, which was beginning to take its first steps at this time. He gave it certain trade protection by his *Ordonnance* of 1673, and he gave it steady sources of supplies of those tropical crops that could not be grown in even the warmest parts of France.

The fruits of the great seafaring explorations of the nations on the Atlantic coast of Europe were preserved in a number of writings that took stock of the plant wealth of the newly discovered lands. We have mentioned Linschoten's *Itinerary* and da Orta's great study of Indian medicines. European interest in the East and the spice trade yielded other catalogs as well. F. Martin left *"Une Description et Remarque de Quelques Animaux, Epiceries, Drogues, Aromatiques et Fruits que se trouvent aux Indes,"* published in 1609; Francois Pyrard left a *Discours du Voyage* (1611) on southern India; Fr. Michael Boym made a *Flora Sinensis* (1656), based on his observations around Macao; and Nicolas Monardes, a Seville physician, cataloged the plant wealth of the New World.

The Influence of the Spice Trade at Home

What were the effects of this growing trade with the East? From the late Middle Ages onwards, we find a growing development of the European sense of style and refinement, leading eventually to the brilliant growth of the modern European perfume industry.

Since Venice led Europe in the number of contacts with the East, it is not surprising that it was there that we first find this increasing refinement of manners. One observer noted that in the city:

> Everything was scented, gloves, shoes, stockings, shirts and even coins. As if this were not enough, people kept objects made of scented pastes on their persons and held ambergris crowns in their hands, bone cups with perfumes . . . not out of devoutness but for pleasure.[7]

Italian pomander, opening in eight sections. This piece is from the seventeenth century, done in a style common to the preceding two centuries. The section visible reads "Neroli," which is still the term used in the fragrance industry for the distilled oil of orange blossoms. Other openings are inscribed for mace and caraway seed, though ambergris was one of the most commonly used aromatics in such pendants—the word "pomander" is derived from pomme d'ambre. *Such pomanders were kept by physicians and confessors who ministered to victims of the plague. Courtesy of The Metropolitan Museum of Art, Gift of Mrs. Arthur Curtis James, 1920*

Silversmiths wrought elegant orbs that they filled with musk or ambergris. From the French words for these objects, we call them today "pomanders"—*pommes de musc* and *pommes d'ambre*. Ladies wore these pendants among the cut-velvet sleeves that were the fashion in Venice during the late medieval period. Potpourris were blended from the herbs grown in apothecary gardens. Diners cleaned their hands with scented waters, until the custom of the knife and fork came into general use in Italy in the sixteenth century.

With the dawning of the Renaissance, Italy retained her lead in perfumes and cosmetics. Leonardo performed experiments with infusions of flowers and herbs in *acquarzente* at the court of Ludovico il Moro at Milan. He also attempted experiments with the enfleurage of orange blossoms in almonds, pressing the nuts to create a perfumed oil, much as the Indian perfumer pressed sesame. Jasmine, oranges, and roses had been introduced into Italy by this time as a result of the long trade with the East.

Rosewater was as popular in Italy as it had been in Persia. The Medici patronized the Monastery of Santa Maria Novella, famous for its fragrant preparations. The Frangipani family (*frangere*, "break," *panis*, "bread"), who had sold the bread to the Papal See, became renowned for their distinct perfume. Giovanni Roseto published his *Secreti Notandissimi dell'Arte Profumatoria* (1555) for the enrichment "of body

DE' SECRETI
DEL REVERENDO
DONNO ALESSIO
PIEMONTESE,
PRIMA PARTE.
CON LA SVA TAVOLA
Per trouar le ricette con ogni commodità.

In 1557 Ruscelli of Viterbo published his Secrets of the Reverend Father Alexis the Piedmontese, *"for both soul and body," at Venice. This was one of the many manuals of beauty which began to appear in the sixteenth century in Italy. From the collection of Florence Wall*

and soul," and in 1557 Ruscelli of Viterbo published *The Secrets of the Reverend Father Alessio Piemontese* in six books, a work expressly on perfumes, later reprinted in Milan, Paris, Lyon, Rouen, Antwerp, and London. In her *Experimenta* (published at Forli in 1525), Caterina Sforza described the scents she had compounded; Isabella Cortese published her *Secreti* in 1561 at Venice; and the *prima donna*, Isabella d'Este, described her fragrances in her collected letters. The pharmacists who served the Medici possessed the richest stock of formulae known anywhere in the early Renaissance.

Botanicals were stored in handsome majolica pots from centers of production such as Urbino, Faenza, and Savona, and waters were kept in phials of Venetian glass. Genoa and Bologna were centers of soap production, and by the end of the sixteenth century tobacco from the New World was being perfumed and ground for snuff in Florence. Another Italian specialty was the mixing of ground gum resins and spices with clay to hold flowers at a banquet; these were called *buccheri*.

France was not wholly without sophistication in these matters. Nobles had employed *coussines*, small sachets worn in the clothing, and made *oyselets de chypre*, fragrant molds much like the *buccheri*. In general,

Silver ecclesiastical censer, Italian, eighteenth century. Originally, the early Christians hesitated to make use of incense in their liturgy because of its associations with the state cults, but this puritanism eventually passed away, and incensing became an important part of Byzantine and Roman ceremonies. In the West, however, the condemnation of scent in church was revived by the reformers of the sixteenth century. Church incense continues to use exactly the same clean and resinous-smelling aromatics as used by the ancient Greeks and Romans—Arabian frankincense and myrrh. Courtesy of The Metropolitan Museum of Art, Gift of William C. Breed by exchange and Gift of Irwin Untermyer, by exchange, 1980

The flower and full plant of the Florentine iris. Northern Italy has been a center of the cultivation of this plant since Renaissance times. From George Nicholson, Illustrated Dictionary of Gardening, *London, 1888*

however, French skill and finesse lagged far behind those of Italy in the sixteenth century. But the momentous sojourn of François I in Italy, culminating in his capture at Pavia in 1525, led to an "Italianization" of all aspects of French culture. On his return, the Italian taste in arts, cosmetics, gardens, and architecture took the country by storm. The king had negotiated with the Medici Pope Clement VII for the marriage of his son Henri II to the Pope's niece, Caterina. The marriage took place in 1533, and this led to a second wave of Italian influence. Caterina brought with her all the arts of the Florentines. Her perfumer, Renato Bianco, joined her in Paris and set up a shop on the Pont au Change, and her alchemist Cosimo Ruggiero made her powders—and most likely her poisons (arsenic was the poison of choice among the Medici).

Henri IV (1553–1610) resisted the new Italian ways, which he considered foppish, but contemporaries said of the king that "he stank like carrion." Europe continued to resist bathing. Part of the reluctance came from a fear of colds and fever; the climate in France, England, and Germany is not that of Baghdad. Perhaps the scourge of syphilis, one of the drawbacks of the globalization of trade at this time, had its effect as well, along with the fear of water-spread contagion since bathing was still conceived of as a public practice.

Nevertheless, the movement toward better care and adornment of the body slowly continued. Anne of Austria, the wife of Henry's successor, confessed to her contemporaries that she was *"fort difficile"* when it came to bad odors, and they told her that at her death she would be carried off to hell in fresh linens and smelling of perfumes.

Louis XIII (1601–1643), Anne's husband, introduced the custom of wearing the wig, the *perruque*, supposedly to cover injuries to his scalp and natural head of hair. The world of fashion soon followed suit, sporting black or brown curls of other people's hair, or of horsehair for the less affluent.

Louis XIV (1638–1715) was supremely sensitive to odors. His perfumer, M. Martial, composed a special perfume each day, and the Sun King had orange trees planted in tubs for delectation on the *parterres* in the summer and within his orangerie in winter.

The tuberose as depicted in the Chinese Mustard Garden Manual, *a seventeenth-century book of wood-blocks.* Polianthes tuberosa *was originally found in Mexico, where it was known as the "bone flower" because of the shape and color of the bud. The Spaniards brought it to Europe and to the Far East (initially the Philippine Islands) at about the same time. Its scent is used in the most expensive perfumes and reproduced in many others. The single variety shown here is more odorous than the double.*

Soapmaking was encouraged by Colbert; by raiding the Italian soap industry and promising workers better pay in France, he succeeded in seeing fourteen concerns at work in Provence. The orange tree had been planted in several places for Provence's largest center of soapmaking, Marseilles, but as the number of factories was increased, the need for fragrance material grew as well. This boded well for the improvement of hygiene.

Grasse had long been a center of the glove-making industry. Goats grazed on the hills around the town, and their hides were tanned and fragranced for the highly scented kid gloves worn by the nobility. Anne of Austria left no less than three hundred and forty pairs at her death.

It is often said that Caterina de Medici sent one Tombarelli to Grasse to establish the perfume industry there, based on Italian models. It is true that Italian influence had always been strong in Grasse; for centuries the town had been allied to the nearby Republic of Genoa. But records show the existence of Tombarellis from the early 1300s, long before Caterina left her native land. Thus although Grasse had a perfume history from the Middle Ages, it was destined to metamorphosize with the increasing interest in fragrances that arose during the age of Louis XIV.

Besides goats, Grasse produced olive trees, and several soap factories there made use of olive oil, which was pressed by windmills. Perfumery actually began in Grasse as a kind of offshoot of glove-making, but the market for it steadily increased. In March of 1673, Colbert's Ordinnance of Commerce put the industry of *gantiers-poudriers-parfumeurs* on a more stable footing as part of the *Six Corps*, the six most powerful business societies of the day, with privileged access to products from overseas. Grasse grew by supplying this business; it became a kind of link between the new Atlantic world and the earlier Mediterranean culture of Italy and Levant. Italy had no Colbert to protect its industry and to assure herself of supplies from overseas, nor did she have a centralized court that adorned itself by means of unlimited funds. Thus in the seventeenth century Italy's precedence in perfumery waned and France's became strong. But even today the Monastery of Santa Maria Novella retains its *officina di farmacia e profumeria*.

Grasse's prominence was not without rival within France itself. Montpellier was another southern town with a tradition of herbiculture reaching back into the twelfth century. The fields around the city were redolent with medicinal herbs as well as carnations, violets, lavender, jasmine, roses, and (by 1670) the tuberose, which had been introduced into Europe from Mexico. The two cities remained sparring partners throughout the seventeenth century. Only in the next century did events grant Grasse the lead that she has retained to this day.

England was not without fragrance during the Renaissance and the seventeenth century. One of Elizabeth I's great fascinations was the pair of scented gloves from Italy presented to her by the Earl of Oxford in 1573. She was also proud of her cloak of perfumed Spanish leather and fond of adjourning to the stillroom where various fragrant waters were compounded for her and her ladies. One Ralph Rabbards, a "gentleman studious and expert in Achemical Artes," sent Her Majesty a letter advertising his "waters of purest substance from odors, flowers, fruites and herbes . . . clere as crystal, with his owne onlie proper vertue, taste and odor contynuinge many years."[8]

Shakespeare frequently alluded to the rose, which may have been his favorite flower, but he mentions violets, marjoram, mint, civet, lavender, and musk as well. He spoke of the "casting bottle" (similar

Seventeenth-century English silver-gilt ewer and basin for rose water. In Tudor times, food was still eaten with the fingers, but the hands were washed and scented with rose water after each course. Courtesy of The Metropolitan Museum of Art, Gift of Irwin Untermyer, 1968

to the Persian *gulabdan)*, used in Elizabethan times to fragrance a room with fragrant waters. Herbs in his day were sold in Bucklesbury Street, the district that was synonymous with clean fragrance. Soap was not manufactured in Britain until 1641, and bathing was not at all popular. When Cromwell overthrew the monarchy and inaugurated the Commonwealth, all perfuming went overboard. However, the Restoration of Charles II in 1660 brought with it all the manners of the court of Louis XIV.

Among the frills imported from France was the powdered wig. Powder rendered these headpieces artifacts of fragrance. Oakmoss *(Evernia prunastri)* appeared frequently in wig powders, and powdered orris root and rose petals were also used. Two famous blends were the Poudre à la Marechale, named after the Marechale d'Aumont, and Cyprian powder. In the reign of Louis XV, the French returned to a white or a gray wig that was less elaborate than those worn by either Louis XIV or Charles II.

The Great Plague had several effects on seventeenth-century manners in England. For one thing, it finally made bathing more common. The custom of taking tobacco, particularly snuff, was encouraged because it was believed to ward off pestilence, and after the Great Fire, London was rebuilt in such a way that air could circulate and staunch the sources of infection. Evelyn even suggested that large areas of London be planted with plants "such as yield the most fragrant and odoriferous flowers and are apt to tinge the air upon every gentle emission at a great distance."[9] The plan was not adopted, and the world is still waiting for the introduction of fragrance into urban planning.

7

The Eighteenth Century

The last years of the reign of Louis XIV were marked by pomp and solemnity, but after his passing, France entered into the Rococo period, marked by lightness, not gravity, intimacy, not monumentality, and an interest in the little pleasures, not the pomps, that beautiful materials could give the beholder. A wave of Chinese influence swept in, with an emphasis on the tender and fugitive joys of taking tea in a garden, of listening to a small chamber concert, or of talking with friends in an informal, *sans gêne*, manner. *Goût*, good taste, was everything. The heavy cut velvets of the earlier century were abandoned for shimmering silks in light colors; massive furniture gave way to creations of almost ethereal grace; and the apartments of Versailles were done over, deemphasizing kingly grandeur and stressing intimacy and charm. The worst of the former sanitary abuses of the palace were remedied, and more attention than ever before was paid to elegance of grooming, fragrance, and hygiene. Versailles became *la cour parfummée*: the world of Boucher, Watteau, and Fragonard. The minister of finance observed wryly that "for the French, taste is the most fruitful of businesses."[1]

Of all European countries, the Rococo style is linked most intimately to France, particularly to the personalities of Jeanne Antoinette Poisson, la Marquise de Pompadour, to her successor, the Comtesse du Barry, and to Marie Antoinette. Madame Pompadour, above all the rest, encouraged every phase of the decorative and minor arts with her generous patronage, guided always by her exquisite and unerring taste. The producers of Grasse, and indeed of all Europe, owed much to her interest in fragrances, and in this period the industry evolved from a craft to a near-industrial phase.

What were some of the products produced for the glittering markets at Paris and Versailles? Gloves remained important until the end of the century. In 1700 the glove-makers had sought to entirely differentiate themselves from all other tanners, and by 1724 their lobbying proved efficacious. Seventy firms were recognized as creating products more allied to luxury than to utility: the *gantiers-parfumeurs*. The twenty-one manufacturers that were located at Grasse met regularly in the Convent of the Augustinians to review the quality of their materials, the news of the fragrance crops (particularly the orange trees), and reports from their agents at the capital. The most famous scent of fine kid gloves at that period was "Neroli," from the blossoms of the bitter orange, named after the Duchess of Nerola. Scented gloves remained one of the major fragrance products until in the 1760s, when the government initiated a series of efforts to raise revenues by setting high imposts on hides. Try as they may, the associations could not thwart these ill-advised taxes.

Montpellier had so invested in this one fragranced product that it went under completely. The Fargeon family had been important to the perfume industry in the seventeenth century, but when Montpellier collapsed, Jean-Louis Fargeon went to Paris, where he became perfumer to the king, and Jean-Jacques-Mathieu Fargeon went to Grasse, where he set up a fragrance house. With this sudden demise of an ancient perfumed artifact, the association dropped the first part of its title and became simply *"parfumeurs."*

Wigs continued in popularity during the eighteenth century, and by

A French perfumery of the eighteenth century—the proprietress uses a balance to weigh out a formula, a man decants, and a boy works the still crowned with a Moor's head condensing cap. From Father Polycarpe Poncelet, La Chymie du Goût et de l'Odorat, *Paris,* 1766. *From the collection of Florence Wall*

the eve of the revolution, some of them had become ridiculously elaborate. The Terror put a final end to the fashion, although the custom of wearing wigs survived for a while in England.

As bathing became increasingly commonplace, scented vinegars were used to tone the skin. The scented fan was also used as a weapon of flirtation—sandalwood was especially desired, imported by the ships of the *Compagnie des Indes Orientales*. Pomades were made by enfleurage of jasmine, violet, jonquil, carnation, or hyacinth, or by maceration of orange blossoms in hot fats. In the eighteenth century the pots that held these emollients were thick-walled to withstand the journey by mule train to the market cities. But now we find an increasing standardization of pottery sizes, reflecting the rationalization of the industry.

"Bergamotes" were little papier-mâché boxes that incorporated the fragrant rind of bergamot, *Citrus aurantium, ssp. bergamia*. The earliest mention of these little boxes from Grasse dates from 1745, but the custom did not last beyond 1832.

Potpourris were very popular in the period, and the increasing trade with the East gave the compounder a more lavish use of spices than was ever before possible. The rose was the central element of such blends, reinforced with the deep-blue lavender, spices, silvery wisps of oakmoss, and powdered orris root. White flowers did not dry well, turning brown and retaining little of their scent, but the blue and red anthocyanin pigments of the roses and lavender flowers made them attractive visually as well as olfactorily.

But what made a potpourri particularly charming was the eighteenth century's discovery of Chinese porcelain, which, like glass, would not react with the essential oils of a plant. The name "porcelain" came from the Portuguese at Macao, who gave the word *porzella*, "little pig," to a kind of lustrous, milky-white shell they found in Chinese waters. They used this term for the ware they encountered at Macao and Canton, and the name held. Great quantities of porcelain made their way to Europe through the Straits of Malacca and around the Cape of Good Hope, but the Europeans wanted to reproduce the material themselves, not merely import it. A German alchemist working at Meissen was the first to reproduce the ware, and soon Meissen and Sèvres were producing high-quality chinaware. The rarer Chinese porcelains were fitted with flowing ormolu mounts, creating potpourri jars or *brûle-parfums*—a marriage of the best of East and West.

Matching pommade jars of porcelain, French, eighteenth century. Scented pommades were made by placing such flowers as lilies-of-the-valley, violets, jonquils, jasmine, and tuberose upon pure white lard. The animal fat absorbed the essence and could be used as a fragrant emollient, much like modern cold cream. Courtesy of The Metropolitan Museum of Art, Gift of R. Thornton Wilson, 1950, in memory of Florence Ellsworth Wilson

A potpourri jar done at Meissen in hard-paste porcelain. Böttger, the alchemist, was the first to discover there the secret of recreating in Europe the much-envied Chinese porcelain. The bronze mounts are French, belonging to the Louis XV period. Courtesy of The Metropolitan Museum of Art, Gift of Mr. & Mrs. Charles Wrightsman, 1974

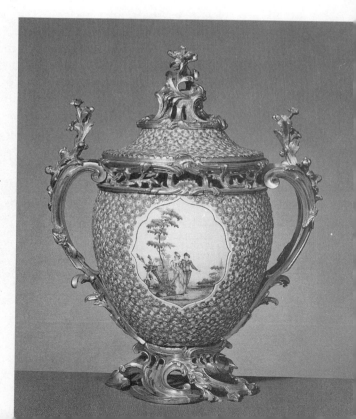

The greatest scent of the age was not made in France, but its reputation was made by its wholesale adoption by French nobility. The origins of eau de cologne actually reach back to Italy. A barber, Gian Paolo Feminis, born in Val Vigezzo near Santa Maria Maggiore, left his homeland to seek his fortune in Germany, and in 1709 he began marketing a highly distilled "water" fragranced with several herbs, well-known to the Italian tradition. His *Aqua Admirabilis* was made of a highly rectified grape spirit (which conserved some of the fruit notes of the grapes), oil of neroli, bergamot, lavender, and rosemary. The product was well received by his customers in Cologne, and Gian Paolo soon summoned another member of the family north to help in the business. Giovanni Maria Farina (1685–1766) came to Cologne, set his uncle's formulation into writing, and in 1732 took entire charge of the business. Farina's fragrance was advertised as a veritable panacea good for the skin, the stomach—the alcohol of that time was not denatured and could be quaffed as well as splashed—the gums, and even recommended for veterinary uses. As business expanded, so did the Farinas. Numerous manufacturers appeared in the city, each one claiming to be authentic descendants of Feminis, each with the true formula. French troops stationed in Cologne during the Seven Years' War brought back this wonderful "water," which they dubbed "*eau de cologne*." The scent was particularly irresistible to Madame Du Barry, who spent a fortune on the light, clean, and fresh scent.

Other perfumes of the eighteenth century usually consisted of one note, such as jasmine, neroli, and ambergris. Marie Antoinette was fond of the traditional rosewater and of a water of violets. Millefleurs was one of the few perfumes compounded from several essential oils, extracted from an enfleurage *au bouquet*, or *au pot-pourri*.

Technically, perfumers experimented with extractions made with various oils, including almond and apricot seed. Enfleurage techniques were improved, and a literature of the French industry began to appear. At the very end of the seventeenth century (1698), Sieur Barbe published *Le Parfumeur François*, which promised to "teach all the means of obtaining odors from flowers, and to make every kind of perfume composition." The following century saw the *Chimie du Goût et de l'Odorat, ou Principes pour composer facilement, et les Eaux de senteurs* (1755) by Poncelet; the *Traité des Odeurs* in 1764 by M. Dejean, and in 1771 Buc'hoz published his *Toilette de Flore*, which promised instruction in concocting emollient creams, rouge, powders, distilled essences, and

Europe had a long tradition of mounting precious objects—relics, jewels, nautilus shells—in precious or semi-precious metals. Chinese porcelain, with its shell-like surface and bell-like tones, seemed like such a treasure to the French of the eighteenth century, and thus this potpourri jar was fitted in a mount of gilt-bronze (ormolu). The porcelain is from the Ch'ien-lung period (1739–1795) and the mounting is from around 1745–1749. Such a container would be filled with dried roses, sandalwood chips, and ground spices. Courtesy of The Metropolitan Museum of Art, Charles Wrightsman Fund, 1972

waters. In 1774 the *Nouvelle Chymie du Goût et de l'Odorat* appeared, by Larbalestier Petit, promising to teach "at little expense" how to make both liqueurs that could be imbibed and perfumes that could be smelled. Around the same time Diderot completed his great *Encylopédie*, which left a wonderful record of such distilling in the last half of the century.

A section of the Hôtel de Cabris, Grasse, at the Metropolitan Museum of Art, New York. The elegant oak panelling uses the theme of incense burners (visible on the doors seen in the mirror) as a tribute to the local industry of Grasse, which by the end of the eighteenth century had outstripped Montpellier, its sole rival as perfume center of Europe. The potpourri jars on the table were standard accessories to such aristocratic apartments at the end of the ancien régime. Courtesy of The Metropolitan Museum of Art

Eighteenth-Century Bottles

The technology and sophistication of making and designing perfume containers also increased along with the development of the fragrance industry. *"Allons a cette porcelaine/Sa beauté m'invite, m'entraine,"* went a French verse of the time. Madame Pompadour was enamoured of porcelain potpourri jars at her numerous chateaux, such as Bellevue and Choisy. A French craftsman took this art of Sèvres to England, where the medium was also employed for making perfume flacons. From 1760 on, a series of harlequins, maids with full skirts, birds, animals, flowers, and Chinese mandarins were the shapes of choice for Chelsea scent bottles. The English also manufactured bottles of wedgewood in black basalt with gilt borders and flacons in blue jasperware; France had no monopoly on elegance and style during this age.

Glass technology also made great strides. A dictum of the Bourbons was *"la noblesse se perd dans la trafic"* ("The nobility loses caste if engaged in business"). But an exception to this limitation on the nobility in the domain of crass business was the art trades, where great refinement was brought to an industry such as glass manufacture.

Pochet et du Courval is a firm that continues a brisk trade in perfume bottles today but whose origin goes back to a patent to the Sieur du Courval on January 9, 1623. It was later sold to the Marquis of Senarpont. The royal glass factory of Saint Gobain originated in 1665 with a grant from Louis XIV, and this firm also continues to make thousands of bottles for the perfume trade as well as more massive objects of industrial glass. Usually these early establishments were set up within close range of a forest, for they were notorious consumers of firewood. The beautiful Forest of Eu is still the background for the factories of Pochet in Picardy.

During the time of the Sun King, Bernard Perrot at Orléans rediscovered the technique of blowing glass into a mold, and cameos and other insignias meant to flatter His Majesty appeared on his scent bottles. Glassware became increasingly important in the eighteenth century due to the consumption of luxuries at Versailles—especially mirrors and chandeliers—and the wine industry. In 1767 the *Verrerie de Saint-Louis* was founded, the first such plant to break the British monopoly on lead crystal. Around the same time, the glassworks of Sainte-Anne was established, which would in the following century (1822) become the *Cristallerie de Baccarat.*

Chelsea scent bottles, from the mid-eighteenth century. These porcelain bottles have been cast in the shape of bouquets of flowers, but the openings are at the top. Porcelain, like glass, will not react with the essential oils of a perfume. There was considerable experimentation with this material in Europe after the secret of man-ufacturing hard-paste porcelain in the Chinese manner was finally mastered. Porcelain will contract a great deal more than glass in cooling, however, so glass has remained as the most suitable container for alcoholic perfumes. Courtesy of The Metropolitan Museum of Art, Gift of Irwin Untermyer, 1971

The flacons created in the age of Louis XIV were usually made of tinted green glass, and often they were undistinguished. But by the period of his grandson, they had reached great refinement. Beautifully cut crystal flasks were frequently capped with stoppers of gold and held in *nécessaires*, or cases, made of tortoiseshell, sharkskin, wood, leather, or porcelain.

Before drawing the accomplishments of the eighteenth century to an end, it is worth mentioning some of the important names of British perfumery. In 1708, Charles Lillie (or Lilly) of London introduced scented snuffs and such perfumes as Orangeflower, Musk, and Civet Violet. In 1730, an emigrant Spaniard, Juan Floris, set up a business in wigs and hairdressing, selling scented powders, scents, and potpourri. His concern is still operative today. Thomas Yardley of London received a charter from George III in 1770, and in 1780 he brought out his famous lavender scent, which is probably, in soap form, one of the world's most popular fragrances.

At the initiation of Madame Pompadour, Louis XV adopted the Chinese imperial custom of plowing the first furrow of spring. Louis XVI did the same, but the gap between toilers and consumers had widened beyond bridging. The French revolutionaries of 1789 wanted nothing to do with perfumes, luxuries, or anything that recalled the Bourbons. For a woman to dress with style was to court imprisonment or death. Wigs went out for good, and the followers of Robespierre, men and women, cut their hair in the severe, short "Titus" cut.

The perfume set of Madame de Pompadour—six bottles of rock crystal, a cup for coffee, and bonbonière. Jeanne Poisson, Marquise de Pompadour (1721–1764), gave enormous encouragement to perfumery, as well as to all the decorative arts. The scents contained in the bottles would have included eau de Cologne, rose, lavender, mille-fleur, *and orange blossom waters, and the coffee and sweets served to revive the user fatigued by the* soins de beauté. *Courtesy of The Metropolitan Museum of Art, Gift of Mr. and Mrs. Charles Wrightsman, 1976*

The perfume industry—like the crafts of Sèvres porcelain, Lyons silkgoods, and Parisian cabinetmaking—went into decline and would have become extinguished were it not for the efforts of the artisans to maintain their skills despite the tempests of politics. Napoleon gave these trades assistance by numerous commissions, and by permitting the return of the old noblesse. However, it was only by 1835 that the French perfume industry was doing a volume of trade commensurate to that of 1789.

Container for soap or sponge, French, eighteenth century. Europeans were very reluctant to bathe until the eighteenth century, unlike the ancient Egyptians, Greeks, Romans, and unlike their contemporaries in the Muslim world, India, China, and Japan. Soap, a product of Islamic science, was at first something of a rarity—chiefly known in the Latin civilizations, where the availability of olive oil and aromatics made it more common than in northern Europe. Soap was molded into balls and kept in such boxes, with a matching one for the sponge. Courtesy of The Metropolitan Museum of Art, Rogers Fund, 1924

8

The Nineteenth Century

France Under Napoleon

Tragic as the Revolution had been for the luxury trades, perfumery among them, one benefit it brought was the abrogation of all the guild structures that had been in effect since the late Middle Ages, as well as the granting of special privileges. Thus the nineteenth-century industry would be governed by the ebb and flow of the market alone. Anyone with a new idea who could find sufficient backing would be free to try it. In practice, however, this laissez-faire developed more slowly than at the mere penning of a decree, for the perfumers, glass makers, soap makers, cabinet makers, ceramicists, and silkweavers retained the old rules and standards in secret, like a freemasonry, fearing a loss of quality and control.

Napoleon Bonaparte represented a counterbalance to the radical democracy of the Revolution. The emigrés were allowed to return, the church was reestablished, and in 1802 he was crowned emperor. Fashion was no longer dangerous. But Napoleon was republican enough to create a new nobility, one of talent, and he financed scientific research and rewarded all scientific talent. With this encouragement, French technology made enormous gains. The organic chemistry that revolutionized perfumery and the related soap industry in the nineteenth century owed much to the Little Corporal. But fortunately he brought more immediate gains as well. Napoleon was almost neurotically fastidious about cleanliness and good scents. He washed with the British soap, Brown Windsor, made with bergamot, clove, and lavender oils, and his favorite scent was Farina's Eau de Cologne—often consuming several bottles a day. Elegance, coupled with a certain republican restraint, dictated the imperial style for men, and the increasing concern for cleanliness became a mark of the bourgeoisie class in France and throughout Europe.

One of the events that marked the reappearance of perfumery in post-revolutionary France was the founding of a shop of the Farinas in Paris that purveyed the emperor's favorite scent. However, the venerable Jean-Marie soon found that a client of such importance invited other producers, and France saw a proliferation of "Farinas." *"Ils étaient deux alors—ils sont mille aujourd'hui—tous 'seul', tous 'Jean-Marie'"* observed one wag.[1] ("First there were only two, but now there are a thousand—each one 'the real one'; each one 'descended from Jean-Marie Farina.'") The stalwart Jean-Marie Farina did legal battle with his competitors. His own product made use of the finest grape spirit and required aging for a full year; much was at stake, but his name was successfully defended. Jean-Marie finally retired to Italy, homeland of all the true Farinas, and the formula was sold to Léonce Collas, who found that he too had to continue the defense of his formula. In 1862, Collas sold the original formula to the firm of Roger et Gallet, which today has rightful claim to the Parisian Eau de Cologne. The branch of the family that remained in Cologne found that the popularity that Napoleonic patronage brought to their product brought with it the same rival claimants. By 1865, faced with thirty-nine competitors, the German heirs to the authentic formula identified their company as *"Gegen dem Jülischplatz über"* and consumers were warned that they should only buy the products from the house at this address. To be the world's oldest continuous perfume and its most popular has not been an easily won distinction.

Eau de Cologne was compounded from bergamot oil, lavender, and rosemary oils in a highly rectified grape spirit—thus, it could be ingested as a liquor, as well as splashed on the skin. Denaturing of alcohol was only practiced at the end of the nineteenth century. Here an advertisement from about 1825–1830 touts both internal and external uses of one brand of the world's most popular fragrance. From the French National Library, poster collection

The year 1809 saw the publication of *Le Parfumeur Impérial* by C. F. Bertrand. There was no longer a "royal" perfumer, but the actual substance of Bertrand's book contained material similar to that discussed by eighteenth-century handbooks, such as how to make pomades of hyacinths, roses, jonquils, and mixed flowers *(pommades de pot-pourri)*. Bertrand also contributed to the raging controversies by suggesting his own recipe for eau de cologne.

The illustrious house of Antoine Chiris, founded in 1760, managed to survive the Revolution as did the ancient house of Tombarelly d'Escoffier although no longer known as *Parfumeur de la Cour*. The former was among the first to start floral plantations in the soon-to-be-established North African colonies; to this day Morocco and Algeria remain important producers of fragrance materials. The house of Antoine Artaud of Grasse weathered the political storms and the firm of J. F. Houbigant which had enjoyed a brief patronage from the nobility (the house was established in 1775) and then sold fragrance to the Bonapartes. The firm of Pierre-François Lubin was actually begun under Napoleon with a shop whose sign bore the title *Aux Armes de France*. The firm fortunately fell into the arms of a generous client, the beautiful Princess Borghese, who allowed her name to be linked to the Lubin creations. The house of Lubin was the first to solicit the North American market, aiming particularly at the plantation culture of the South.

Another name that remained important in the nineteenth century was that of Louis-Toussaint Piver, who succeeded Guillaume Dissey in 1813, the proprietor of a shop called *La Reine des Fleurs*.

Napoleon was important for thus permitting the restoration of the traditional luxury industries of the old culture as well as for setting forth an ideal of personal cleanliness and good grooming. Not all revolutions have been followed by such moderating spirits. But where Napoleon permitted the reestablishment of the old courtly ways, his consort Josephine actively promoted them. She had been married to a noble of the old regime and had barely survived the Terror with her life. Once the all-clear was sounded, she openly advocated the cultivation of all the graces of an earlier France.

Fashion Under Josephine

Josephine set the tone for the daring and yet elegant fashion known as the *Empire* style. She, as well as the beautiful Madame Recamier and Madame Tallien, embodied a fashion reminiscent of the bare-armed Cleopatra (inspired by Napoleon's Egyptian campaign) or evocative of Grecian maidens. White was the color of the new style, but unrelieved white could be very monotonous. The answer to this minor problem appeared in the Indian shawls that Napoleon had brought back from the souks of Cairo. Colorful and scented, these Kashmiri wraps added the perfect blaze of color to contrast with the white dresses of the new fashion and provided a measure of warmth, for the climate along the Seine was not the same as that along the Nile, not even for even the most enthusiastic orientalist.

These shawls (from the Persian *shal*), worn by both men and women from the earliest days of the Mughuls, were made from the precious

Nineteenth-century factory of the firm of Antoine Chiris where the new method of solvent extraction was successfully applied at the turn of the century. The architectural style is the Moorish-Saracenic, so popular in France during that period.

underfleece of the Tibetan mountain goat *(Capra hircus)*. The wool was so fine that these cashmeres could be drawn through a thumb ring. An intricately designed shawl could take up to eighteen months of labor, and the weavers protected their work by shipping it in boxes filled with the leaves and stems of dried patchouli, which served as an insectifuge. Fine carpets were also preserved in this way. The protein of the wool, like human hair, retained the scent tenaciously, and when European manufacturers sought to capitalize on the new fashion for these shawls by producing copies of the paisley pattern, they found the market reluctant to buy. The scent as well as the material was attracting the consumers, and when the source of that clean, resinous but unfamiliar odor was finally identified, the textile houses of France and England avidly bought up the tropical mint. Once known, patchouli became a popular scent in French perfumes in the middle of the century. Patchouli, then, is the fragrance to imagine wafting up from the wrappings of the beauties in the paintings of David, Ingres, Gérard, and Gros.

Josephine is also famous for her association with the rose. Her retreat at Malmaison was ringed by rose gardens, which included every known species available. The painter Pierre-Joseph Redouté immortalized her collection by painting the portraits of each one. Josephine was also fond of musk, a heavy, languorous scent that Napoleon could not abide. When the emperor spurned her in favor of Marie-Louise, Josephine took her final revenge by saturating the imperial apartments in musk, which she knew was one of the most retentive of scents.

Marie-Louise was also linked to the history of perfumes. Following her estrangement from the vanquished conqueror, she retired to Parma in 1817, where she became enamored of the violets that were a characteristic feature of the local flora. She became the champion of the violet as Josephine had been of the rose. She encouraged further plantings and the distillation of violet water at the monastery of San Giovanni Evangelista. The nineteenth century saw the creation of many violet perfumes—Parma violets were popular cut flowers and manufacturers tried to capture this popular fragrance. North Americans are often mystified by the "violet" odor because their common violet *(Viola canadensis)* is odorless; the scented Parma violet can only grow in a Mediterranean climate.

At the end of the century when violet-toned synthetics were discovered, the labor of picking these small flowers became cost-prohibitive. The plant is still a part of the perfumer's palette, however, because at almost exactly the same time it was discovered that the leaves (which

The violet (Viola odorata) *has always been part of the perfumer's repertory, but today it is the leaf that is treated by solvent extraction, rarely the flower. The florentine orris root possesses almost the same odor note as the violet flower, but does not demand the same laborious effort to harvest. The shiny, blue-green leaves have a cool green note, somewhat like the smell of a freshly cut cucumber. From George Nicholson,* Illustrated Dictionary of Gardening, *London, 1888*

are more easily harvested) could be treated by solvent extraction to yield an arresting green note similar to the scent of a sliced cucumber. Roger et Gallet's Vera Violetta created in 1892 was a beautiful violet perfume but it made use of the synthetic violet scents as well as the natural.

Josephine had pulled fashion out of its revolutionary slump, but once her influence had waned, it sank into a slump of another kind. The age of the middle class had dawned, and the bourgeoisie were eager to display their new wealth and, at the same time, demonstrate their moral superiority to the old noblesse. Styles became prim and, for women, encumbering. Scents, if worn at all, had to be light—especially in England and Germany—and musk and patchouli were entirely tabooed in those countries.

However, at this time men's styles received the imprint of Beau Brummell (George Bryan Brummell, 1778–1840), the British arbiter of fashion who introduced the style for black cloth set off with immaculate linen. He decreed that macassar oil from the East Indies was the fit dressing for the hair. Because the oil tended to stain, women crocheted antimacassars to protect sofa and chair backs. The oil, from the seeds of *Schleichera oleosa*, had a bitter-almond odor. Brummell set the stage for the masculine ideal of cleanliness and well-bred understatement. Only certain colors and certain scents were "correct," an image that would persist, by and large, until the youth explosion of the 1960s, when men's styles burst into colors and textures such as had not been seen since the days of the Stuarts and the Bourbons. Even today, after the Mod styles have come and gone, the well-brushed, understated look set by Brummel in the first half of the nineteenth century remains an important hallmark of male style.

The Glittering Second Empire

Feminine fashion made a dramatic recovery with the figure of Empress Eugénie, wife of the second Napoleon. The Spanish-born Eugénie de Montijo de Guzman (1826–1920) was, like the wife of the first emperor, a striking beauty, whether in a ball gown of full crinolines and off-the-shoulder sleeves or in the equestrian attire of the *lionnes* of the Second Empire. Her sense of style was aided and abetted by the first of the great modern couturiers, the Englishman Charles Frederick Worth. Worth, the son of a ruined lawyer, came to Paris to seek his fortune. Within ten years he was so famous and sought after that only Eugénie could call upon him without an appointment. Clients had to be recommended as they would for application to an exclusive club. Worth created the authority of the couturier that has been so traded upon in perfume merchandising. The Worth perfumes were initiated by Jean-Philippe, son of the founder, as a free presentation to clients of the

Empress Eugénie (1826–1920), a Spaniard and the consort of Louis Napoleon, re-introduced good taste into French life, much as Madame de Pompadour and Empress Josephine had done in their periods. She patronized all of the traditional fine crafts that had been associated with the throne, and saw to the creation of the Musée des Arts Decoratifs at the Louvre. The House of Worth provided her dresses, and the House of Guerlain her fragrances. Courtesy of Guerlain, Inc.

dress house, but the success of Dans la Nuit soon proved that the perfume was an entity of its own. Today more people know the name of Worth through its perfumes than its fashions.

Eugénie's sense of style and her delight in ornamentation ensured the development of perfumery in France while Queen Victoria was suppressing these trends in England. Another factor in the promotion of perfume was the wave of orientalism that swept Paris in the 1850s, 1860s, and later, which was due in part to France's increasing colonial activity in Muslim lands.

Eugénie patronized the house of Guerlain, and it was for her that the famous Eau Impériale was created in 1861. The Maison Guerlain still preserves a letter of gratitude from the Empress.

Guerlain, one of the most important names associated with the history of perfumes, was the creation of Pierre François Guerlain, who came from a family in Picardy engaged in manufacturing pewter. He and his father did not get along, and Pierre left France for England, where he worked for a small soap firm. He was later sent back to France as a sales representative, where he began to make better soaps than the ones he was supposed to sell. In 1828 he struck out on his own, opening a shop on the Rue de Rivoli where he sold perfumed soaps, scents, and smelling salts. Smelling salts revived the tender blossoms of the age who were always wilting; Guerlain provided them with strong inhalations of lavender and ammonia. In 1848 Guerlain had so prospered that he was able to move to *rue de la Paix*, the fashion center of Paris and the same address as the House of Worth. Whatever lingering scruples remained as a result of associating perfume with easy virtue were put to rest by the fineness of Guerlain's fragrance, the distinction of his packaging (with the imperial crest upon a bottle molded with the Napoleonic bee emblem), and above all, by the nod of the Empress.

At the International Exhibition at Paris in 1867, perfumery and soap were displayed in a section of their own, not, as in previous exhibitions, as stepchildren of pharmacy and chemistry. The French, with their delight in fragrances and scented soaps, wines, and silks, were amused by Queen Victoria's choice of exhibits—a model farm, a school, a church, and a presentation by the Bible Society.

Louis Napoleon was responsible for finally separating perfumery from pharmacy by passing a law requiring that all pharmaceuticals list their ingredients on the label. Naturally the contending makers of eau de

Eau Impériale was created by the House of Guerlain for the Empress Eugénie in 1861—and remains one of the longest-lived perfume creations of all time. The bee, symbol of the industrious Napoleonic house, has been used in the molding of the bottle. Mid-nineteenth-century labelling dominated a considerable area of the bottle surface, but subsequently became increasingly abbreviated. Courtesy of Guerlain, Inc.

cologne were not about to tip their hand, although up to this point the assets of the liquid for the stomach had been touted as well.

It was during the Second Empire that the perfumer Eugene Rimmel (1820–1887) wrote the first chronicle of the perfumes of mankind, *The Book of Perfumes*. Rimmel knew the scent of each of the materials that he discussed, and he had studied the long history of perfumery in non-Western cultures as well as in Europe. The book was published in both London and Paris, and printed on perfumed paper. In the middle and late nineteenth century, the label was usually markedly larger than it is today in the twentieth century. Rimmel, with his wide-ranging knowledge, created some of the most tasteful of such labels for his perfumes, soaps, and sachets, many of them with images drawn from the history of fashion.

The period also saw the rise of the house of Bourjois, founded in 1863 as a compounder of theater makeup but soon expanding into

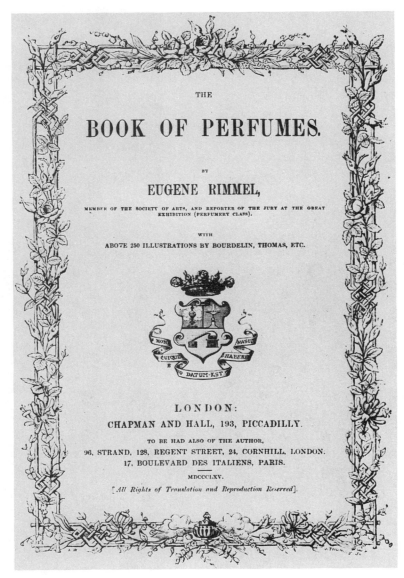

THE

BOOK OF PERFUMES.

BY

EUGENE RIMMEL,

MEMBER OF THE SOCIETY OF ARTS, AND REPORTER OF THE JURY AT THE GREAT
EXHIBITION (PERFUMERY CLASS).

WITH

ABOVE 250 ILLUSTRATIONS BY BOURDELIN, THOMAS, ETC.

LONDON:
CHAPMAN AND HALL, 193, PICCADILLY.

TO BE HAD ALSO OF THE AUTHOR,

96, STRAND, 128, REGENT STREET, 24, CORNHILL, LONDON.
17, BOULEVARD DES ITALIENS, PARIS.

MDCCCLXV.

[*All Rights of Translation and Reproduction Reserved*].

Eugene Rimmel's Book of Perfumes *appeared in 1865 in London, and almost simultaneously in a Parisian edition. The work by this writer-perfumer was the most accurate and clear presentation of the industry to appear at that time. The book was especially clear on the use of perfumes in the East—a subject that was beginning to pique the European imagination— and the paper used in the printing was itself perfumed. From the collection of Florence Wall* other cosmetics and perfumes. The firm of Edouard Pinaud was founded in 1840 under the sign of *"La Corbeille Fleurie,"* reaching its apogee under the Second Empire. The house created an Eau de Toilette de l'Impératrice Eugénie and a Bouquet de l'Exposition Universelle 1867. The firm had its own printing shop for production of the labels and posters it needed, and it established a worldwide network for distribution. The United States was a prime market, and many American men are familiar with the Lilac Vegetal of Pinaud, one of the fine aftershaves used by men's barbers.

A number of other new houses did a flourishing business in the encouraging climate of the Second Empire. In 1849 the house of Molinard set up a firm in Grasse to sell perfumed waters. As the Riviera began to attract wealthy visitors, the firm served them. Frédéric Millot's house had begun in 1839 and expanded steadily. It was this company that commissioned the celebrated Hector Guimard to design the flacons of the perfume made for the 1900 Paris Exhibition. Hermès was the famous saddlery and leather goods house established in 1837, heir to a long European tradition of tanning and scenting gloves. Gellé Frères succeeded the enterprise of Jean-Louis Fargeon, who had been perfumer to Louis XVI, the Queen, and the Count d'Artois. This firm received numerous prizes at the various industrial fairs that characterized the period.

In Grasse alone, four important contemporary suppliers sprang up in the mid-nineteenth century: Roure Bertrand Dupont, Robertet et Cie., and J. B. Lautier; Eugene Charabot took over the older company of Hugues Aîné around 1900. Tournaire and Company was a different type of supplier; since 1833 they have made the stills, water baths, vats, and containers necessary in processing the essential oils.

The Second Empire was to end with the humiliation of the Franco-Prussian War and the violence of the 1870 Commune. However, Paris was soon healed of these wounds, and the *Belle Epoque*, which was to witness a veritable explosion of perfumery, was ushered in. But before we survey the creations of that time, let us examine the technical progress of the decades that preceded it and contributed to its successes.

Grasse—factory of the former firm of Hugues Aîné with its twin alembics crowning the facade and (on the right) *the town house of the Count of Mirabeau. The old factory has been designated the site of the French national museum of perfumery.*

Progress in Science

During the Revolution, the great chemist Antoine Lavoisier (1743–1794) had been told that the Revolution had no need of savants. Fortunately Napoleon soon gave the lie to this arrogant taunt. His patronage assured a steady stream of talented scientists who contributed both to France and to Europe as a whole. Bertrand's manual of perfumery at the beginning of the century reflected the advanced craft status of the eighteenth-century industry, but the amount of technical changes from the age of Napoleon until 1900 were so many that the entire character of perfumery was drastically transformed.

Organic chemistry made enormous strides: In 1818 J. J. Houton de la Billardière discovered the chemical pattern underlying the fragrant oils: the famous terpene rule, with the ratio of carbon to hydrogen in the proportion of five to eight. His investigations were made with spirits of turpentine, hence the "terpene rule." His work was built upon by J. B. Dumas (1800–1884), who looked into the makeup of many of the other essential oils; each analysis was published in Liebig's influential *Annalen de Pharmacie*. He devoted particular attention to those oils that congeal at room temperature, such as camphor and menthol. Later Marcellin Berthelot (1827–1907) studied the hydrocarbons in the essential oils. In 1835 H. E. Robiquet made the first successful experiments in the extraction of the essential oils in flowers that could not withstand distillation: solvent extraction.

Germany, inspired by the example of Napleonic France, embarked in the early nineteenth century upon a Golden Age of chemistry. In 1818, Romershausen, the apothecary of Aachen, performed the world's first distillation under a vacuum—an operation that is duplicated daily in the modern perfume and pharmaceutical laboratory. In 1838 J. Liebig and F. Wohler identified benzaldehyde, the aldehyde responsible for the fruity fragrance of the peach kernel and bitter almonds. Liebig was also responsible for a discovery that has been used many times in cosmetics: the synthetic color alloxan, now known in the trade as "blush pink."

Another German genius, F. August Kekulé (1829–1896) tortured over the contradictory chemical nature of benzene, which had defied every model of formulation. Finally he fell asleep, and in a famous dream beheld myriads of serpents whirling around and around, finally catching hold of their own tails. Kekulé awoke to solve the problem

Early perfumer's scale, Grasse. The nineteenth century saw a complete meta-morphosis in perfumery from a highly developed craft to a modern industry, making use of improved technologies of extraction and of developments in organic chemistry. But the first decades of the century were times of trial and error, without the assured clientele of the old noblesse. Courtesy of Colette Hoffman

by describing the ring nature of benzene, now one of the most familiar images in organic chemistry, extremely important in perfumery which is so frequently concerned with the aromatic benzene–ring chemicals. Another German scientist, Otto Wallach (1847–1931), did so much research on the essential oils that he was dubbed "the Messiah of the terpenes" by the pharmacist Fr. A. Flückiger. F. W. Semmler (1860–1931) was another pioneer whose structural analyses paved the way for the creation of a synthetic fragrance chemical based upon the structure of the natural molecule.

In England William Perkin, discoverer of the aniline dyes, also syn-thesized the man-made odor chemical, coumarin (1868), which has the same fragrance as new-mown hay. Others followed: synthetic musk

Le Trèfle Incarnat was created in 1898 and was one of the first perfumes to use amyl salicylate, a recently discovered synthetic, to create the odor of clover. Courtesy of Marylène Delbourg-Delphis

(1888), synthetic vanilla (vanillin) in 1890, ionone, the synthetic violet scent, in 1893, and synthetic camphor in 1896. In addition, the analysis of natural essential oils had reached such a stage that certain elements of the oils could be removed and used as isolates with their own particular odor note.

Improvements in Soapmaking

Essential-oil chemistry was not the only area to expand in this golden age of science. Soapmaking became infinitely cheaper as a result of work done in France. Just before the Revolution, the Duke d'Orleans financed the efforts of Nicolas Leblanc to find a means of synthesizing the caustic soda necessary for the saponification of the fats. Previously wood ash had been used, but the number of trees that could be sacrificed for that purpose was limited. Leblanc was successful, but his backer, the Duke, fell victim to the revolutionaries, and Leblanc himself perished as a suicide in 1806. M. E. Chevreul built upon Leblanc's discoveries by determining the exact ratio of soda to fat and went on to do epochal work on the nature of fats and oils between the years 1811 and 1823. The invention of the steamboat in the early part of the century made vast stores of vegetable fats available to the burgeoning soap industry (the tropical palm and coconut oils) and by 1850 soap was no longer a rarity. The soap industry had become what it remains today, one of the largest consumers of essential oils. The old producers—Castile, Provence, and Liguria—saw their products change from standard to luxury products.

Distilling technology was also advanced by the invention of the *chauffe-vin* by Aimé Argand in 1780, which was subsequently applied to the distillation of fragrance alcohol. The principle was simple and elegant. Instead of using cold water, the wine to be distilled was used as the coolant of the condenser. Then it was introduced into the still having been preheated, thus saving fuel. And with Napoleon's advocacy of the sugar beet, the French industry had another source of sugar to be converted into ethyl alcohol.

During this time, developments in agricultural science and thinking spread to the European colonies that cultivated aromatic crops. The scented-leafed geranium (*Pelargonium graveolens*) had been discovered in South Africa, and British botanists at Kew Gardens worked on hybridizing strains with the highest oil content. The French established plantings of the geranium on the plain of Mitidja in Algeria in 1847 and later in Morocco and on Réunion Island. Today few essential oils are as important as rose geranium.

Another essential oil that is also used extensively because of its extremely low price is that of eucalyptus. Labilladière first discovered the *Eucalyptus globulus* on the island of Tasmania in 1792, and it has been widely planted in Australia for its sharp and medicinal leaf oil; the oil is used in perfumery, flavorings, and in medicine.

The Dutch performed sophisticated research into all tropical botany, including the cultivation of spice plants, in their botanic garden at Buitzenborg (now Bogor) on Java. Ylang-ylang (Tagalog for "flower of flowers") was discovered on Ceram in the Indonesian archipelago by Captain d'Etchevery in 1770, but the systematic exploitation of these heavy-scented blooms was not made until a German, Albertus Schwenger, was shipwrecked on the island of Luzon in the Philippines. He fell in love with the sweet perfume of these cream-colored flowers and decided to try to distill them. His efforts were a success; the ylang-ylang was one of the few flowers that came through the process with a scent faithful to the original flower. Another German, F. Steck, one of the many German apothecaries in the islands, further rationalized the growing of ylang-ylang, and samples of the new fragrance material were exhibited at the Paris World Exhibition of 1878. By 1893 this crop was introduced to Réunion, and it has become one of the mainstays of French perfumery. The finer grades of *Cananga odorata* are called "oil of ylang-ylang," and the less desirable are called "cananga oil," more suitable for soaps.

Bois de rose was another product unknown to earlier perfumery; it is a rose-scented oil distilled from chips of the tree *Aniba rosaeodora*. Wild trees were felled and floated downstream to Cayenne for billeting and shipment to European distilleries. The first *bois de rose* appeared in the European trade in 1866.

The southern United States produced cedarwood oil, distilled from the familiar fragrant reddish wood used in cedar chests. The tree is actually not a cedar but the *Juniperus virginia*, related to the *Juniperus communis* of Europe, which yields the juniper berry used in flavoring gin. Cedarleaf oil is another cheap American oil, first used in the nineteenth century and distilled from the leaves of the *Thuja occidentalis*. The extensive planting of oranges, lemons, grapefruits, and tangerines in the United States also assured the international industry of a readily available source of citrus oil as a by-product of fruit production.

A different type of oil was petroleum—the first "gusher" of modern times had erupted in Pennsylvania in 1859. This new resource was increasingly exploited by organic chemists as a source of synthetic odor chemicals, but equally important was the suggestion of Hirzel in 1874 that petroleum ether, not benzene, become the solvent of choice in the floral solvent-extraction process. Louis Roure was the first manufacturer to exhibit commercial samples of floral concretes, and in 1898 Léon Chiris built a large extraction factory at Grasse. Charles Garnier carried the process to Bulgaria, Egypt, and the French possessions of Algeria, Morocco, and Réunion.

Further Advances in Glass Manufacture

Another technology upon which perfumery depends is glass manufacturing, and while the perfume industry grew, so did glassmaking. French winemaking stimulated experiments with the mass production of bot-

A nineteenth-century British toiletries box of smoky agate containing five perfume bottles, files, and an ivory piece for the writing of small messages. Courtesy of The Metropolitan Museum of Art, Gift of Admiral F. R. Harris, 1946, in memory of his wife, Dena Sperry Harris

tles, and this had repercussions for the smaller containers used for colognes and perfumes. By 1886 the final assembly-line mechanization of blowing molten glass into molds had been achieved.

Two important names in perfumery glass were that of Baccarat, established on earlier foundations in 1822, and Verreries Brosse, founded in 1854. Perfume glassmakers such as these tended to standardize the design of molds in the last third of the century, not through any lack of imagination but because of the increased importance of the printed label. As trademarks became more important at the turn of the century, the trend was reversed and the glass container began to undergo a myriad transmutations while the label became increasingly inconspicuous. Clear glass remained the norm, although tinted glass was widely available.

The cosmetic jars that were made for the trade at Grasse before the coming of the railway in 1863 were heavily buttressed to withstand the vicissitudes of animal transport over the hills to the northern market centers. However, after that date they became lighter and more elegant, reflecting the change in transport technology.

La Belle Epoque

All these factors—new chemicals, new fragrance crops, new means of extracting old fragrances, easier access to supplies and new markets because of better transportation, more sophisticated production of alcohol and glassware, and a growing middle-class clientele—added up to the explosion in the perfume industry during the final years of the nineteenth century. Among the great perfumes of this Belle Epoque

Jicky was taken from the nickname used in the Guerlain family for the young Jacques Guerlain, and was created by his uncle Aimé Guerlain in 1889. The blend combined the then-new products of solvent extraction—the floral absolutes—with orris and lavender, allied with some products of the burgeoning field of organic chemistry. It was conceived as a man's toiletry, but was almost immediately lionized by the female leaders of the Belle Epoque. Courtesy of Guerlain, Inc.

were Fougère Royale, created by Paul Parquet for Houbigant in 1882, the first perfume to make use of a synthetic, coumarin. The scent was used both as a soap perfume and as a perfume in its own right and was tremendously successful in both forms. In 1889 the House of Guerlain produced Jicky, a truly family affair. The perfume was created by Aimé Guerlain, named for the young Jacques Guerlain ("Jicky" was his nickname), and presented in a bottle designed by Gabriel Guerlain working with the glassmakers of Baccarat. The scent made use of the new absolutes, the products of solvent extractions as well as synthetics, backed up with orris, bergamot, and lavender oils. Although its name seems to indicate a masculine market, Jicky was quickly taken up by the *grandes dames* of the period. To this day Jicky is sold in Paris. In 1890 Aimé Guerlain brought out Cuir de Russie, and in 1895 the Guerlains created Le Jardin de Mon Curé in a flacon by Baccarat. In 1898 the House of L. T. Piver brought out Trèfle Incarnat ("Red Clover"), created by Jacques Rouché, a man of many talents who later became the director of the National Theater of the Opera at Paris. Rouché used amyl salicylate, a synthetic, to create the perfume's soft, sweet-hay note.

9

The Twentieth Century

The year 1900 was the apotheosis of the dazzling Belle Epoque. *Le Tout Paris* turned out for the lavish Universal Exposition held that year. Women of fashion and leisure filled the cafés dressed in the flowing lines of Jacques Doucet and the younger Worth, like the buxom beauties portrayed in the posters of Jules Chernet. The art of living was raised to a sophistication never seen before, and perfumery entered upon its golden age. In this same period the couturier, Paul Poiret, linked perfume inextricably to fashion design, and François Coty began his long career by the use of the flourishing Art Nouveau style that was sweeping France.

The Paris Exhibition was commemorated by the creation of a special perfume by Houbigant, Coeur de Jeanette, created by Paul Parquet, making use of some of the new materials produced by the research of the late nineteenth century. In 1903, the flacon for Les Violettes was designed by the master glassmaker Emile Gallé, and in the following year, Guerlain celebrated the life of the boulevards with Champs Elysée, in a flacon made by Baccarat.

Paul Poiret (1879–1943) initiated the conception of the couturier fragrance by creating Parfums Rosine, a company (named for his daughter) which would produce fragrances that would be fitting accessories for the fashions of this genius of pre-World War I style. Poiret had grown to maturity in the world of Sarah Bernhardt and of Eduard Vuillard. His ideal of woman was elegant, luxurious, free of the constraints of the earlier bustle and corset, and sheathed in fluid lines and dazzling oriental colors. He served an apprenticeship with both the houses of Worth and Doucet, but soon set up his own shop with his wife, Denise, serving as the exemplar of his new look. His style became the rage of Paris when the Countess Greffulhe (Proust's Duchesse de Guermantes) appeared at her daughter's wedding in a gown by the new designer. Poiret drew upon the artistic wealth of the time: Raoul Dufy, Sonia Delaunay, Paul Iribe, Georges Lapape, Edward Steichen, Man Ray, and Erté. His perfumes were created with the collaboration of the perfumer-glassmaker M. Schaller, and later with the celebrated Almeras. The packaging of his perfumes resembled the look and materials of his fashions, emphasizing brilliant colors, opulent textures, and harlequin and lampshade patterns. The very names of these perfumes evoke the exotic image Poiret espoused: Le Fruit Défendu, Nuit de Chine, Shakhyamuni, Borgia, and Le Balcon.

The trend Poiret started in 1910 turned out to be one of the most important in the history of the twentieth-century industry; it meant the coming together of two of the oldest of the French luxury arts—fashion and fragrance.

In 1912 three important perfumes were introduced, which are still part of the contemporary scene: Houbigant's Quelques Fleurs, blended by Robet Bienaimé, assistant to and protégé of Paul Parquet; Caron's Narcisse Noir by M. Daltroff, based on and using the scent of that spring flower of Persia and China; and Jacques Guerlain's L'Heure Bleue, employing incense resins, labdanum, and balsam of Peru along with several of the newest synthetics.

Perfume bottle done as an individual piece by the Art Nouveau glass-maker Lucien Gaillard. Gaillard, unlike René Lalique, did not work with perfume firms in mass production. Courtesy of The Metropolitan Museum of Art, Gift of Mr. and Mrs. Lloyd Macklowe, 1981

A fin-de-siècle Russian noble-woman enjoys the perfume of White Violet, a scent of the firm of Rallet and Company. Founded by a Frenchman who had settled in imperial Russia in the 1840s, the company was closed by the Revolution of 1917. Ernest Beaux, the creator of Chanel Number 5, was one of the many creative emigrés from Russia to come to France, and his work in perfumery began with Rallet. From the French National Library, poster collection

A belle of the pre-World War I period swirls in a sea of Pravia, a perfume by the firm of Pinaud. She wears the "lamp-shade skirt" and harem pants popularized by Paul Poiret. From the collection of the Cooper-Hewitt Museum

Although La Feuilleraie only lived nine years as a commercial product, this 1911 illustration exemplifies the hobble skirt and egret feather popularized by Paul Poiret before World War I. Poiret was the first couturier to initiate a perfume. Courtesy of Marylène Delbourg-Delphis

Georges Lepape, "Woman at the Red Mirror," 1919. Lepape did fashion posters for Paul Poiret, as well as designs for textiles. From the Museum of Grasse.

Coty

Unlike the house of Poiret, the firms of Houbigant, Guerlain, and Caron were primarily created to formulate and retail perfumes. The most celebrated phenomenon among these kinds of houses that sold fragrances exclusively was François Coty. Coty (1876–1934) was born Frances Sportuno on the island of Corsica to a middle-class family. He gravitated to France and became secretary to a political figure of the day, Emmanuel Arene. On his way to and from his duties, he struck up an acquaintance with an apothecary who enjoyed compounding fragrances, which he sold in unimaginative apothecary jars. This craft was interesting enough to captivate the young Corsican and he became obsessed with perfumery.

Coty made a pilgrimage to Grasse and became affiliated with the ancient firm of Antoine Chiris. He learned the nuances about each of the flowers and herbs grown there, from cultivation to the stills and the new solvent extractors. We are uncertain as to the extent to which Coty created his perfumes himself or simply selected samples, but he had a highly developed olfactory sense and could identify every element in a compound.

At one point Coty wished to create a perfume from one of the cabbage roses that was popular during the Belle Epoque, La Rose Jacqueminot, named after a famous general. With backing from his family

François Coty (1873–1934) revolutionized the perfume industry. He had an acute olfactory sensitivity, knew the perfumer's materials intimately, set his products in the finest of containers, and sold smaller quantities at cheaper prices in order to involve new sectors of society in the use of fragrances. Coty collaborated with the master glass-maker, René Lalique (1860–1945), who shared his conviction that mass production did not necessarily involve a deterioration of quality. Courtesy of the Coty Division, Pfizer Corporation

and several of the wholesale houses, he created a fine perfume, using attar of rose enhanced with one of the new synthetics, ionone, with a violet note. Despite the fineness of the fragrance, breaking into the world of Parisian style in 1905 was not easy. It is said that Coty, piqued by the lack of interest in La Rose Jacqueminot in the department store *Le Louvre*, flicked a bottle of the perfume onto the tile floor, where it broke and the scent was released. Soon everyone wanted to know "what that was" and Coty's career was launched. His first store was at 61 *rue de la Boétie* but he was soon able to move the House of Coty to the stylish *rue de la Paix*. By 1910 Coty was considered *the* perfumer of Paris; clients included the czar and czarina, who commissioned fragrances for their daughters.

There were several reasons for this meteoric success: Coty's keen olfactory sensitivity and his knowledge of the primary materials; the care that he took in the packaging of the perfume product; and his marketing sense. While Coty sold to the *grandes dames* and grand duchesses, he was one of the first to down-price his product to reach the pocketbook of the Parisian shopgirl. He sold smaller bottles so that perfume could be an affordable luxury for an entirely new market, and he dispensed samples with largesse. Coty also recognized the importance of the American market and actively cultivated it at a time when the French firms who were trying to reach it left their affairs to representatives, who were often nonchalant.

Coty's packaging was distinguished by its links with another innovator, René Lalique (1860–1945), an association that began in 1907. Lalique had begun his career as a jewelry designer, working for Cartier and Boucheron. His clients included the "divine" Sarah Bernhardt. But in 1895 Lalique began to experiment with another medium, glass; its plasticity accorded well with the Art Nouveau style he had espoused. His own home was designed in the new style, and Coty and Lalique agreed that Art Nouveau would become the mark of the flacons they would develop together. Coty demanded that the art glass be capable of mass production, in accordance with his concept of a wider market, and yet remain a work of beauty. Lalique employed a variety of motifs for his perfume bottles: flowers, ferns, cicadas, Grecian maidens, and medallions. Lalique's factory at Saint-Denis in the northern suburbs of Paris also produced pieces for Worth (Je Reviens), Roger et Gallet (Le Jade), Houbigant (La Belle Saison), Molinard (L'Ile d'Or), and others, but the association between Lalique and Coty is the most well known, and the two artisans left the pefumery industry greatly changed.

Coty's interest in the quality of the presentation even extended to the paper of the label on the bottle and the boxes containing his powders and soaps. His wife's uncle was an engraver, and the two men spent many hours in determining the color, weight, and texture of the paper and the sharpness of the printing. Poiret was not the only creator affected by the orientalism that swept France before World War I; Coty commissioned Léon Bakst, designer of the sets for *Schéhérazade* by the *Ballets Russes*, to design the box for the powder sold with his fragrances, using paper of red, black, and gold. The explosion of color set off by the *Ballets Russes* (themselves influenced by the Thai dance troupe that had previously visited St. Petersburg) helped to create the vogue for lipstick, which has since become a major fragrance product. Prior to Poiret, lipstick and mascara had been considered garish and vulgar, but now they became part of the oriental chic. By 1924 American women alone were using up three thousand miles of lipstick a year.

The final phase of the Belle Epoque came to a brutal halt with the War of 1914. The advances of the late nineteenth and early twentieth

La Rose Jacqueminot was the perfume of 1902 that assured the success of François Coty. It was his re-creation of a famous horticultural variety of rose, famous for its color and fragrance. Shown here is the 1907 bottle, done by Lalique. Coty used violet notes to give the rose scent an added resonance. Courtesy of Marylène Delbourg-Delphis

century were applied to warfare and France and England first witnessed all the horrors of chemical weapons. Fashion and all its accessories were of the most minor interest during the awful years between 1914 and 1919. The north of France was ravaged although Provence, the region of perfume production, had been spared.

Cessation of hostilities brought giddy relief to those who survived and a sense of disbelief, ushering in the *années folles* of the next decade. The twenties were to be an age of heady freedom—the age of jazz, automobiles, smoking and drinking, the flapper, and of bobbed hair. Far from having been forgotten during the years of the War, fashion, and with it fragrance, came back with renewed ardor, and Paris remained more than ever, the center of style—although styles changed dramatically.

The advertisement for La Rose France was designed by Mucha, the renowned affichiste *of the Belle Epoque. The perfume was created in 1911 by Paul Parquet for Houbigant, and was named after* La France, *a variety of rose that enjoyed great popularity at the time. Courtesy of Marylène Delbourg-Delphis*

The Designers of the Twenties—Perfume Is Wedded to Fashion

The trend that Poiret had begun before the War rapidly expanded during the twenties. Every major couturier had to have a fragrance as well. This meant growth by leaps and bounds for the industry of Grasse because an entirely new approach to style emerged after the War and numerous important designers appeared as its representatives.

The most important of this new wave was Gabrielle (Coco) Chanel (1883–1971). Chanel was diametrically opposed to the exotic ideal espoused by Poiret. She abominated his egret feathers, flowing skirts and harem pants, plush fabrics, and Levantine colors. Chanel loved the Spartan, well-bred look of the British aristocracy. It was her genius to transpose the boater's hat and the jersey and pullover from England to France, and from male use to feminine chic. The khaki of the doughboy became a prominent color in the Chanel collection—it is said that she bought fabric from army and navy surplus houses to transform into dresses. Her personal color preference was for somber black, and her dresses and suits were divested of every superfluity—the "deluxe poor

Gabrielle (Coco) Chanel brought forth a new style by adapting masculine apparel and accessories to feminine use. This technique was even utilized in her famous Number 5, where a bottle of a man's cologne was transformed into the severe chic of a classic feminine perfume. Courtesy of Chanel, Inc.

look" which remained her hallmark. Chanel and the other designers of the twenties preferred a "boy-girl" (*garçonne*) style that suppressed the hips and chest and did not emphasize the waist.

This same knack of transforming male-associated wear to feminine style characterized the packaging of her famous Chanel Numero Cinq which appeared shortly after the War, in 1921. Gone were the rich colors of Poiret's boxes: the cartonnage was executed in gray, and the label in severest black and white. The flacon was sharp and rectangular, an adaptation of a bottle of a men's cologne but as elegant as a cut diamond. Even the name was spare: five was Chanel's lucky number.

The perfume itself broke new ground in perfumery as well as in packaging. The formulation was the daring creation of Ernest Beaux, an emigré from Russia who had worked with the House of Rallet in

Moscow prior to the 1917 revolution. A sharp and ringing synthetic, an aldehyde, was used as the topnote, but softened and bolstered by a sensitive use of costly naturals—ylang-ylang, jasmine, rose, and animal notes. Numero Cinq broke new ground in perfumery (the aldehydic type) as Chanel's designs became the model of the new age of fashion.

Another great creator of the twenties' style was Jean Patou. After serving in the French army, he set up a courturier house in Paris, which further developed the new spare look initiated by Chanel. He worked with Jean Almeras, the perfumer who had begun with Poiret, but Poiret's house had not survived the changed look of the twenties.

The first Patou perfume was Amour-Amour which was a great success of 1925. This designer created the first suntan cosmetic (Huile de Chaldeé) two years later, capitalizing on the vogue for sunworship encouraged by Chanel who returned to Paris bronzed from her cruise on the yacht of the Duke of Westminster. In 1929, Patou's Le Sien was touted as "a masculine perfume for the outdoors woman," who "plays golf, smokes, and drives a car at 120 (kilometers) an hour."[1]

In 1930, Jean Patou's perfumer created a kind of "bar" of perfumes called Cocktail Dry, but the creation most intimately linked to the name of Patou is Joy, created in 1931. The object of this perfume was to be free from all vulgarity, "cost what it may." And cost it did. Joy made use of Bulgarian rose and absolute of jasmine, two of the most expensive ingredients known even now, along with unusual synthetics, likewise expensive and difficult to make. The perfume was an immediate success. Joy was originally purchased by subscription in limited editions, and much advertising capital was made out of its distinction as "the world's most expensive perfume." Patou set his brother-in-law in charge of his perfume line, and the Patou fragrances were created in-house.

Captain Edward Molyneux, an Irishman, was the third leader of the twenties' style. He openly copied Chanel by naming his own fragrance Le Cinq de Molyneaux (1925), an aldehydic with a soft base of oakmoss. This fragrance won renown later as the scent worn by Edith Piaf. The scent well repaid the couturier, and several others soon followed— Charme (1929), Vivre (1930), and Le Chic de Molyneaux (1932).

The fourth famous name of the post-World War I period in France was that of Jeanne Lanvin. She began her career working as a designer for the *Maison de Haute Couture*, founded in 1889. Her lines were new but lacked the severity of Chanel. Like Chanel, however, Jeanne Lanvin was interested in the active artistic life of the time; Armand Rateau created the furnishings for her residence, and the dramatic *Boule Noire* of My Sin (1925) was designed by Paul Iribe. The Lanvin logo depicts Mme. Lanvin and her daughter dressing for a ball. The fragrance was a mixed floral type; the name was originally Mon Peché, which had not caught on in France. It had been sold in the United States as My Sin, and it succeeded at home with its new English name. André Fraysse was Lanvin's chemist-perfumer. In 1927 he created the famous Arpège, named after the musical arpeggio, which it imitated in olfactory terms. Arpège is rich in jasmine and other florals, a warm attractive composition.

For the couturiers who followed Poiret by linking fragrance with their fashions, a new need was in evidence. Perfumery was new to them—they had no experience in the nuances of top notes, body notes, base notes, the differences between a chypre and an oriental, and the complexities of the fatty aldehydes. Chanel and Patou retained perfumers but most did not and were in danger of floundering. Louis Amic of the Grasse house of Roure Bertrand Dupont saw their needs and worked with this new couturier/perfume merchant to chart a way through unfamiliar waters. Jean Amic was the son-in-law of Louis Maximilien Roure, the first to exhibit the industrial use of the new floral absolutes. His son, Louis Amic, set up a working relationship between Grasse and the Paris of fashion following his appointment as head of the firm in Paris in 1928.

Although the twenties witnessed this great growth of couturier fragrances, those houses whose only *raison d'être* was perfume were equally active. François Coty had watched with amazement the buying-up of perfumes by the returning American servicemen after the Armistice, and he set his sights on this new market. His American establishment was created even before his branch opened in London.

In 1921 Coty sent Jean Despres to New York. Despres was the son of one of the professors of Coty's own son. Despres's operation was soon doing an enormous trade for the perfume house in Paris. The firm wisely shipped the essential oils and the art packages to New York but had the perfumes assembled with American alcohol, thus avoiding the finished-goods duty. In 1925 his L'Origan sold for one United States dollar, the same price one would pay in France. Coty had tapped the most lucrative new market in the world.

Coty's scents included the classic Chypre (1907), L'Origan (1907), named for wild marjoram, and Jasmin de Corse (1911), named for his birthplace. In the twenties the oriental Emeraude appeared (1923), and L'Aimant (meaning both "magnet" and "lover"). The flacon for Emeraude was designed to look like a square-cut emerald, an experiment that resulted in much breakage in manufacture for the glass was almost paper-thin around the shoulders of the bottle. Coty died a rich man in the height of the Depression (1934). He owned a large chateau called Longchamps that was near his factory, the "City of Perfumes" at Suresnes by the Seine.

The House of Guerlain was also extraordinarily active after the War. Jacques Guerlain created Shalimar in 1925. With its rich base of sandalwood, ambergris, musk, and civet, this perfume has become the archetype of the modern oriental type. The bottle evoked the fountains of a Mughul garden, a creation of Raymond Guerlain and Baccarat. Mitsouko was created during the War and released soon after it (1919). Mitsouko was the name of a Madame Butterfly in love with a British naval officer, characters created by the novelist Claude Farrère. In 1929 Guerlain brought out Liu, named after the Chinese slave girl in Puccini's opera who stabbed herself rather than betray Princess Turandot. For all the toughness of the jazz age, or perhaps because of it, there was still a real market for make-believe and the romance of faraway places— if only to judge from the perfumes of the day. Nor should it be imagined that all presentations espoused the ascetic understatement of a Chanel No. 5. The majority employed a romantic label and poster display.

Parfumes Caron, of the *rue de la Paix*, was a house created exclusively for scents by Ernest Daltroff in 1904. Tabac Blond, created in 1919, had a soft, sweet, leather scent, and Nuit de Noël, created in 1922, had a striking black flacon. This perfume used a classic eau de cologne top note on a base of vanilla, rose, orris, oakmoss, and ylang-ylang. Bellodgia (1927) and Fleurs de Rocaille (1935) were other famous fragrances created by Daltroff. Mme. Félicie Bergaud collaborated in the design of the Caron flacons.

In general, the houses of perfume produced more perfumes than the couturiers; for the houses, perfumes were their stock in trade, but clothiers usually had to job out the creation of a new perfume. In her book, *Les Sillages des Elégantes*, Marylène Delbourg-Delphis has stressed that women used to look to new perfumes as they did new fashions in dress. But with the rise of the couturier fragrances, fragrance became an anchor amid the changing styles. This tendency prevailed, and after 1929 the tempo of perfume creation began to diminish. The semi-

LE RÉVEIL DE L'ÉGYPTE
B. Nessler PARFUMEUR PARIS

The twenties saw a longing for distant places, far from the day-to-day existence; and perfume, like the genie from the bottle, was a means of wafting one away. Le Reveil de l'Egypte was not an important fragrance, but it illustrates a major theme of the times. Courtesy of Marylène Delbourg-Delphis

annual rhythm of the fashion showings, however, served as ready-made opportunities to advertise their perfumes.

The Thirties

The *garçonne*, or "boy-girl," look of the twenties had freed women from stereotyping, but by the thirties another voice was insisting that "the

La Normandie, created for Patou, the couturier, in 1935, commemorated the debut of the illustrious luxury liner. Fragrance advertising romanticized the automobile, ocean liners, and airplane travel in the twenties and thirties. Courtesy of Marylène Delbourg-Delphis

body must never be forgotten." Elsa Schiaparelli was not afraid to reveal the curves of the frame, restoring the suppressed waist and hips. This Roman designer, whose shop had opened at the end of the twenties, was both aristocrat and rebel. She chose the finest fabrics and draped them beautifully, but she also loved "to set off cascades of fireworks." Like Poiret, she designed dresses that would light up and did not keep to the beige and black that had been the hallmarks of Chanel. "Shocking pink" was her favorite color and so Shocking was the name she chose for her perfume that appeared in 1937. The idea for the bottle came from a torso in plaster that Mae West had sent Schiaparelli from Hollywood, portraying the Venus de Milo. Schiaparelli was amused and decided to make a bottle based on the torso. The fragrance had a warmth from its use of a patchouli base and a top note of hyacinth. Salut (1931) was French for "Hi!" and her Snuff (1939) was presented in a crystal pipe in a cigar box. Schiaparelli associated with the Surrealists and shared their love of the offbeat. She made buttons out of lollipops, paperweights, and miniature guitars. One of her hats was an enormous shoe, another a lamb chop; a stream of lobsters adorned one of her evening gowns. Handbags played tunes when they were opened, and she created phosphorescent jewelry. As with Poiret, fashion almost became theater.

Schiaparelli spent the World War II years in New York; her "de-

Elsa Schiaparelli's Shocking of 1937. Madame Schiaparelli was a great supporter of the surrealists of the 1930s, and used their typical blend of art and clowning. The poster is by Vertes. Courtesy of Marylène Delbourg-Delphis

cadent art" would not have appealed to the Nazis. But the year after the War, she had Dali design her Roi Soleil flacon, and in 1948, back to her old tricks, she named a new perfume Zut, a rather fresh word from French slang. Chanel closed her doors during the War years, but, like Elsa Schiaparelli, she was still indomitable and would later present new collections.

The Depression years were a time of difficulty in France, as elsewhere, yet creators continued to produce many classic fragrances. Tabu (1931), formulated by Jean Carles for the Spanish firm of Dana, was sumptuous and oriental, the prototype of the later Youth Dew and Opium. Vol de Nuit (1932) by Jacques Guerlain incorporated the idiom of the aldehydes into the language of the Guerlains. The bottle was entirely different: a glass defined by the shape of the French Air Force wings. The theme played upon the fascination of the thirties for air travel. In 1933 Dana produced Twenty Carats—perfume in lieu of the money so few possessed—and in 1935 Isabey launched Grand Slam, another common wish in those years of poverty.

Coty died in 1934, but his successor, Henri Robert, created Muguet des Bois in 1936 to immortalize Coty's custom of presenting his employees with bouquets of lily of the valley every May first, taken from the grounds of his Chateau de Puy d'Artigny.

Vol de Nuit, 1933, was named after the novel by Antoine de Saint-Exupery, and bears the impress of the French aviator's wings. The scent is a blend of many components, including spices, orris root, aromatic wood oils, and oak moss. Courtesy of Guerlain, Inc.

Dior and the Postwar Revival

The War years were dark for all those French industries that appealed to play, fantasy, and heightened imagination. Very few fragrances were created; France was cut off from needed supplies from India and the East Indies and from traditional markets in America and Britain. Nevertheless, Chantilly (1941), Replique (1944), and the innovative Bandit (1944) by Mademoiselle Cellier made their appearance. Edmond Roudnitska, who was soon to become the perfumer to Dior, created Femme in 1944, and Jacqueline Fraysse created Antilope, released in 1945, for the House of Weil.

Just before the Depression, couture had been France's second highest export; after the War, the government decided to intervene and recover the losses in this once-fertile area. In 1945 it helped finance a *"Théatre de la Mode"* at the *Musée des Arts Decoratifs*, displaying the works of many new designers such as Pierre Balmain; Hubert de Givenchy; the Spaniard, Cristobal Balenciaga; and Christian Dior. But this was only the first round of the battle to recover lost territory. The French textile firm of Boussac gave extensive financing to Christian Dior with which to launch the "New Look." In one stroke, Dior abolished the practical, efficient look of the war years. Indeed, the sweeping skirts that appeared on that morning of February 12, 1947, when his new collection was inaugurated to a stunned public, seemed to reach back to a period that predated even Schiaparelli and Chanel. Back came the full hips, full bust-line, thin waist, bare shoulders, and high gloves of a nigh-forgotten era. To British and American supply boards, conscious of acute shortages of materials, this seemed another example of French naughtiness, and the British government demanded a boycott of the new Parisian style. To these critics, and to the liberationists who saw Dior taking women on a retrograde path that negated all the gains of the twenties, the designer could only express the sentiment: "I thank heaven I lived in Paris in the last years of the Belle Epoque. They marked me for life. My mind retains a picture of a time full of happiness, exuberance and peace, in which everything was directed toward the art of living."[2] But the New (or old) Look swept all before it, and manufacturers in London and New York could not even give away dresses cut in the pre-Dior style.

Dior's work was meticulous, reminiscent of the House of Worth, bringing joy to the tailors and seamstresses who examined his materials; new techniques and forgotten ones were used. The world was tired of depressions and wars, and the New Look was a complete coup for France. Paris took orders while the rest of the textile world resisted or tried to catch up. All of its traditional prerogatives returned with a vengeance after the eclipse of the war.

Perfumes, of course, rode on these coattails. The New Look coincided with the beginning of two decades of unprecedented prosperity in the West. Dior's own Miss Dior, created by Roudnitska at his laboratory at Cabris, appeared in the same year as his fashion offensive. The elegant posters for the Dior perfumes were done by the *affichiste* René Gruau. The Dior perfumes (financed by the Moët group) were advertised by posters depicting the Dior woman as an aristocratic swan with a trailing black bow. Diorama appeared in 1949 and Diorissimo in 1955. Balenciaga's Le Dix was presented in the same year as the New Look, and that fashion house did Miss Balmain in 1958 and Ivoire in 1979. Robert Ricci designed the famous twin doves of L'Air du Temps in 1948, with its note of spice and flowers. In the next decade L'Interdit, inspired by Audrey Hepburn, was created for Givenchy; he had designed many of Hepburn's film costumes. In 1959 Madame Grès asked her perfumer, Omar Arif, to create a fragrance that would evoke her trip through the Spice Islands; the result was Cabochard, a perfume which has become a classic.

France and the Sixties

The late fifties and sixties witnessed a prosperity throughout the Western world that was without precedent in world history. The terrible scars of war were healed by the diligence of European industry and political leaders aided by the enormously successful Marshall Plan of the United States. The French luxury industry had had the daring to make a bold sweep with the elegance of Christian Dior New Look which made enormous profits on the American and reviving European fashion markets. French gowns trailed across the silver screens of the American movie industry, and France's authority in all things elegant was secure.

But the sixties proved to be an unsettling, though exciting, new decade. The great master had died, suddenly, in 1957, leaving the fate of the House of Dior on the slender shoulders of the twenty-one-year-old Yves Saint Laurent. The young couturier suffered several nervous attacks due to the stresses thus imposed—luxury goods accounted for a sizable proportion of France's export market—and eventually Saint Laurent was to sever his relations with the House of Dior. The career of a couturier in the sixties was not going to be easy, for the great baby boom of the war years had produced in those years the youth explosion that was to question all authorities. The generation that had grown up with the confusion of the war years in its infancy and the unheard of prosperity of its adolescence was not ready to accept anything simply because it had always been so. The Algerian War in France, as well as the Vietnamese War with its French and American phases, created a climate of disdain for conventional leaders and of efforts to form a counter-culture. Rock and folk music gave expression to this rebellion, and the centers of fashion and anti-fashion were wherever youth congregated—Berkeley, Haight-Ashbury, New York, Liverpool, and London. Mongolian shepherd blouses, dashikis, Nehru jackets, Indian pyjamas, and flowing Moroccan burnouses rapidly succeeded each other as the style of the hour. Men sprouted beards, stuck flowers in their hair, and wore love beads, sandals, and the ubiquitous blue jeans. Commercially too, France began to experience the maturing of the United States as a center of luxury goods. The American fashion, cosmetic, and fragrance industries were beginning to spawn their own, not unsophisticated, products.

Faced with this rebellion among consumers and competition from the growing American beauty industry, a number of couturier houses closed, as did Balenciaga in 1968, or else, tried as best to ride the trends which they were no longer initiating. Courrèges brought out a see-through dress, Saint Laurent dressed models in white baby-doll vinyl boots, skirts went way up and down to the ground, and Op and Pop styles were tried. Fashion leaders tried to meet the consumer half-way by entering the ready-to-wear (*prêt-à-porter*) market. In many ways this tarnished the image of the couturier with its links to the great crafts of France which had developed under the patronage of the court. No ready-to-wear garment could ever hope to have even a fraction of the fine handwork that made every Dior gown such a revelation to seamstresses and tailors, works of art avidly acquired by museums. However, it did give traditional French fashion a way of living with the changed world of the new generation. As part of this, beginning with Pierre Cardin, many fashion leaders began to license their names to a vast range of consumer goods—leathergoods, stationery, furniture, sports goods, housewares, and every conceivable fashion accessory. With this we see the transition of the couturier to the designer. This metamorphosis was of greatest importance for understanding the selling of fragranced products today, because just as *haute couture* had given perfume such a new lease on life by its wholesale adoption of fragrance in the twenties, the seventies and eighties would become the period when designers began to set new records in the sale of scents.

The chaos of the sixties did not last forever. "Do your own thing!" did not remain the watchword of the seventies, and many consumers began to feel a need for arbiters of style. On the other hand, the world of fashion had to recognize that there were many choices in matters of taste, and that its mandate was often to simply add good design to trends in beauty that originated anywhere in the world. But, as we shall see, Paris has continued to remain an important center of the contemporary world of fashion and its countless fragrances.

10

Perfumery in America

France and the United States are by far the major consumers of fragrance in the world today. We have seen the development of the industry in France; now let us look at how the American perfume industry evolved into its present state.

In the seventeenth century the English men and women who sailed for the rocky coast of New England were not likely to pursue the craft of perfume. The Puritans frowned on self-adornment, and we find, for example, heavy fines for wearing long or powdered locks at Harvard in 1636. However, a few decades later fashion had reared its head even in Boston, where the laws of the Massachusetts Colony permitted the use of silks, lace, and simple cosmetics to members of the trading elite and forbade them to the lower classes.

In the eighteenth century Philadelphia, New York, Williamsburg, and Charleston became seats of British colonial administration, and the gubernatorial courts followed fashions from England. Cromwell and the Puritans were defeated by 1660 and the wig carried the day in America as it had in Restoration England; soon every army officer carried a campaign box filled with shaving gear, cologne, a wig, and powder. The first style in wigs was that of the Stuarts—long brown curls; but after the continental Hanoverians assumed the throne in 1714, the lighter periwigs became the order of the day.

The fragrances used in the colonies resembled those used in Europe: Hungary Water, Orange-Blossom Water, Lavender Water, and Eau de Cologne. In the South, the Elizabethan tradition of making sachets, pomanders, and potpourris was retained. Since horticulture there was popular, as in England, the women of the plantations had a full repertoire of herbs and flowers to work with.

Perfumery among the colonialists was one of the most dimunitive of American industries, but the background technology was developing. John Winthrop, Jr., son of the Massachusetts governor, was the first to possess contemporary European laboratory equipment. In the eighteenth century, the Scotch-Irish immigrants brought with them their practical knowledge of distillation. One John Lucena was granted the first patent to manufacture castile soap in 1761. The first manufacture of fine glass was by Henry Stiegel, near Lancaster, Pennsylvania, in 1767. These beginnings were the precursors of the vast American distilling, soap, and glassmaking industries—all to be linked with perfumes.

The Early Firms

In 1729 the first American pharmacy opened in Philadelphia. In 1752 Dr. William Hunter, an English pharmacist, settled in Newport, Rhode Island, and opened a shop where he sold drugs and perfumes. When the American Revolution flared up, Dr. Hunter cast his lot with the Tories and died in the attempt to suppress the uprising. His widow sought to escape confiscation by the Revolutionaries by registering the firm under the name of Charles Feke, one of her husband's clerks, and the ruse worked. The business flourished, selling to the Newport shipping families who were growing rich on the China trade. After Feke's death, ownership passed to Rowland Hazard and Philip Caswell. With the inclusion of a Canadian partner, the firm became Caswell-Massey. Today Caswell-Massey, since removed to New York, can claim to be the oldest retail firm of "chemists and perfumers" in the United States.

The wholesale essential-oil house that can lay claim to the oldest continuous business is that of Fritzsche, Dodge and Olcott of New York. Its origins lay with Robert Back, who in 1798 opened a drug and import business at 128 Pearl Street, selling essential oils, soaps, and perfumes. By 1840 the firm had become Dodge, Cuming and Company, and by 1861 Dodge and Olcott. They specialized in extracts of sandalwood, nutmeg, clove, and bay. The company later merged with Fritzsche Brothers, which had begun as an American offshoot of Schimmel and Company of Leipzig, a continental firm known for patronizing the organic chemistry of essential oils.

While New England culture did not encourage the arts of adornment, it did encourage the arts of commerce. Wealth was viewed as proof of membership in the covenant of the elect, and Yankee traders learned to make a sale out of the least promising of situations. After the Revolution, the Napoleonic Wars gave the new republic, a neutral in the war between France and England, a golden opportunity to trade; and at home, domestic manufacturers flourished.

American chemists followed the developments of research into soaps and essential oils that followed Napoleon's patronage of French science. William Colgate was among the first outside of France to make use of the work of Chevreul in his factory, which produced soaps, candles, and starch from 1806 onward. In 1837 Procter, an Englishman, and Gamble, an Irishman, joined forces in Cincinnati in the soap business. The Palmolive Company of Milwaukee, also engaged in soap manufacture, was founded later (1864).

With the opening of the Pennsylvania oil wells in the mid-century, the United States began its long love affair with petroleum and petroleum products. Another "mine" of synthetics was opened in 1857 when S. Warren began the commercial distillation of coal tar.

Two of the most highly noted American soap perfumes were Ivory, with its strong note of oil of citronella, and the floral, powdery Cashmere Bouquet, originally created as a perfume but transformed by William Ungerer into one of the most popular and long-lived soap fragrances.

In 1878 the Mennen Company was founded in Newark, New Jersey, with a line of personal-care products. In 1882 the Andrews Soap Company, which later became the Andrew Jergens Company, was established in Cincinnati. Its Jergen's Lotion, redolent of oil of bitter almond, was an important early cosmetic in the United States. Lever Brothers was founded in England in 1885 and brought to America in 1895. Bristol-Myers was founded in the same year, and Johnson & Johnson dates from 1887. Cleanliness was close to godliness in nineteenth-century America, and soap companies remain one of the great consumers of essential oils in the United States today.

At the end of the nineteenth century almost every supplier of essential oils was located in a narrow area around the docks at the tip of Manhattan island. On South Street the bowsprits of the merchant ships practically touched the warehouses. Here the essential-oil firms received crude spices for distilling, processed oils, and finished perfume compounds from Paris, for many of them also served as representatives for leading French houses. Because the French companies suspected their American agents of using some poorer quality essential oils to extend their fragrance compounds, there was a tendency to rotate representatives. This was the pitfall that Coty sidestepped by sending his own representative to oversee production and to actively cultivate the market in the United States. After the boom of the twenties, most of the houses of Grasse and Paris had permanent daughter establishments in the United States.

Some of the early essential-oil houses in America that continue to this day include J. Manheimer, Inc.; D. W. Hutchinson and Company; Magnus, Mabee and Reynard, Inc. (now a part of Crompton and Knowles Corporation); Norda, Inc.; Polak's Frutal Works, Inc.; Ungerer and Company; Florasynth, Inc.; and Felton International, Inc. International Flavors and Fragrances developed from Van Amerigen-Haebler, Inc., founded in 1929, with antecedents in the Netherlands. Under Ernest Shiftan and Henry G. Walter, Jr., this company has grown to be the largest supplier in the world, the only essential-oil house on the stock exchange in New York City. Givaudan Corporation in American was the affiliate of L. Givaudan et Cie, S. A., of Geneva, begun when the Swiss company acquired the American firm that had represented it prior to 1924. This company is also one of the world's largest, a great deal of its revenue having derived from the scenting of many items of American manufacturing, such as textiles, rubber goods, and printing inks which have disagreeable or even nauseating odors of their own.

The Beginning of the Cosmetic Industry in America

The first American to enter the cosmetic field in a major way was Richard Hudnut, the son of a New York druggist, whose father's very ordinary store was on the corner of Broadway and Ann Street. After Richard Hudnut graduated from Princeton, he became fired with the idea of visiting France. There he was astounded at the beauties of the Belle Epoque and the ease and abandon with which the French used perfumes, cosmetics, and rouge; he decided that these adornments were not cheap or risqué but accoutrements that should be introduced to American women. Upon his return, he transformed the family drug concern into a shop with floors of black and white marble parquet and chandeliers which rivalled Versailles. The new Hudnut shop became a tourist attraction, seductive to both eye and nose. Eventually Hudnut's products became so popular that he closed the glittering store to concentrate on wholesale orders. His products were Violet Sec Toilet Water, Du Barry Beauty Preparations, and compounds entitled Yankee Clover and Three Flowers. He also carried a line of products for the hair. In 1916 Richard Hudnut sold his successful business and retired—to France.

If Hudnut could be called the father of American cosmetics, Florence Graham—Elizabeth Arden—was the mother. Her professional name derived from a book Miss Graham had read and liked: *Elizabeth and Her German Garden*. She was a Canadian nurse, convinced that skin would respond to cleansing, toning, and nourishment. She had been quite impressed by the beauty of New York women, who spent considerably more time on grooming than was customary back home in Woodbridge, Ontario. After years of waiting and planning, she finally opened a beauty shop in 1910, selling hair and skin care products and fragrances. The fame of her salon soon spread, and similar establishments shortly opened their red doors in Boston, Washington, and Chicago. Graham was fond of flowers and plants, and her most famous perfume was named for the sight from her Virginia retreat: Blue Grass.

Another woman important to the early history of American cosmetics was Helena Rubinstein. She left Kracow in Poland to open a salon in London in 1907 and subsequently came to the United States. Charles Jundt came to New York in 1919 and opened his salon at the Ritz Carlton, becoming Charles of the Ritz. His company specialized in custom-blended powders, perfumes, and soaps.

The California Perfume Company founded in 1886 became, in the thirties, Avon Products, Inc., of Suffern, New York, with a large line of sold-at-home products that included soaps, after-shaves, baby products, and fragrances. Avon has become one of the most successful of mass-market firms retailing beauty products.

Men's toiletries included Bay Rum which was originally West Indian rum mixed by various distillers with the oil of *Pimento acris*. This plant is a close relative of allspice, not of bay laurel, the bay leaf of cookery. Florida Water was another American product compounded of classic eau de cologne to which several spice oils had been added. Pinaud's Lilac Vegetal was another men's product dispensed in American barbershops at the turn of the century.

After-shaves became important because of the clean-cut look which replaced the beards of the nineteenth century. The trend was aided by the 1906 removal of the American tax placed on perfume-grade alcohol. The Denatured Alcohol Tax Regulation recognized the difference between beverage and industrial use of ethyl alcohol. The Williams Company's Aqua Velva appeared in 1917. In 1935 Canoe became another large seller in this category. The fragrance had originally been formulated for women but later discovered its true market. Old Spice (1938) was another formulation, originally entitled Early American Old Spice, designed for women. But Shulton, the manufacturing firm, asked the perfumer at Dodge and Olcott to reformulate the perfume for men, and it was made more citrusy. Old Spice was sold in a container which was cream-colored, like an eighteenth-century rose-petal container, decorated with an East Indian motif. It became an enormous success.

World War I gave many American women salaries of their own, and the rising film industry popularized the use of cosmetics. As a result, sales surged during the twenties. American troops returning from Europe after World War I with numerous bottles of French perfume had also helped create a greater market for fragrances. Even the Depression did not wholly curtail the sales of fragrances and cosmetics—perfumes lasted long and remained gift items, and soaps and cosmetics were affordable.

One important company born in the Depression was Revlon. Charles Revson (1906–1975), son of an immigrant from Russia, went to work in a Seventh Avenue dress house and then began selling nail polish for a distributor. His flair for selling was so apparent that he and his brother decided to create their own business along with a chemist, Charles

Lachman. Lachman was responsible for the "l" in "Revlon." Capital in 1932 was hard to come by, and the three-hundred-dollar loan they took out was given at a rate of twenty-four percent interest. Lachman developed a creamy opaque nail polish, which Revson took to beauty salons. In 1939 the polishes were color-combined with lipstick, and after World War II, cosmetics, creams, and fragrances were incorporated into his beauty line. By 1967 the cosmetics and fragrances accounted for ninety-one percent of the company's earnings.

Revson's first fragrance was named for the American designer Norman Norell. It had been developed for Revlon by a wholesale house which specialized in essential oils. Associates voted against his choice of the seventy-one-year-old designer as the guiding inspiration for the fragrance but Revson's wife Lynn wore his clothes and her vote carried the day. Norell himself was given authority over the packaging, and a lavish promotion inaugurated the new perfume at Bonwit Teller's in 1968. Revson grossed a million dollars in sales from Norell in the first year, and the figure tripled in the next.

Estée Lauder and her husband Joseph founded a company that has always been Revlon's rival. Her corporation was begun in 1946 after the War to market preparations developed by her uncle, a cosmetic chemist. In 1953 Estée Lauder brought out her Youth Dew, one of the all-time fragrance bestsellers. The fragrance was an oriental, with notes of frankincense, patchouli, vetiver, clove, and musk. It was sold in a novel form. Youth Dew was a bath oil, not a typical alcoholic perfume, and had a greater concentration of essential oils—three times that of the most popular perfume being sold at the time. The format was clever and timely, for although most women still considered perfume a luxury for a night out, a bath oil could be applied every time a woman took a bath.

The name Youth Dew struck a responsive chord in women—it was a good fragrance, it promised youth to a mature clientele with money to spend, and the lotus bud shape of the bottle was appealing. It has become one of the three major sellers in the United States, and its sales remain impressive. Its success has generated a number of competitors. Aramis was launched by the Lauders as a companion men's fragrance to Youth Dew, in 1964. It, too, has been enormously successful, and Estée Lauder, Incorporated, a private company, has sales which approach the one billion mark.

Norell, Youth Dew, and Aramis are in the category that the French call "grand perfumes" *(les grands parfums)*. In concluding, it should be noted that it was the Yankee genius for selling that saw that fragrances could be sold equally to enhance a furniture polish, diapers, soap flakes, baby lotions, antiperspirants, and rubber toys and dolls. Even today French fragrance manufacturers have learned to "see" a new market considerably below the world of fashion and elegance. The poet Baudelaire's *calme, luxe,* and *volupté* were not what Americans usually required, but cleanliness was. As a result, the American essential oil grew up closely allied to the soap industry and developed extensions into many other home products as well.

Having taken a look at the historical rise of the perfumery industry and its recent history on both sides of the Atlantic, let us assess the life of the industry today: where its supplies and materials come from, how they are handled industrially, and what are some of the ways in which they are sold.

PART

III

PERFUMERY TODAY

II

Sources of Supply for the Modern Industry

If, as Napoleon said, an army marches on its stomach, the perfume industry marches on its supplies. Wholesale houses still quake when they read about typhoons in the Spice Islands, political changes in jasmine-growing regions, or fluctuations in the availability of petroleum extractives. We have seen how the animal, botanical, and synthetic sources of fragrance have come to be used historically; here we will look at these sources and see how they are supplied to today's growing industry.

Animal Sources

As we have seen, ambergris is a secretion of the sperm whale, *Physeter macrocephalus*. It was an important part of the Arab-Chinese trade nexus;

the Chinese associate it with aphrodisiac properties. This myth has remained fairly green, for the advertising copy for many of the perfumes of the twenties underlined their "amber" qualities, said to inspire love; indeed the odor of ambergris is not unlike a woman's natural scent. Today only the Soviet perfume industry and, perhaps to some degree, the Japanese make use of this precious substance. The rest of the world has voluntarily agreed to stop killing this endangered species. Currently the ambergris note must come from synthetics for 99.9 percent of the world industry, although it is conceivable that if the slaughter of these mammals soon ended, they might be scientifically "herded" for the score of valuable products they yield.

Natural musk played an important role in perfume history but today is much less significant. While the odor of musk is more popular than ever, its source is synthetic. It is soft, sexual, and somewhat akin to the human skin odor, which made it a great hit of the sixties when "sensuality" was discovered. Nevertheless, musk continues to be one of the most popular single-note scents.

In the mountains of Anhui Province in central China, efforts have been made to encourage the deer, *Moschus moschiferus*, to mate on game farms, with encouraging results. The first tries were dismal failures, with the deer frequently dying, but studies were made of their habits to better determine the plants that furnished their diet in the wild. Dandelions and honeysuckle proved to be two of the plants they browsed on. Once the herd was surviving, the next step was to ascertain whether or not the musk could be extracted without slaughtering the animal. It was discovered that animals can be operated on for their musk three times. Musk is reproduced each time and the animal continues living. Formerly it took the lives of a hundred and forty deer to produce a kilo of musk. By following safe and scientific ways of preserving the flocks of musk deer (and even increasing them) and equally safe ways of removing their products, we may be able to reverse the decline of natural supplies of musk.

Castoreum is a by-product of the Canadian and Siberian fur trade, a secretion of the beaver *(Castor fiber)*. The castoreum-producing scent glands are found between the genitals and anus of both males and females, where an oily substance with a warm, pungent, leathery note is secreted. The secretion of the Canadian beaver is considered finer than that of the Russian beaver. As with all such animal products, castoreum has wonderful fixative properties and is widely used in modern perfumes.

Nineteenth-century Chinese certificate of quality for Szechuanese musk. The musk deer's original range extended all over China, but the sweet scent from the scent glands of the male animal made the deer a rarity except for in the wilder areas of western China on the Tibetan border. Today, the animal is being bred in captivity by the Chinese, and is no longer killed for the removal of the musk pod.

Civet is a secretion of *Viverra civetta*, and it is also found in the Indian *Viverra zibetha* and the Indonesian *Viverra megaspila*. The most commonly used species for perfumery is *Viverra civetta*, from Ethiopia. In that country civet-raising is a state monopoly. The cat is drained of this product once a week; it is not killed, although the method of extraction is not pleasant. The cats are caged, goaded with bamboo rods to produce the flow of adrenalin and of the civet. Then the civet is extracted through the anus. The odor of this glandular secretion is unspeakably fecal and repugnant. However, in dilution it becomes warm, sexual, and leathery and will exhibit remarkably tenacious fixative qualities.

Animal sources are extremely few in number compared to the vast array of essential-oil–bearing plants and the ever-increasing synthetic aroma chemicals that can be derived from petroleum and coal. Nor does there seem much likelihood of many other animal oils being added to the list. It is possible that the European wild boar, *Sus scrofa*, is a source of animal odors akin to the ones secreted by the human male body. The scent Andron contains the animal steroids androstenone and 5-alpha-androstenol, but the exact source of the scent is a company secret. The skunk produces a powerful odor, and certainly many individually unpleasant essences can become agreeable when used in minute amounts in careful blends, but to date this has not happened to this animal's secretions.

Essential Oils Derived from Plants

Plant aromatics have certainly dominated the perfume story, and despite the great importance of synthetics, they continue to play a central part in perfume work. A fragrance deficient in the natural oils becomes shrill and tinny, almost headache provoking; the plant oils give a composition softness and roundness. Also, the plant oils have given a language for the description of the newer synthetic odor chemicals. Very few perfumers will describe a fragrance as "methyl phenylacetate-y" or as having a lovely "2-methyl-2-pentyl-cyclopent-2-en-l-one note," and certainly no writer of perfume ad copy will. A perfume will have a "rosy" note or a hint of "pine" or "peach."

We will list the major plant oils and their salient characteristics under the following headings: florals, herb oils, leaf oils, spice oils, root oils, citrus oils, resins, and fragrant woods. We will talk briefly about each oil and mention the countries that produce them today, for perfumery has become irreversibly cosmopolitan.

THE FLORAL OILS

The rose was the earliest of the flowers to be distilled and therefore one of mankind's most widely used essences. The industry today differentiates between two types of rose: *rose bulgare (Rosa damascena)* and *rose de mai (Rosa centifolia)*. *Rose bulgare* has a deep, intensely roseate note, and it is still principally a distilled product, whereas *rose de mai* is both distilled and widely treated by the newer method of solvent extraction. It too has a sweet odor, reminiscent of the flower but somewhat lighter than the damask rose.

The *Rosa damascena* was the rose celebrated by Sufi poets in Iran and Turkey, and it was a Turkish merchant who introduced it to Bulgaria. It has found a home for itself in the Valley of Kazanluk, which runs east and west across Bulgaria, protected from winds and weather by hills to the north and south. This nation is the world's largest producer of this incredibly costly oil. After the absorption of Bulgaria into the Soviet orbit following World War II, producing attar of rose became a state monopoly. Each *koncoum* (vase) of rose oil is stamped with the *Bulgarska-rosa* seal and accompanied by a certificate of purity.

Turkey remains the second greatest producer of this kind of rose oil today; most of the plantations are located in the Isparta region. Some production exists in the Soviet Union near the Black Sea, and in Syria and India, but Bulgaria and Turkey outdistance all the others. Bulgarian rose oil is rated the world's finest, but the Turkish oil is not far behind in quality.

Attar of rose is expensive for several reasons. To start with, the rose is not a low-maintenance plant and requires much pruning, fertilizing, and spraying to conserve its condition. New fields must be started by cuttings from healthy plants, but an old field will produce for as many as forty years if carefully tended. When the flower is to be processed, the petals must be wholly separated from the green sepals at their base; green floral parts would give a green, not rosy, note to the distilled oil. Distilling the flowers requires cohobation, i.e., a second run through the still, as rose oil separates from water only with great difficulty, unlike most essential oils. Sometimes a third distillation is necessary, costly in terms of fuel and labor alike. The yield in oil is only one kilogram per four thousand kilograms of flowers. Nevertheless, the Bulgarian peasants are noted for their skill at distillation and their ability to wring every molecule of oil from their crops.

The Frenchman, Charles Garnier, brought equipment for solvent extraction to Bulgaria in 1904, but water distillation remains the preferred method. The Bulgarian government is subsidizing research into further refinement of the traditional process.

Price is the only limit to the use of this fulsome material; even trace elements of attar can soften and transform a perfume creation. The oil of damask rose can also serve as a flavor, such as in *locoum*, Turkish Delight. It is also likely that it is used in some popular soft drinks to add roundness and fruitiness.

Rose de mai has always been a specialty of the Grasse region, but the acres there under cultivation have steadily diminished since World War II. Today Morocco is the largest source, its plantations spread out between the High Atlas range and the Djebel Sarro. The rose of Marrakesh is a sub-variety that is extremely popular in Morocco, but there are other types as well; the plant is known for its ability to hybridize. Moroccan oil is an extremely important part of modern perfumery; its price is half that of Bulgarian oil.

If the rose is the queen, the jasmine is the king of fragrance. Since Muslim times, jasmine has been diffused from Persia and Kashmir throughout Europe, Asia, and North Africa to be used in cosmetics, hair dressings, religious garlands, and as a perfume for tea. The jasmine was associated with the rise of European perfumery in Italy during the Renaissance, and when Italian ways were transposed to France, the cultivation of this flower was included. Today French jasmine from around Grasse is indubitably the finest, although very little is produced. Italy also produces a superlative absolute of jasmine. But it is Egypt that is responsible for eighty percent of the world's production.

Charles Garnier also brought solvent extraction apparatus to northern Egypt in 1912, and from that beginning the Egyptian industry has burgeoned. Jasmine requires plenty of sun and warm summers. Because the winters in the south of France are frequently cold enough to harm the plants, the *Jasminum grandiflorum* is grafted upon rootstocks of *J. officinale*. In Egypt both the *officinale* and Arabian jasmine (*Jasminum sambac*) forms are grown.

Each flower must be picked by hand, a reason the crop has diminished in France. Upon picking it can be treated either by the ancient means of enfleurage or by solvent extraction. The absolute costs over $1,500 a pound.

Jasmine exudes its most exquisite perfume at dawn, the hour Paracelsus called the "time of balsams" (*balsamiticum tempus*). In Egypt this is when teenage children pick the blooms, not because there is any wish to exploit the children (who then go to school), but because the low height of the bushes makes the task backbreaking for adults.

During the period of *La France Outre-Mer*, plantings were made in Algeria, in the valley of the Mitidja, and in what was then French Syria, near Beirut. These are not major producing areas today. Future rivals to Egypt may well be India and China, where manual labor is still extremely cheap; jasmine is grown in both countries now.

Not one of the *grands parfums* is without jasmine. Its complex and wholly attractive scent is as popular today as it has always been. Synthetic jasmine is easily manufactured, but even to that a little true jasmine absolute is added to remove harshness.

The tuberose *(Polianthes tuberosa)* receives its name from the tuberous nature of the root from which it sprouts in the spring; it has nothing to do with "rose." The plant is a native of Mexico, where it was known to Aztec apothecaries as *omixochitl,* "bone flower" from its bone-white blooms. However, during the period of global exploration, tubers first reached Europe the long way around. They had been exported from Acapulco to the Philippines and thence to the East Indies. Simon de Tovar, a physician of Seville, received the plant in 1594, and from Spain it was taken to France and Italy. For many centuries the flower bloomed at Pégomas, Auribeau, and Madelieu, near Grasse, but today the production in France has been reduced to a fraction of what it was at the turn of the century. Morocco is the leading producer of this indispensable floral; India has also obtained the best extractive apparatus from the Grasse house of Tournaire and produces an excellent tuberose absolute. The Indian name, *rat ki rani,* "mistress of the night," was the inspiration for its first botanical name in Europe: *Amica nocturna,* "friend of the night."

Like jasmine, the plant can be extracted by enfleurage and solvent extraction because both plants have the unique ability to create fragrance even after they have been picked. The odor of tuberose is intensely sweet but with a curious camphorlike note. The *absolu d'enfleurage* has a fatty note due to minute residues of lard, and the absolute of solvent extraction has a touch of greenness picked up from some of the constituents of the floral parts.

Sometimes an absolute is made from unused flowers from the cut-flower trade. These flowers are usually double, although for perfumery use the single-flowering variety is more odorous.

The cost of tuberose oil is one of the highest in perfumery: $2,000 a pound. The tuberose note is important in fragrances such as White Shoulders and Chloë.

As a crop, tubers cannot be grown in a field for more than two years, but they do have the ability to tolerate soils with a high salt and alkali content—soils that would be spurned by far less aristocratic plants.

Broom *(Spartium junceum)*, or Spanish broom, is known in the perfume trade as *genêt*, taken from the old Latin word *genista*. The Plantagenets *(planta genêt)* took their name from this plant. The flower resembles the sweet pea in structure as it is a member of the same legume family; the leaves are long and rushlike, hence the name "broom." The perfume is sweet with notes of hay. Spanish broom blooms bountifully across the hills of Provence and Languedoc; this prolificacy makes it one of the cheaper of floral absolutes, only $1,200 a pound. It has been grown for the perfumers of Montpellier and Grasse since the sixteenth century, and France continues to be a major producer of genêt, one of its traditional floral crops that has not had to look for a new home elsewhere in the face of rising real-estate development. Spain and Italy, old perfume lands, also continue to produce absolute of broom. The absolute is sometimes used to give a richness to fruit flavors, and an old specialty of Provence is broom-flower honey. The absolute is used to tone down some of the brashness of the synthetic aldehydes.

The old way of preparing broom was to macerate the flowers in hot oil. Today it is wholly a product of solvent extraction. The flowers must be sent to the extraction centers right after harvesting; otherwise the odor quickly deteriorates.

Another leguminous plant is cassie *(Acacia farnesiana)*, a New World plant that became one of the attractions of the famous Villa Farnese at Rome during the Renaissance. Today it is grown in southern France and Northern Africa. The closely related *Acacia cavenia* is also used for its own flowers, or as rootstock for the more desirable *Acacia farnesiana*. *Mimose* in perfumery refers to the *Acacia dealbata*, a flower raised in Provence for the cut-flower and perfume trades. The concrete has an attractive beeswax odor.

The Amaryllidaceae produce the following members of their perfume family: the jonquil *(Narcissus jonquilla)*, considered the finest in terms of odor; the paper-white narcissus *(N. tazetta)*; and the poet's narcissus *(Narcissus poeticus)*. The authorities Y. R. Naves and G. Mazuyer have scant praise for the last two narcissus perfumes. The paper-white's scent is "violent, crude, savage," and that of the poet is "clearly fecal."[1] What is so offensive to those august authors is the intense greenness that comes through the solvent-extraction process. But this same greenness can be used as an asset by a skilled perfumer.

Jonquil absolute has a deep, sweet note, with something of a green undertone. It resembles tuberose. These flowers are grown in France; an absolute has also been made from various narcissi in Holland as a by-product of the bulb and cut-flower industry.

The carnation *(Dianthus caryophyllus)* produces a heavy, sweet, honeylike absolute that only begins to resemble the fragrance of the living plant in extreme dilution. It is produced as a complement to the cut-flower trade of France and Holland, and about thirty kilos a year are produced. The essential oil is present in the petals only in small amounts. A good percentage of the absolute contains eugenol, the same molecule found in oil of cloves. Although the two species are in no way related, the carnation has been identified popularly as the "clove pink."

Oil from the hyacinth *(Hyacinthus orientalis)*, favorite flower of the Marquise de Pompadour, is obtained by solvent extraction. The flowers have also been used in a novel method whereby the scent of the hyacinth is made to cling to silica gel or charcoal in a cylinder through which carbon dioxide or nitrogen has been introduced. The hyacinth note is extremely popular, but the natural oil is used only in the costliest of perfumes. It is floral and green.

Actually not a floral extract but a flower bud extract, *cassis* is drawn from the common black currant *(Ribes nigrum)*. The concrete contains sixteen percent of an oil that has a strong fruity fragrance and a wonderfully intense flavor. Small doses can give a fragrance an interesting fruitlike cachet. France (Burgundy) is the greatest producer as well as consumer of this product.

Chamomile is one of the oldest of the European medical herbs. It was widely grown in monastery gardens. As a tea, it has always been used as a remedy against fevers. *Matricaria chamomilla* is cultivated in Hungary, Yugoslavia, Czechoslovakia, the Soviet Union, Germany, and Spain. The flowers are used for extraction, but since they are so small, many stems are processed as well. The oil can be distilled or a tincture made by steeping in alcohol. The scent of chamomile is part of the bouquet of such ancient liqueurs as D.O.M. and Benedictine. The distillate is an unusual blue color; at first it was believed to be a product of the copper laboratory apparatus, but in 1664 the oil was distilled in a retort of glass and the same color came through. The first commercial distillation of the oil was in 1822 by the Hungarian pharmacist Franz Steer of Kaschau. Today it is used to give a sweet, herby-fruity note a fragrance that remains through all stages of evaporation.

Ylang-ylang is one of the most commonly used of the floral oils because it blooms with tropical abandon. The flower is native to the Indonesian and Philippine archipelagoes, where it is still produced as an article of commerce. It is also grown for the perfume trade on Réunion and as an ornamental plant in Cuba, the Dominican Republic, and Puerto Rico. Nossi Bé and the Comoro Islands, off the coast of Madagascar, also produce a fine commercial ylang oil.

The flowers yield two grades known to the industry as "ylang-ylang," the finer, more floral oil, and "cananga" (taken from the scientific name for the tree, *Cananga odorata*), which is coarser. Climatic and botanical differences account for these gradations. The flowers are yellow at maturity, and drooping, with narrow petals. They bloom on trees that can reach up to eighty feet in height, but the trees are usually cropped where cultivated. Wild plants are constantly disseminated by birds that eat the fruit and drop the seeds over a broad range.

In rural areas of the Philippines and Java, simple water stills, which look exactly like those portrayed in the distillers' manuals of the sixteenth century, extract the oil. Where capitalization of the native industry has taken place, larger steam stills remove the essence from the flowers. The high cost of fuel has given great viability to the simpler type of stills throughout the tropics. The distilled oil is pale yellow and has a powerfully sweet odor that has an almost bananalike note. Cananga oil is heavier than the ylang but more tenacious.

Boronia absolute is a delightful oil rich in the violet notes of beta-ionone. The top note is fresh, the body notes extraordinarily rich and warm. It is expensive, costing about the same as jasmine absolute, and one of the few florals to come from Australia. The plant grows in the swamps of the southwest, not far from Perth. Its wet habitat has protected boronia from the forest fires that are the scourge of the region. The Forestry Service does not permit uprooting of the plant, and to conserve the local ecology, only the blossoms can be taken. Boronia grows in such tannin-rich bogs that when used as a cultivated plant, Australians have found that it responds well to dressings of spent tea

The champac flower possesses a heady, gardenia-like perfume. For centuries it has been used in India and China—today its oil is being extracted by modern techniques for use in the highest-quality perfumes.

leaves. The first concrete was exhibited at the British Empire Exhibition of 1924, and since then boronia has become a part of the world perfumery.

Champac *(Michelia champaca)* is another unusual floral oil, produced in India and China by solvent extraction with petroleum ether. It has a velvety, heavy scent and blends well with rose, carnation, and sandalwood. Although the blossoms are only one and a half inches long, and a half inch in diameter, champac exudes a powerful perfume. It is likely that this flower will become more and more used in the modern industry.

European perfumery has always made great use of lavender. The flower played its part in herbalism, lent its name to a color, and found its way into nursery rhymes. Mitcham in Surrey was the center of the English lavender production; it still raises such a fine lavender that the product is entirely consumed at home and no English lavender is exported.

France, too, is linked to this plant, but there the export of lavender oil is a major enterprise. The classical *Lavandula officinalis* ("officinal," i.e., "pharmaceutical") lavender is now more properly styled *Lavandula angustifolia*. It has received much attention from modern hybridists, having been crossed with the wild spike lavender *(Lavandula latifolia)* to produce a new crop: lavandin *(Lavandula hybrida)*. Today lavandin oil production outdistances that of true lavender oil: 140,000 metric tons as opposed to 7,000 metric tons yearly. Both, however, are extremely important components of the economy of the south of France. Five cultivars of lavandin have been developed, with varying nuances in the final oils: the "Abrial," "Super," "Grosso," "Standard," and "Maime Epis Tête" strains. Part of the reason for the interest in developing variant strains is that lavandin has been so profitable and so heavily planted that exhaustion of the terrain has been reflected by poor yields in certain areas.

Lavender's flowering tops and stalks are either steam distilled or (less frequently) treated by solvent extraction. Lavender has a refreshing floral-herbal odor, with agreeable, balsamic undertones. Lavandin has less fineness and more woody undertones, but it is still a delightful material for perfumery work. The lavender note is unexcelled in colognes and compositions with a fresh, sportive, or outdoor note. It is a standard in masculine fragrances.

France is the major lavender producer, but lavender is also grown in Spain, Italy, southern Russia, Hungary, and Tasmania. In the latter area, as in France, much research has been given to the full mechanization of the planting, harvesting, and processing of the crop, with considerable success. This has assured the competitiveness of a very ancient natural product even when grown in the industrialized regions of the world.

SICALAV, the greatest distiller of lavender in France, dries and sets apart fifty tons (U.S.) of lavender flowers for use in sachets and potpourri. No other flower is as popular in this regard. Every family linen cabinet *(armoire)* in France breathes this clean fragrance.

THE HERBAL OILS

Rosemary (*Rosmarinus officinalis*) deserves pride of place among the many herbal oils that are used in perfumery. Rosemary produces healthy, sportive, and clean notes. The sharpness of rosemary oils, however, and the fact that we season food with so many of them, demand skill in their use. Rosemary certainly has been used liberally in both Italian and French cooking, but it has a splendid, strong, fresh, piney note that makes it a wonderful component of men's fragrances and eau de cologne. It is one of the ingredients in the first cologne of Giovanni Maria Farina.

Like many of the members of the mint family, rosemary is a native of the chalky soils of the Mediterranean region. Most Americans and Northern Europeans are familiar with a demure kitchen herb, but in the Mediterranean area and in California, rosemary will become a woody bush, often six feet in height. Commercial distillation is carried out extensively in Spain, Tunisia, France, and Morocco. The leaves, florets, and sometimes the twigs are steam-distilled.

Basil is derived from the Greek word for "king," *basileus*. Oil of basil is sweet-spicy, with woody undertones. It is grown for the fragrance and flavor industry in France, Italy, Spain, and North Africa. A basil closely related to this, *Ocimum basilicum*, is the "Réunion basil" grown in Réunion and the Comores Islands. The exact botanical distinctions between the two are disputed, but the Réunion oil has a more herbal note. Basil is also steam-distilled.

Clary (or sclary) sage belongs to the same family as basil. Although it has been used in flavoring liqueurs and wine essences, it is particularly dramatic as a perfume ingredient. *Salvia slarea* has a wonderful winelike odor, but it is fresher and more volatile than the scent of wine. Among the plant oils, clary sage is considered one of the closest to ambergris. It is one of the most interesting of the perfumer's oils and is used in colognes and chypre blends.

Thyme (*Thymus vulgaris*) is distilled in France and Spain for its brownish red oil. It is rich and powerful, with a sweet, warm odor. It makes a welcome addition to soaps that have a medical, hygienic appeal.

Marjoram (*Origanum vulgare*) is also cultivated in France and Spain. The distilled oil is spicy, aromatic-camphoaceous, reminiscent of car-

Flowering top of clary sage. This herb, with its attractive muscatel odor, is distilled for perfume use. It is one of the few primary materials being seriously considered for commercial planting and harvesting in the United States.

damon, and adds a piquant note to colognes and orientals. *Origan* in French perfume parlance refers to *Thymus capitatus*, another strong herbal oil, grown in Spain.

Several mint oils are used in perfumery. Natural menthol is extracted by steam distillation from the field mint *(Mentha arvensis)* grown in Japan and Brazil (principally by descendants from Japanese immigrants accustomed to its culture in Japan). China is also an increasingly important source of these crystals. Like camphor, solid crystals will form on top of the distillate. The addition of menthol gives lift and freshness. It is sometimes used in lipsticks for its cooling effect. Peppermint *(Mentha pipirita)* and spearmint *(Mentha spicata)* can each be used in perfumery for lift and greenness, but these are small fractions compared to their vast use as two of the world's most popular flavors. Most of these double mints are grown in the United States. Pennyroyal *(Mentha pulegium)* has a strong, almost harsh mintiness and is used for extraction of menthol and industrial odorizing. It contains pulegone in great amounts, which is toxic and allowed only limited flavor use and is banned entirely in some countries. It is produced in North Africa and Spain.

Thujone is another toxin, contained in *Artemesia absinthum*, wormwood oil. Its flavor use is also monitored. It is interesting (the flavor of the familiar vermouth) but harmful in large doses (the French *absinthe*). For fragrance work, the distilled oil has a note that is herbal, warm, and deep. The thujone can be removed from the oil to create a similar but unique herbal note to various perfume blends.

Oil of bay laurel is strong and spicy and blends well with citrus oils, spice oils, and pine. It is a native of the Mediterranean and is grown in France, Italy, Turkey, North Africa, and the Soviet Union. Leaves of *Laurus nobilis* were the crowns of victors in ancient Rome. Even the wood is scented and has been used for marqueterie work for that very reason. Its uses in *haute cuisine* are legion.

Coriander oil is distilled from the seeds of *Coriandrum sativum*, native to southern Europe and Asia Minor. Its odor is pleasant—spicy, sweet, and somewhat woody. *Coriandre* is a modern perfume (Courturier, 1973) named after this agreeable scent. Coriander blends well with clary sage as well as with floral notes in jasmine and lilac blends. The flavor use is much more extensive than for fragrance; most of the world's crop is raised in the Soviet Union.

The umbellifers are so called for their characteristically umbrellalike floral parts. Queen Anne's lace (actually a wild carrot) is the most common example of the umbellifers, growing almost everywhere. Most of the oils in this family are seed oils and have a strong family resemblance. Celery-seed oil (from *Apium graveolens*) is such a material. It is used frequently in perfumery but only in small amounts. It can impart warmth to a scent and is extremely tenacious. The oil is distilled commercially in one town above all others: Saint Rémy-en-Provence. Dill oil (*Anethum graveolens*) is used even less; it has a closely related odor, slightly more pungent. Caraway oil (*Carum carvi*) can be used in small amounts in jasmine bases or in tabac perfumes; it can also be used as a mask in insecticides. Both plants grow well in the cooler parts of Europe. Cumin (*Cumimum cyminum*) can also be introduced in trace amounts for green and spicy notes. The oil from the seeds of the carrot

(*Daucus carrota*), distilled in France for perfume use, can add an interesting warmth to a composition, bringing out certain more conventional odors such as that of rose.

Angelica oil can be distilled from the seeds or the roots of *Angelica archangelica*, one of the largest of the umbellifers, an enormous herb that grows to over the height of a man. The seed oil is fresh, light, and peppery; the root oil, earthy and herbal, with animal undertones. Oil of angelica root contributes to the bouquet of Cointreau liqueur. It is first mentioned as an article of commerce in the Frankfurt Ordinance of 1582, listing the prices apothecaries might pay for drugs. The oil distilled from the aerial parts of the plant was first mentioned in Brunschwigk's "Big" *Book of Distillation*, the second of the two he produced.

THE LEAF OILS

The leaf oils play the part of the heavy artillery in perfumery. With a few exceptions such as violet leaf and labdanum, Mother Nature produces ample leafage with a high essential-oil content in every blade, and these leaves can be used freely as materials in their own right or as botanical mines from which to extract specific fractions that are more desirable than the whole oil.

Lemongrass (Cymbopogon citratus) is a good example; fifteen hundred tons a year are produced, setting it among the ten largest essential oils of the world. Although the grass is native to India and Sri Lanka (Ceylon), it is now grown commercially in Central America, the Comores, the Malagasay Republic (Madagascar), Brazil, and China. The fresh or partly dried leaves are steam-distilled or distilled using the water-and-steam method.

As the name suggests, lemongrass has a strong lemon odor, due to the eighty percent citral content. In perfumery this is usually isolated from the other contents of the oil, and in turn it can be used as the starting material for choice ionones. It is interesting that lemongrass also serves as the starting material for the manufacture of Vitamin A. Lemongrass Cochin is from a related species, *Cymbopogon flexuosus*, grown in southern India and also used for citral isolation.

Cymbopogon martini is the scientific name for palmarosa, with a sweet, floral-rosy odor and varying undertones, depending upon the age and quality of the oil distilled. Not an expensive oil, it is suited for soap use and as a starting material for the extraction of geraniol, an isolate with a rosy odor. The material is very important in perfumery and takes its name from the rosy-leafed geranium, another leaf-oil source, and not from the more familiar *Pelargonium* varieties grown as pot ornamentals.

Palmarosa is grown in India, Brazil, Java, and the Seychelles. Leaves, stems, and flowering tops are cast into the stills. The oil is produced by means of simple, direct-fired stills situated close to the fields.

Two other *Cymbopogon* species are important perfumery materials: *C. nardus*, citronella Ceylon, and *C. winterianus*, citronella Java. The West discovered citronella in the later part of the last century (although it has long been used in Indian and Sinhalese cultures) and has made it an important part of the manufacture of soap. The first samples were exhibited at the World's Fair at London's Crystal Palace in 1851. The citronella Ceylon is grown exclusively in Sri Lanka; citronella Java is grown in Indonesia, Central America, China, and Taiwan. The Java type is somewhat fresher and sweeter than the Ceylon oil and is used as a source of citronallal and its derivatives.

What botanists called the "Indo-Malayan" center has produced another important leaf oil that is certainly more aristocratic than the *Cymbopogon* oils: patchouli. Fine as it is, this oil from *Pogostemon cablin* is used so extensively in the perfume industry that China has devoted increasing crop space to its cultivation in recent years. Other major producers include Indonesia, India, Malaysia, Brazil, and the Seychelles. This tropical member of the mint family is steam-distilled from the leaves and stems. The process may take as long as twenty-four hours, after which the oil is set aside to age to remove harshness and greenness.

During the 1960s patchouli oil became a mark of the hippies, who used its herbalness to mask the tarry odor of marihuana. Since the oils they used were not of the best quality, today many grownup hippies have a poor image of this oil. But in the words of author-perfumer Steffen Arctander: "Patchouli oil (native distilled) is a dark orange or brownish-colored viscous liquid possessing an extremely rich, sweet-herbaceous, aromatic-spicy, and woody-balsamic odor. An almost wine-like, ethereal-floral sweetness in the initial notes is characteristic of good oils."[2]

Arctander also notes that patchouli "is used so extensively that it is hardly possible to specify its field of application."[3] Actually patchouli is used in orientals, chypres, and powder perfumes, and it blends well with sandalwood, rose, lavender, and bergamot. Famous blends with patchouli notes include: Jicky (1889), Tabu (1931), Shocking (1935), Miss Dior (1947), Aramis 900 (1970) Bill Blass (1970), and Polo (1978).

Unlike many essential oils that must be distilled immediately after the harvest of the crop, patchouli actually improves with drying and aging. The essential-oil houses in Grasse, London, and New York would regularly await ships carrying baled, dried leaves rather than drums of oil and then distill on their own premises. The U-2 boats of World War I put a stop to this, and producers faced with stranded gluts of patchouli took to distilling the oil in the East Indies. Today very little oil is distilled in the West.

European explorers who scoured Cape Province in southern Africa in the seventeenth century discovered the now-familiar geranium in the six hundred species that abound there. Botanists at Kew worked with the plants until they had hybridized such familiar ornamental plants as the *Pelargonium x hortorum* and economical plants such as the rosy-leafed variety, *Pelargonium graveolens x Pelargonium radula*. Because of this background, propagation of horticultural and commercial geranium plants is always vegetative; seed will produce genetic "sports." The first plants grown for the French perfume industry were planted in Algeria in 1847; in the 1880s extensive plantings were set out on Réunion. Today these areas have been joined by Egypt (one of the fastest-growing areas for *all* essential oils), Morocco, and China. As with every botanical, each *vin de pays* must indicate its provenance because local geography and weather affect the odor note of each oil. For example, oil of geranium Bourbon (from the old name for Réunion) is known for its powerful leafy-rosy odor and the rosiness of its dry-out note.

The geranium oil glands are liberally distributed over the surface of the soft, hairy leaves, which are treated to one and a half hours of distillation in small field stills. Seven hundred grams of oil can be extracted from two hundred and fifty kilograms of freshly cut leaves. Geranium oil is used in every type of fragrance work but not in flavorings.

The same plant family (the *Geraniaceae*) also produces zdravets *(Geranium macrorhizum)*, with a lively odor reminiscent of clary sage. It finds use in perfume, as a solvent extract, and in the *materia medica* of Bulgaria.

Eucalyptus oil is produced in copious amounts by the blue gum *(Eucalyptus globulus)* of Tasmania and Australia. The blue-green leaves are both rounded and lance-shaped. Commercial topping of the trees occurs in Spain, Portugal, and India, and the tree has been planted everywhere in the tropics and subtropics.

The leaves are steam-distilled for the oil, which has a familiar pharmaceutical fragrance and flavor. It is used in numerous formulas for low-cost perfumes, as in a mouthwash, and in industrial preparations where a clean, strong odor is called for.

The leaves of the West Indian *Pimenta acris*, a thirty-foot tree, produce the oil that gives the familiar scent of bay rum, oil of bay, or oil of pimenta. It is fresh and spicy, with a hint of the medicinal, and dries out with a soft, balsamic afterglow. The men's toiletry called "Bay Rum" was first made in the Virgin Islands (then the Danish West Indies) by the distillation of rum with leaves of *Pimenta acris*. Today processing is done by means of steam or water distillation to which salt has been added to lower the boiling point. Today Bay "rum" is no longer made with rum but of oil of bay and regular perfumery alcohol.

The leaves and twigs of several conifers are used for the pine note. *Tsuga heterophylla* is distilled to get "Western hemlock oil." "Spruce oils" represent blends of *Tsuga canadensis, Picea mariana*, and *Picea glauca*—Eastern hemlock and black and white spruce oils. The odor is fresh and balsamic; the oil is used in pine fragrances, soaps, and cleansers.

Balsam fir (*Abies balsamea*) is steam-distilled to obtain a colorless oil with a Christmas-tree smell. This fir grows throughout the United States and Canada. *Abies sibirica* produces the Siberian "pine" with a similar note.

Thuja occidentalis, the American white cedar, is the source of cedar-leaf oil. *Cedrus atlantica*, from Morocco, is cut, chipped, and steam distilled for its pinelike oil. Its close relative, the cedar of Lebanon, has now become so endangered that it is no longer distilled for its fragrant oil, one of mankind's earliest perfumes.

Also conifers are the Virginia cedarwood, actually a *Juniperus virginiana*, and Texas cedarwood (*Juniperus mexicana*); both produce fragrant oils that are low in price and used in perfumery, especially in soaps. Juniper berries come from *Juniperus communis* , a small tree with fruits that are crushed and steam-distilled. Juniper oil has a fresh, pine-needle odor and is used in colognes, chypres, and after-shaves. This European product is often seen emblazoned on the labels of gin bottles.

The word for gin actually comes from *genièvre*, the French word for these berries that give the liquor its characteristic bouquet. Not all of these conifer oils are leaf oils, but they are treated together for the sake of order; as it is, the disparity between the names is bewildering: "spruce" oils from hemlocks, and "cedarwoods" which are given the name of *Juniperus*.

Camphor is produced today, as in the past, in China, Japan, and Taiwan. Leaves, twigs, roots, and branches can be distilled as well as the chipped wood of felled trees. Pure camphor (d-camphor) is crystalline; other fractions include white camphor oil, brown, and blue oils. Blue oil is the heaviest and is used as a mask for objectionable odors and in inexpensive soaps. Pure camphor has a clean, ethereal scent and is tonic in the extreme; a sense of coolness, akin to the perception of pure menthol, follows inhalation. The brown oil consists mainly of safrole, which is isolated to produce heliotropine. Camphor trees grow to one hundred feet in height; by weight the pure camphor is 0.8 percent of such a tree, and 0.4 is the percentage of the remaining liquid oils—white, brown, and blue.

The island of Taiwan was once renowned for its virgin stands of majestic camphor trees with their aromatic foliage. Before World War II, distillation was an important island industry, but with the appearance of synthetic camphor and the industrialization of the economy after 1949, this industry has declined. Individual trees of great antiquity, however, still stand at major Taoist and Buddhist shrines. The People's Republic of China remains a major producer of this essential oil. China is also a major producer of *Litsea cubeba* (in the laurel family), used for the isolation of citral and its derivatives.

The following oils are leaf products produced by the kilogram and not the ton, therefore unable to be ranked among the *grosse artillerie* of perfumery. Violet-leaf oil is extracted by the solvent process from *Viola odorata* to create an interesting material that is intensely green with the sharp scent of a crushed leaf. It is expensive, but carefully used, adds an unusual vibrato to floral and chypre perfumes.

The violet plants are grown under the shade of olive trees in France and Italy; Egypt is also now raising this delicate crop. Violets are suitable for the cut-flower trade but too expensive to be used in perfumery today.

Artemisia pallens is distilled in India for the pungent oil of davana; rue oil is distilled from the leaves of this Spanish oil with its peculiar cat-spray odor. The botanical name is *Ruta graveolens*; in Western herbalism it has been known as "herb of grace," said to halt the inrush of witches and evil spirits. A sprig of the plant adorned the sheriff's bench at Guildhall to avert the jail fever of the accused.

The myrtle (*Myrtus communis*) was one of the most beloved of scented plants in the gardens of Baghdad, Damascus, Granada, Cordoba, and Isfahan, and it is still used in modern perfumery. The distilled oil is very fresh and strong, camphoraceous, and spiced—material for the lift of a top note but without the heaviness of a fixative material. The attractive and compact plant, with its fine, evergreen foliage, is grown commercially in Spain, Morocco, France, and Italy. The biblical Queen Esther took her name, *Hadassah*, from the Hebrew word (*hadas*) for this shrub, and Greeks and Romans awarded their poets the myrtle branch, signifying that their fame would remain ever green.

Labdanum is another plant that has been esteemed for several millennia. The leaves of *Cistus ladaniferum* exude a viscous resin that covers leaves and branches with the sticky labdanum. Dioscorides relates the manner in which this substance was collected on Crete: shepherds and goatherds would send their flocks into the brambles and then comb the sticky labdanum from their fleece with a *ladanisterion*, a kind of double comb. Tournefort witnessed the same process during his travels through the Levant in 1718. Today the bushes are cropped and the leaves and branches boiled in water. The resin rises as a dark mass, which is skimmed off and poured into wooden molds; the water flows off and the gum hardens. Blocks of ten kilograms are cut out and set aside to age. An alcoholic extract is made from the crude gum, and generally an inert solvent is added to enable pouring of the material. Solvent extraction can also be used. The Spanish word for labdanum, *jara*, is derived from the Moors; its use was part of the culture of Spain in Muslim times. Spain and France are the major producers of labdanum today. Labdanum's scent is sweet and agreeable in the extreme. It is honeylike and slightly musk-animalic. It is widely used in perfumes and expensive soaps.

Oakmoss is included with the leaf products by stretching the term "leaf" a bit. Actually it is a lichen (*Evernia prunastri*), a combination of a fungus and alga, not even a higher plant. Its trailing thallus (the true term for its extension, remotely resembling leaf tissue) hangs off of the trunk or the branches of various oaks and other deciduous trees. It resembles Spanish moss, although the two are not even distantly related.

Oakmoss too is of very ancient lineage, having been used since pharaonic times. The odor accounts for its long popularity; it is suave, full, and honeyed. It reminds one also of powder and of new-mown hay. It has been one of the main components of the classic chypre. Indeed, one of the reasons for the choice of the name (the French word for Cyprus) is because this material grew there. Today oakmoss is grown in Yugoslavia, France, Italy, and Morocco. Solvent extraction is used.

Mousse d'arbre, or tree moss, is a less refined material from similar lichens that grow on pines and spruces in central and southern Europe: *Evernia furfuacea* and *Usnea barbata*. These lichen retain the pine turpentine notes from the trees upon which they are found; the odor is sharper than that of oakmoss. ("Moss" is, strictly speaking, a misnomer, only so called because of similarity in appearance. It should be called "oak lichen," but that term has never been heard in perfume circles.) Other lichens exhibit fragrance, including the *Cladonia rangiformis*, the staple of the reindeer of Lapland, and at times other species wind up in the sack of the collector.

THE SPICE OILS

Many people mentally relegate the spices to the food area, never dreaming that these powerful aromatics have an important part to play in perfumes. All of the spices used for flavor serve as fragrances as well. A few of them are used whole or ground as elements of potpourri or sachet blends, but the great majority are distilled for pouring into perfumery compounds or vats of soap.

Cloves come from the undeveloped flower buds of a tree that grows to a height of thirty feet. The botanical name is *Syzgium aromaticum*; the earlier name was *Eugenia caryophyllata*, whence the name for the main constituent of oil of clove: eugenol, the smell of a dentist's office.

The exact origin of the tree is probably the Moluccas in Indonesia. During the derring-do days of the Dutch conquest of the East Indies, all clove trees were uprooted by law save for those on Amboina, and a strict monopoly was maintained on cultivation. Much blood has been spilled over this homely spice.

Pierre Poivre, at great risk to his life, succeeded in spiriting clove seeds away from the Dutch colonies and planting them in the French possessions in the Indian Ocean. Next, the British obtained seed and found a ready home for it in the two islands twenty-five miles off the East African coast: Zanzibar and Pemba. The climate was perfect, and the Arab businessmen found plentiful labor in the slave system that prevailed on the islands. The Dutch monopoly was definitively broken by 1818, and today Zanzibar and Pemba account for almost all of the world's supply. Madagascar is the only other producing area. Indian sellers have taken over the role of brokers in Zanzibar, and Chinese merchants in Madagascar.

The unopened clove bud must be handpicked to distill the fine "bud oil," but the leaves also contain essential oils, the "clove-leaf oil." A tree will bear five years after being set out from the nursery and may continue bearing for a century. Clove-bud oil is used in perfumery for its sweet-spicy note; it adds richness to rose and other sweet florals. The leaf oil is rougher and is used in soap blends and as a source of eugenol, an anaesthetic used in dentistry and a germicide used in pharmaceuticals.

Cinnamon (*Cassia zeylanicum*) originates on the island of Ceylon, and Sri Lanka is still the principal producing country. Like clove, cinnamon has had a colorful history. The Portuguese seized Ceylon in 1505 and forced a huge tribute in this spice from its rulers. When the Dutch took Ceylon, they enforced a monopoly, which was finally broken by the British in 1796. When Ceylon passed into British hands during the Napoleonic wars, the amount of land under cultivation of this spice was extended to forty thousand acres. Today the acreage is just under that figure.

The dried inner bark provides the cinnamon oil of commerce, but the leaves are also distilled for an essential oil. The bark oil has the familiar sweet cinnamon note and is also used to isolate eugenol and convert it into vanillin, synthetic vanilla. Small amounts of the oil add force to oriental blends; the flavor use of cinnamon is well known. "Quills" are strips of the bark used in the food industry; the same bark is broken up prior to distillation for its oil.

"Chinese cinnamon" is the related cassia, *Cinnamomum cassia*, a product of Kuang-hsi and Kuang-chow provinces in southeastern China. Oils can be distilled from the bark, leaves, and stems of this tree, with varying nuances of a cinnamon bouquet. Cassia is often used in flavors, particularly in those of the cola beverages, but much less frequently in perfumery. The oil can easily cause discoloration in soaps.

Nutmeg oil is widely used in men's fragrances and in small amounts in other blends. It is a pale yellow oil that has a fresh, light, and warm odor, distilled with steam from the seeds of *Myristica fragrans*. The same tree produces mace, which is the shiny red aril that surrounds the nutmeg itself; it has a more pungent odor.

The name nutmeg comes from the medieval spice trade; in 1158 *nuces muscatorum* ("nuts from Muscat") were being traded in Genoa. When the British broke the Dutch monopoly by occupying the Moluccas from 1796 to 1802, they introduced the trees into Malaya and Grenada in the West Indies. Today Indonesia, Grenada, Ceylon, and India are major producers. Connecticut became known as the "Nutmeg State" because local sharpies whittled wooden nutmegs to sell among the true.

The monoterpenes present in nutmeg oil are sensitive to heat and tend to become gummy or to produce ill-smelling compounds. So a terpeneless oil is prepared to obviate these problems. The nutmeg itself is made up of about ten percent essential oil and nine percent in mace.

Allspice is one of the few spices native to the West, not to the East Indies. Most of the world's crop is grown on Jamaica. The berry of the *Pimenta dioica* tree is steam-distilled for an oil with a general spice note that blends well with oil of ginger, rose geranium, lavender, patchouli, and orrisroot oil. The top note is fresh and the dry-out note is tealike.

The alternate name for the product—pimento oil—comes from the Spanish *pimienta*, "pepper," because the berry resembles the peppercorn. The tree is dioecious, meaning that some trees are wholly male (non-fruiting) and others wholly female (fruiting) instead of having the male and female parts that are usually present in the same flowers of the one plant.

Vanilla is another word derived from the Spanish conquistadors, the diminutive of the word for "bean," *vaina*. The Spanish encountered the dried bean of the orchid, *Vanilla planifolia*, in Mexico, where the Aztecs used it to flavor their *chocalatl*.

Vanilla, whose flavor use is obvious, can be prepared for fragrance use by solvent extraction of the pods or by percolation in a hydroalcoholic solution. Vanilla adds sweetness and depth to floral bases and blends well with sandalwood and spices in oriental compositions. It has great tenacity. Although vanillin is available at only a fraction of the price, the exquisite nuances in natural vanilla and concern for the safety of synthetics (coumarin, the first synthetic, proved to be very toxic) make the yearly demand for vanilla greater than the world's total supply.

Vanilla is the only orchid to find perfumery use, although many of this family have wonderful and varied odors. It is not truly a "spice" and is placed among the spices only by its association with the spice trade.

Mexico is the home of the vanilla orchid, but today the island of Madagascar produces most of the world's crop. Réunion, Java, Tahiti, and the Seychelles are other producing areas.

The history of vanilla away from its native Mexico is interesting—it was relatively easy to transplant the vanilla orchid. But in its home, the flowers were pollinated by hummingbirds and bees of the *Melipona* genus, and these could not be taken with the plant. Consequently vanilla plants in Réunion, which had come from Mexico, grew luxuriantly but never bore the all-important pod, for the flowers were never fertilized. However, a freed slave, Edmond Albius, perfected a method in 1841 for the hand pollination of the floral parts, and today a worker can transfer the pollen to the pistil of the vanilla orchid on as many as three hundred flowers a day. This Réunion method is today followed everywhere—including Mexico—for it is more reliable than the birds and bees.

Pepper (*Piper nigrum*) is extracted with alcohol or acetone or distilled for its warm, dry, woody note that is used for highlights and effects. The main producing lands are in the region of its botanical origin: India, Indonesia, Malaya, Thailand, and the nations of Indochina.

Ginger oil is distilled from the tuberous rhizomes of *Zingiber officinale*. The spice originated in the Indian Ocean region, but today is grown throughout the tropics; the oil finds a limited use in men's spice blends. Cardamon is a closely related member of the ginger family. The oil of this plant (*Elletaria cardamomum*) is not processed from the rhizomes, but from the pungent seed capsules. High quality cardamon oils have a pleasing, fresh spiciness; cheaper oils have a harsh, medicinal, and eucalyptus-like odor.

THE ROOT OILS

Valerian (*Valeriana officinalis*) is the most disreputable of the aromatic roots, having a rank, Limburger-cheese smell so powerful that tradition says the Pied Piper of Hamlin had valerian in his back pocket when he charmed the town's rats. Isovaleric acid is responsible for this objectionable note, but underneath it lie layers with musky-woody, balsamic tones that can enhance certain compositions if well used. The flowers of this plant are known as "garden heliotrope" and have a pleasant odor. Commercial plantings are in the Soviet Union, the Baltic states, Belgium, Germany, and France. "Kesso root" is a Japanese variety (*V. officinalis var. latifolia*). The oil is extracted by drying, crushing, and distilling the roots. The older the root material, the higher the proportion of the vile-smelling isovaleric acid.

Vetiver has a rooty odor that is sharp and distinct but not unusual; it is somewhat like the smell of a sliced potato. The thin, wiry roots of *Vetiveria zizanoides* are distilled in India, Java, Réunion, Haiti, and Brazil for a viscous oil that is extensively used for its own distinct freshness and its amazing fixative quality.

Orrisroot has a very different note. It resembles the perfume of the violet flower, with fruity undertones that are warm and tenacious; it is also quite fixative. The rhizomes of *Iris germanica, var. florentina*, and *Iris pallida* are dried and stored for two or three years and then distilled or extracted with volatile solvents. This beautiful material has been esteemed for centuries. The Greco-Roman herbalists knew it—Theophrastus, Dioscorides, and Pliny—and the plant was grown in the gardens of Kashmir, where the Persian name for it was *bihk-i-banafshah*. Today the village of San Polo in Tuscany is a major source of orris, as is Morocco. It is a costly material ($25,000 a pound), for each rhizome must be stripped of its brown skin to reveal the creamy interior, and the entire crop must be cured for many months.

THE GUMS AND BALSAMS

Frankincense and myrrh are still produced in Arabia Felix, the Arabia considered "blessed" by the Romans for the occurrence of these two gum resins. Less-fine species occur in Somalia. Frankincense is extracted by steam distillation, and the product is known commercially as oil of

The rhizomes of the Florentine iris (Iris germanica, var. florentina) *contain glands of essential oil with a violet-flower scent. The full perfection of this note requires months of drying, and careful paring of the outer brown skin. The dry, decorticated roots were ordinarily milled in the eighteenth century for use as a powder for wigs, or as a fixative for potpourri. Orris root is still used in potpourris, but it is more commonly distilled for use in fine perfumes. From George Nicholson,* Illustrated Dictionary of Gardening, *London, 1888*

olibanum. A resinoid can also be prepared, using hydrocarbon solvents. Myrrh can be treated in the same ways. Both continue to delight mankind as they have for ages past.

Benzoin resin is steeped in alcohol to obtain the sweet balsam note, reminiscent of vanilla. The Indochinese *Styrax tonkinense* is finer than the Sumatran *Styrax benzoin*.

Galbanum is another resin, one which is excreted from the base of the shoots and leaves of *Ferula galbaniflua* and processed for a powerfully green and woody fragrance used in chypre, pine, and moss blends, but always with great discretion. The gum can be dissolved in alcohol, distilled, or treated by solvent extraction.

Balsam of Peru is an exudation from the bark of the *Myroxylon balsamum, var. Pereirae*, a tall tree from the "Balsam Coast" of Central

America in El Salvador. The area was a place of transshipment of Peruvian goods to Europe, and the product was lumped in with other goods, although it did not occur at all in Peru.

The odor is balsamic: rich, soft, sweet, and tenacious. As is, the balsam will dissolve in perfume alcohol. Balsam of Tolu (*Myroxylon balsamum*) is a related tree from Columbia and Venezuela with a similarly suave odor.

THE WOOD OILS

Bois de rose (rosewood) is another product of the forests of northern South America. *Aniba rosaeodora* is chipped and distilled for its essential oil, which is principally used for the isolation of linaloöl, constituting seventy percent of the oil. *Bois de rose* has a sweet, woody odor by itself, and the linaloöl is used in lily-of-the-valley and neroli compositions.

Sandalwood (*Santalum album*) is one of the oldest perfumery materials, having over two thousand years of uninterrupted use. It is certainly the most important of the wood oils used today. Only India and the island of Timor in Indonesia produce this unusual, semiparasitic tree, which grows to a height of thirty feet and begins to produce the essential oil within the heartwood only after thirty years' growth.

The heartwood is heavy in weight, of a fine close grain, and can be worked to a smooth polish, resembling a kind of botanical ivory. It is so precious that it is a government monopoly in India and eighteen gradients of the material are recognized, even to the sawdust.

The distilled oil is pale yellow and viscous, with an extremely sweet and soft odor note. It remains uniform for a great length of time and is also used as a fixative. Price alone limits its use.

THE CITRUS OILS

The citrus group belongs in a class by itself. Not only are there several important plants—orange, lemon, lime, tangerine, and grapefruit—that form essential oils, but the oils can be extracted from the peel, blossoms, and even the leaves of different plants.

One of the most important of the fragrance citrus plants is one of the generally least known: the bergamot (*Citrus bergamia*). This tree, reaching to about twenty-five feet in height, is grown almost exclusively on a narrow coastal strip in southern Calabria. Some bergamot trees were introduced to Guinea when it was part of French West Africa, but the vast majority of plantings are in southern Italy. The oil is expressed from the peel and possesses an extremely rich, sweet-fruity top note followed by an oily green note and a rich dry-out. It is much used in the classic eaux de cologne and in chypre and aldehydic-type perfumes. The scent is the familiar bouquet of "Earl Grey" tea. It is also used to flavor candy.

One of the constituents of bergamot that must be removed for fragrance use is bergaptan, which is a skin irritant.

Neroli is another citrus product of great importance in fragrance but relatively unknown to the uninformed. This is the oil distilled from the blossoms of the bitter orange, *Citrus aurantium*. An orange blossom absolute can also be made. The bitter orange is native to southern China and Indochina, but today the blossoms bloom in southern France, Italy, Morocco, Tunisia, and Egypt. The scent is light, fresh, with an almost lily-of-the-valley note, infinitely more ethereal than any of the peel oils. Neroli has also been a material of choice in eau de cologne, and it blends well with all the floral absolutes.

Petitgrain is the industry term for the distilled oil of the twigs and leaves of the bitter orange; the oil is also referred to as "Petigrain bigarade." This oil is produced in France, Tunisia, and Paraguay. The term *petitgrain* was French for "little seed," referring to the unripe fruitlets, even though the leaves and twigs are the materials processed. Paraguay produces most of the world's petitgrain, thanks to a peripatetic French botanist, Benjamin Balansa (1825–1892), who began distilling the leaves of bitter-orange trees that had escaped from cultivation and were found growing east of the Paraguay River. Petitgrain is widely used in soap perfumery and citrus blends. It has a somewhat harsh top note with a bitter-floral body note.

The sweet orange (*Citrus sinensis*) is a native to China, but sometimes it is known as the "Portugal orange" due to the many seeds brought back by the Portuguese traders and missionaries at Macao. The peel is expressed for its oil in Sicily, Calabria, Israel, Spain, Florida, California, Guinea, and Brazil. Each locale produces an oil with special characteristics, and perfumers pay much attention to provenance. The oil is used in citrus blends and for isolation of limonene and derivatives. As a flavor, the sweet orange is one of the world's most popular; soft drinks, sherbets, candies, and pharmaceuticals are some of its many applications. In beverages, terpeneless oils are used for their great solubility in water. The bitter-orange fruit (*Citrus aurantium*), which is generally used in the manufacture of marmalade, can be cold-pressed for a similar orange oil.

The mandarin orange has also been used in perfumery. The peel of the fruits of the *Citrus reticulata* can be pressed and the leaves steam-distilled. The first product is called oil of mandarin, the second, petit-grain mandarinier. Calabria is the major center for growing this citrus.

Lemon oil is expressed from the peel of the *Citrus limonia*, a small tree native to southern China. Today lemon production is enormous and has many centers: California, Sicily, Brazil, Israel, and Guinea. The familiar scent is used in colognes, aerosols, and cleansers.

The lime, *Citrus aurantiifolia*, is native to India and Southeast Asia and is the most tender of the citruses. It cannot grow in many of the subtropical regions where other citrus trees thrive. It is also unusual among its kind in producing a peel oil that can be steam-distilled. Some of the fruit is cold-pressed, but very little. This oil is preferred by fragrance formulators as being more "perfumey," like the redolence of the lime itself, but it is rarely used by flavorists. Oil of distilled lime is familiar in the major cola beverages; it blends well with oil of cassia, another prime beverage component.

The grapefruit (*Citrus x paradisi*) can be cold-pressed to produce an oil used to reinforce a bergamot composition. Most grapefruit production is along the Gulf Coast and in California.

This brings to a close our section on the citruses, but it should be noted that there seems to be no limit to the variations possible on this theme. The leaves of the lemon, citron, and grapefruit can be distilled, and cultivars of the most important fruits are constantly being developed by hybridists; these cultivars can be expressed for peel oils of even more variations. The above list, however, embraces the major citrus oils used in the arsenal of the perfumer. The basic citrus note, with all its gradations, has always been extremely popular and still remains one of the most characteristic of notes in men's toiletries.

Synthetic Perfumery Materials

Having looked at animal and vegetable sources of essential oils, we now come to man-made materials. The number of synthetics and their importance to the perfume industry are of utmost importance. In his two-volume work on the subject, *Perfume and Flavour Chemicals*, Steffen Arctander studied over three thousand specific aroma chemicals. Since this edition was published (1969), even more synthetics have been added. The presence of the synthetics is a gauge of the flowering of organic chemistry in the last one hundred years. Many fascinating aromatics have been synthesized by perfumer-chemists working for houses such as Givaudan and Firminich of Switzerland, Dragoco Gerberdeing and Company, Haarman and Reimer Corporation of Germany, International Flavors and Fragrances, and Florasynth of the United States. But many fragrance chemicals have come by serendipity from research in the petrochemical industry, pharmaceutical chemistry, and wood-

Barrels of aroma chemicals, products of the research into organic chemistry made within the last century, await utilization in the warehouses of a major supplier. Courtesy of Dragoco, Inc.

pulp chemistry. To enumerate the names of the various essences thus obtained would make unintelligible reading for all but the organic chemist, but there are significant general remarks that can make the subject more understandable for the knowledgeable lay reader.

These synthetics marvelously extend the perfumer's artistry. We have seen how perfume creation was multiplied geometrically with the incorporation of the first synthetics in a blend: Fougère Royale in 1882. Nor do synthetics fight with the naturals; they enhance them. Santylyl acetate, for instance, will push forward the top note of sandalwood, and benzyl acetate will dramatize the floralcy of one of the expensive absolutes.

The exclusive use of synthetics, however, rarely makes an attractive product. As the authors of the *Fragrance and Flavor Industry* have pointed out:

> Most perfumers and flavorists insist that, to impart life, lustre, body and brilliance to their compositions, and to imitate nature with a high degree of versimilitude, the formula for a fragrance or flavor must contain at least a minimum amount of "naturals." Formulations based exclusively on synthetics can never duplicate the character and appeal of those that contain an appreciable amount of "naturals."[4]

But another fact that must be considered is the question, "How unnatural are the synthetics?" We have seen that the natural essential oils are mined for many isolates, or "semisynthetics," such as citronellal, geraniol, eugenol, isoeugenol, safrole, anethole, farnesol, linaloöl, and thujune. These themselves can be further treated for even more extensive derivatives. Although perfumery consumes only a modest amount of the world's petrochemical supplies, it has still been affected by the dramatic rise in price of those products. It is likely that the chemical laboratory of the living plant will be a perpetual means of obtaining products that can be isolated or recombined in novel ways to produce many man-created fragrance chemicals. The wood-pulp industry too has been a particularly rich source of highly unusual aroma materials derived from cheap and readily available turpentine.

Coal-tar chemistry has produced many valuable aroma chemicals such as benzyl acetate, benzyl alcohol, coumarin, and benzaldehyde. But in a sense coal is natural, betraying its origin as a fossil wood. Whole tree trunks are often found embedded in coal seams, and lumps of coal sometimes bear the imprint of leaves and bark. It was always felt, however, that petroleum was an inorganic product formed by the percolation of various compounds in the early crust of the earth. The "stream chemicals" from oil refineries and cracking plants have produced many important building blocks for aroma chemicals. But now geologists acknowledge the organic nature of even this important starting material. Oil accumulated in the prehistoric earth from minute droplets formed in the bodies of tiny plants and animals, principally microscopic algae and diatoms, and one-celled foraminifera. As the bodies of billions of these living beings decayed on shallow sea bottoms, the particles of oil were squeezed out, most likely with the help of bacterial action. Once free, the drops worked through fissures in the rocks and accumulated in lodes. It was such a reservoir that "Colonel" Drake tapped in 1859, thereby beginning the age of petroleum.

Two petroleum-derived perfume synthetics are paratertiary butyl cyclohyl acetate, with pleasant woody notes and great stability, and "sandela," a product synthesized by Givaudan that smells remarkably like the santalol from the sandalwood tree but bears no chemical resemblance to the naturally occurring molecule.

The aldehydes hit the olfactory sense with great strength but this initial force is quickly lost—chemically the aldehydes are rapidly acetalized. This is where the perfumer must know how to deploy other materials which will build upon, enhance, fill out, and soften initial shock value of the aldehydes. Ernest Beaux used liberal amounts of ylang-ylang, rose and jasmine oils to achieve this secondary effect. As we have observed before, perfumery is an art form, which like music, unfolds within time. Both the synthetics and the naturals have their place in this orchestration. The aldehydes are powerful, highly volatile odor chemicals. Formaldehyde is an aldehyde most people have experienced; it is not a perfume substance, but it gives one an idea of the intensity and pungency of this family of chemicals. Aldehydes can be detected immediately; they give lift to a composition. One cannot perceive the aldehyde topnote in older perfumes, such as in eau de cologne, but aldehydes have been extensively used since they were first incorporated into Chanel Number Five by Ernest Beaux in 1921. These sharp and modern materials are synthetic but are nevertheless described by their resemblance to natural scents. Important perfume aldehydes include aldehyde C7, with an orange scent, aldehyde C10, with a blend of orange, rose, and lemon notes; aldehyde C20, with a fruity, raspberry note. Traces of the aldehydes occur in various plant oils but never in the concentration that can be obtained by synthetic chemistry.

I2

Developments Today
in Perfume Technology

The range of man-made odor chemicals is growing rapidly and the manufacturing processes of existing chemicals are being improved to meet the surging demand for aromatics. Prices in the last ten years have not gone up significantly partly because new resources are being tapped and partly because old ones are being better processed—an anomaly in an economic climate where most manufacturing supplies have skyrocketed in price. An example of this is the production of terpenes from turpentine in the wood-pulp industry which has climbed in a dramatic way. Another trend is an increase in the aroma chemicals coming from the petrochemical industry hand in hand with a decline in those coming from coal-tar sources. Fats such as castor oils have also been tapped as another source for synthetics such as benzaldehyde and styrene.

Nor has the age-old task of obtaining essential oils from the botanical kingdom remained static. In response to the same great demand for fragrance products, there has been a sizable increase in lands under perfume-plant cultivation, particularly in Egypt, India, and China. In each of these regions there is a concern for the planting of the best strains of essential-oil–bearing plants and for using the best agricultural practices (fertilizers, insect control, and irrigation), and the most rewarding extractive techniques.

This has been true in the industrialized areas of the world as well. The United States Department of Agriculture (U.S.D.A.) has funded research on the essential-oil crops as a potential income source for the labor-intensive family farms of the American South. At the Department of Agriculture and Natural Resources, Dr. Arthur O. Tucker has made extensive experiments with many strains of the damask rose, the *rose de mai, Rosa gallica*, the old "apothecary rose," with lavender and lavadin cultivars, clary sage, Greek and Dalmatian sage, the catnip mint, valerian, oregano, the saffron crocus, and other croci that may prove to be substitutes for this most expensive of all the spices.

A similar broadness of interests marks the work of Dr. Brian Lawrence, author of the monthly monograph "The Essential Oils," which appears in the *Perfumer and Flavorist*. Dr. Lawrence has taken in hand the work of developing essential-oil crops for commercial cultivation by the R. J. Reynolds Company. He has made intensive studies of the oil yields of great numbers of the *Labiatae* and *Umbelliferae* families to determine which hybrids are most worth the investment in time, land, and fertilizer. Unlike the U.S.D.A. project, his interests lie in fully mechanized production for large-scale planting rather than for small plots run by families. Fine-quality basil and clary sage are already in regular production from Reynolds' fields in eastern North Carolina. Every year the world's demand for natural essential oils is greater than the supply. Dr. Lawrence foresees American participation in this area beyond consuming oils from elsewhere. Heretofore the United States has been strong only in the production of mint oils, pine products, and oils distilled from stands of native cedars and junipers. He also feels that if sufficiently rationalized, some of the botanical oils of origin might even compete with synthetics in price as well as odor note.

Essential-oil production has received particular attention in other areas too. The Soviet Union has concentrated especially in growing roses, clary sage, and some of the umbellifers. Bulgaria has established large plantings of the rose and some of the lesser-known herbs; Tasmania grows lavender; and Australia cultivates boronia and eucalyptus. In southern France all the traditional perfume crops have been restudied, but lavender and its hybrids have been the object of most research. The *Laboratoire d'Amélioration des Plantes* of the National Institute for Agricultural Research at Antibes has spearheaded examination of every aspect of lavender and the various lavandins, which have come to play an important role in the economy of Provence.

The Tropical Products Institute in London dates back to 1894, when an institute was founded for agricultural problems in the far-flung colonies. Reorganized in 1965, it serves the vital need of linking the industrial world, with its science and its markets, to the Third World of producers. The institute has looked into the cultivation requirements of spice crops and researched the optimal production of some of the fixed oils required by the world soap industry. Fortunately for the Western perfume industry, spice and other tropical oils will remain quite reasonable in price over the next five or ten years. The reason for this is not that attractive, however; it reflects the desperate shortage of capital throughout the nonindustrialized world and the scramble to sell anything in order to obtain it. As Bernard Champon of L. A. Champon and Co., Inc., a leading essential-oil broker, pointed out at the Seminar on the Natural Essential Oils held on June 9, 1983, at the New York Botanical Garden, this situation has resulted in such pathetic occurrences as the abandonment of modern steam-distillation apparatus in Indonesia for primitive wood-fire stills. The lack of cash is so acute that the fuel cannot be purchased to fire a modern (and more efficient) still. The wood is cheap, but the demand for it as fuel results in deforestation and erosion, already a major problem in tropical Asia.

Satellite weather information has been a technological boon to the essential-oil industry. A disproportionate amount of aromatic crops grows in a slim band along the western littoral of the Indian Ocean. The islands of Réunion, the Comores, Zanzibar, Pemba, and Madagascar (the Malagasay Republic) are prone to tropical typhoons. Forewarning could help to save a vast proportion of perfume crops that grow on these islands. The heart of the perfumery industry misses a beat when it hears of storms along the eastern coast of Africa.

The means of extracting the essential oils are also becoming modernized in many areas. In the United States mints can be distilled even while the fields are being harvested, the extraction proceeding while the harvesters lumber through the rows of plants. Tournaire of Grasse and other manufacturers of extractive machinery can make stills that will contain twelve thousand pounds of plant material. Research has also been made into refining the process of distillation itself, especially on the new lavender lands opened up in Tasmania.[1]

Solvent extraction has also been refined for better retrieval of the costliest of the perfume materials. After World War II butane was increasingly adopted in preference to hexane because it could extract the floral oils at a lower temperature; even slight degrees of added heat adversely affect the odor of the jasmines and hyacinths that so attract us when smelled at ambient temperatures.

Perfume chemists have adopted the pharmacists' technique of molecular distillation, which allows separation of elements of varying molecular weight without any change—extremely low temperatures are possible using this technique. Patchouli has been treated to this advanced type of vacuum distilling to remove traces of rust from field stills, without damage to the essential oil.

Recently British perfumers have performed experiments with carbon dioxide in liquid form under pressure; this extracts essential oils with *no* heat at all and without the inclusion of the (non-odorous) natural paraffins and plant pigments.

Other areas in which exciting research is being done vis-à-vis the plant oils is in the study of the biogenesis of these oils, i.e., the pathways by which the plant synthesizes increasingly complex molecules; the hope is that possibly the glands of essential oils might be raised in vitro by tissue culture. In this new development, a callus culture (a mass of growing cells derived from root, stem, or leaf cuttings) is allowed to develop in a nutrient broth and kept at optimum temperature for rapid growth. Secondary plant products such as alkaloids, pigments, tannins, and essential oils have been produced and can be extracted. This area of tissue-culture research is still embryonic, but what has already begun to have repercussions in the essential-oil industry is the ability to clone (from these callus cultures) new plants, each one being an exact genetic replica of the original culture. This type of vegetative reproduction has already been done in India for the *Santalum album*. It is highly desirable to make sure that only the best strains are grown, particularly where the oils appear only after many years' growth (as in sandalwood). Growers must protect their investment of time and money with the guarantee that they begin their cultures with the strains richest in oils.

Perfume zoology has not worked at refining its materials as has perfume botany. As has been mentioned previously, the crude and primitive hunting of the sperm whale may well wind up with the annihilation of the species. However, the Chinese have begun domesticating the musk deer and an Asian species of the civet cat. These efforts are indicative of man's desire for the unique materials of animal origin.

If, as the futurist Marshall McLuhan has pointed out, our technology represents an extension of our bodies, then the "eyes" with which men and women can view the essential oils have become wonderfully sharpened by advanced instrumentation. Earliest men and women could hold a rose petal to the sunlight and see the minute glands of essential oil in the papillae of the petal surface, or they could look closely and see the droplets of oil across the skin of an orange. When means of extracting these oils developed, one could look at millions of drops of oils collected in one glass vial and generalize about the color, odor, viscosity, and other characteristics. When chemistry made its first gigantic steps in response to Napoleon's generous funding in the early nineteenth century, the essential oils were examined and described only after laborious, circuitous tests, known to chemists as "wet" processes. After World War II, however, these methods of determining the composition of an essential oil could be abandoned because of the perfecting of the gas chromatograph (GC) and, more recently, the high-performance liquid chromatograph (HPLC). The principle resembles the modification of regular hydrodistillation invented in the nineteenth century known as fractional distillation, widely used in the petroleum industry. Instead of one condensing surface, as many as thirty separate plates would receive different fractions of the material being distilled. However, GC and HPLC make use of thousands of condensing plates; a million condensing plates are not impossible to this process. These "eyes" can "see" traces in an oil as minute as 10^{-9} gram. Nor does the analyst need huge amounts of an oil to examine its constituent parts; as little as a fraction of a microgram can provide the answer to his or her questions in a matter of minutes. An inert gas—usually helium or nitrogen—sweeps through a long fractionating column only a quarter of an inch in diameter and from six to thirty feet long. As the sample travels along in the solvent, it throws off its constituent elements, beginning with those of lightest volatility. The advantage of the HPLC is that it works at lower temperatures than the conventional GC; although it is more accurate, it is also more expensive. By various methods, the plates are connected to a recorder that registers the relative amounts of a molecule in the oil as a peak; the height of the peak indicates the relative amount. Usually the GC technique is used in tandem with a mass spectrometer, which tells much about the structure of the molecule. Nuclear magnetic resonance (NMR) spectrometry is the most powerful tool for elucidation of the structure of a component, but infra red (IR) and ultra violet (UV) spectrometry are used as well. With these, analysts can determine the unique "fingerprint" of any compound.

These analytic tools have two major applications. The first is in determining the nature of natural products. While this has intrinsic interest, it is also important if the oil is to be rebuilt synthetically. The second application is for quality control. Adulteration (French *coupage*) is a great temptation when crop failures occur and when the prevailing prices reach into the thousands of dollars per pound. A buyer can (and always does) submit a sample of the oil to these forms of analysis to detect whether what has been bought is *truly* one hundred percent Bulgarian rose attar or undoctored davana oil. Nature herself will create some swings of the GC peaks due to yearly fluctuations of rainfall and temperature, but every buyer keeps records of past harvests as reflected on the charts, and if the swings depart too much from yearly alterations, he or she will know that nature has been embellished and extended.

The ultimate in QC, as quality control is known in the industry, is the Research Institute for Fragrance Materials (RIFM). This research operation was set up in 1966 on the initiative of leaders in the American essential-oil industry but is now truly international, with over fifty companies from the United States, France, Britain, Germany, and Japan represented. At their headquarters in Englewood Cliffs, New Jersey, the vast array of animal, botanical, and synthetic raw materials is scrutinized with the "eyes" of the best of contemporary instrumentation. Samples of products are submitted that must reflect actual use, accompanied by their gas chromatograph, UV, or IR curves. These are then subjected to a rigorous examination for safety of use on human skin. To date twelve hundred fragrance materials have been tested for safety of inhalation, allergic reactions, and absorption through the skin. Since 1958 the United States Food and Drug Administration has declared that cosmetics and food products must pass tests that register them as GRAS ("Generally Recognized as Safe"). The RIFM tests are even more demanding—the perfume industry is policing itself—because the discovery of allergic reactions to a fragrance whose development has cost millions of dollars would be catastrophic for a company. Preventing the use of such an allergen in the basic formula is worth more than pounds of cure. The consumer can rest in the knowledge that the margin of safety in using perfumes, after-shaves, and scented soaps is very high.

The American industry has also been a Maecenas to the ongoing research into the psychology of odor perception, funding the numerous human and animal tests underway at the Monell Chemical Senses Center on the campus of the University of Pennsylvania in Philadelphia. While some of the findings have specific value for the development of new products, many more hold out perspectives either for aromatherapeutic applications or for further understanding of the organism-environment relationship that olfaction encompasses. Similar research is being carried on at the Yale-affiliated John B. Pierce Foundation Laboratory in New Haven, Connecticut. In addition to the popular impression of the perfume industry as an enterprise of glamour and fashion, there is a perfumery of organic chemists, natural-products chemists, quality-control analysts, neurologists, botanists, and agronomists. These too, though far less known, are just as much a part of modern perfume as the glitter and romance.

13

The Side We See: The Artistic and Commercial Aspects of Perfumery Today

What are the dynamics of making a perfume? Ultimately this question merges with the greater question of what makes creativity. Ask any perfumer whether a technical background is a requirement of the job, particularly a knowledge of chemistry. He or she will tell you that it is a great help but not a hundred percent necessary. What is, is a sense of art. François Coty, Ernest Beaux, Paul Parquet, and Jean Carles were all perfumers who had not studied chemistry, but each was an artist.

At a perfume conference held in Paris in 1969, Marcel Guillot, the distinguished pharmacist and olfactory researcher, asked the question whether creativity in the making of perfumes was a gift or an acquired trait. The maker of the perfumes for the House of Dior, Edmond Roudnitska, replied that in his experience, "the capacity to create is essentially the ability to imagine."[1] It is imagination that enables the creator to take reality and twist it into the work of art. As Gaston Bachelard notes, imagination is that which is able "to give a new form to the world" by "*deforming* images provided by perception."[2] He likens it to a great tree, at home in both the earth and the sky.[3]

Various perfumers used different perceptions to spark this faculty of forming new images. Roudnitska said that dreams had furnished the material from which his Diorissimo was made; Henri Robert of the House of Chanel kept a diary of fragrance perceptions that he had observed throughout his world travels; memories of Tschaikovsky heard in Moscow before the 1917 Revolution were the *point de départ* for Bois des Iles, created by Ernest Beaux in 1926; André Fraysse found stimulation in the memories of the sights, sounds, and scents of the atelier of Jeanne Lanvin where he had worked as a young man.

Roudnitska in his book on this subject *(L'Esthétique en Question)*[4] is insistent that a perfume distorts and transforms these impressions and memories. Some perfumes may represent a certain flower or plant, but most of them are abstract compositions living an existence of their own. A musical composition, even if named "The Brook," or "The Storm," is never a duplication of those sounds, but leads a life as a complete musical composition, whether titled after something found in nature, or merely identified as "Symphony Number 9."

In order to allow this creative imagination to range fully among perceptions in the present and remember impressions of the past and to fully shape and mold them into something new, Roudnitska declared, "I never do business with people who impose their ideas on me."[5] The wisdom of his philosophy is revealed in the success of the many perfumes he has done for Christian Dior, Marcel Rochas, and for the House of Hermés. He is an independent worker with a laboratory and study at Cabris, outside Paris.

Working on a Fragrance Composition

Given these guiding principles of creativity in work, what are the actual thoughts that go through the mind of the perfumer in the concrete working out of a composition?

The perfumer will work within the context of the client's profile— even Roudnitska works within these parameters. The profile indicates

Lily-of-the-valley was used in the eighteenth and nineteenth century for perfumes, but today its light note is re-created by a combination of synthetic and natural oils. The cost of hand-picking such small blooms is prohibitive. François Coty presented his employees with lilies-of-the-valley every first of May, and after his death, his successor commemorated this custom with the creation of Muguet des Bois. Diorissimo is another fragrance with this note.

the price parameters, his or her conception of the type of fragrance, ideas for the concept, style, package, and the market of the prospective perfume.

The perfumer then works at the tiers and tiers of odorants, blending, sniffing, blending again, starting over again, weighing out each possible combination and amount of material. Endless blotters (*mouillettes*) will be used as he or she observes the behavior of possible arrangements as the combination unfolds in time. Questions come to mind throughout the process, such as, will the fragrance be sharp and pointed or soft and muffled? What tonality will it have? How intense will it be as it rises from the bottle? Intensity can be measured for each of the materials of the perfumer's palette, but there is a difference between the intensity of the material itself and the perceived intensity. Also, different materials in combination attain variant intensities through synergy. All these factors demand the judgment of the experienced craftsperson. Does the perfume seem to have "body"? Is it sufficiently "full," "rich," and "textured" in all permutations of its evaporation? Does it rise and diffuse, or must one draw close to the perfume in order to notice an exhalation? Will the wearer leave a "carrier wave" of the

The concrete produced by solvent extraction of jasmine flowers. This precious substance contains the essential oil of the flowers, solidified in the waxes present in the petals of the plant, that serve to protect it from rain and wind. The entire mass has a bright orange hue due to the additional presence of pigments. These last two elements are of no use to perfumery and must be separated by a process of stirring in alcohol, filtering, and then removing the alcohol from the remaining oil by distillation under a vacuum. The cost of such a concrete is a major factor in the price of a finished perfume. Courtesy of Allen Rokach

perfume in her wake? How does it hold up over a period of time; does it retain its odoricity? These are the questions the artist asks himself while working.

Fortunately the artist will have an art critic ready to judge the work. This critique is the role of the fragrance evaluator. Some are skilled professionals, aware of excellence in perfume and the taste of the market. Others are drawn from off the street if the target is a mass audience, or from the world of chic if the scent is to be up-scale. Their reactions give the perfumer a chance to make a fine tuning. Then, once the customer has given the nod, there will be further work on the perfumer's part in accommodating the new creation to the extension of the product in a line of soaps and cosmetics.

Naming a Scent

Naming a perfume is itself an art. From the depths of the poet-soul a word, a mantra must be born that will join both the essence of the perfume and the imagination of the person "out there" who is to buy

The "organ" of perfumery. The great perfumes of the twenties and thirties were created at consoles such as these, filled with vials of essential oils and products of synthesis, weighed, and evaluated on blotter paper strips. Today, the scale is electrical, and most of the components are assembled by an assistant in an adjoining room. Courtesy of Naarden Corporation

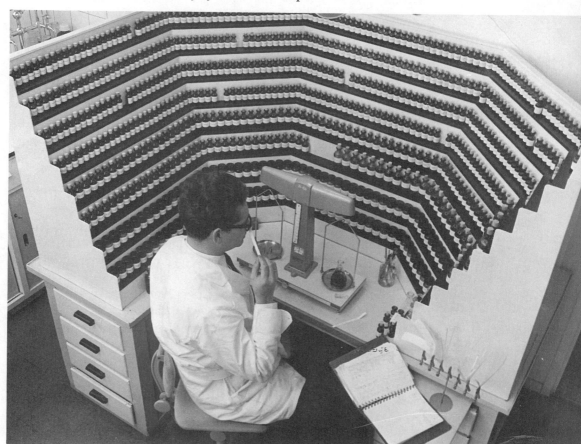

An assistant selects from the enormous wealth of aroma materials at the warehouse of a major supplier of Grasse. Courtesy of Allen Rokach

it. Constantin Wériguine[6] attempted to sort this poetry of perfume names into categories and found that scents were named for flowers, love, history and fashions, evocative symbols (Carnet de Bal, Calèche, Quadrille, for example), abstract names (Chanel No. 5, Y de Saint Laurent). Based on her research into French perfumery from 1889 to the present, Marylène Delbourg-Delphis has greatly ramified these categories into themes that are principally concerned with love, travel, signatures (authorities of fashion or perfumes named for the house), times and seasons, out-of-the-real (dreams, games, rapture), nature, art, contemporary life, myths, Paris life, and femininity.

Just as creative fantasy gives birth to a perfume, the perfume, coupled to its name, gives rise to countless images in the mind of the receiver. No resource has been left untapped in the material of the perfume, and no province of poetry has remained unvisited in the search for its name.

The Jazz Age in perfume advertisement—Lucien Lelong's Tout Lelong, 1927. Here, the name of the scent was a pun on its creator's name. Perfume titles range from the humorous to the dramatic; some even have non-names, numbers, or letters like musical compositions.
Courtesy of
Marylène Delbourg-Delphis

Packaging

Packaging is the third step in the art of perfume presentation. We have seen how perfume grew up in the arms of the glass industry; the essential oils themselves refuse to stay in any container other than glass, which does not enter into chemical liaisons with them. Today dilutions of essential oil in eau de toilette, after-shave lotions, and cologne form will remain in plastic bottles, but perfumes and pure oils are too reactive, and glass remains the container of choice in these areas.

To one familiar with modern perfumery, there is a feeling of utter helplessness in deciding which fragrance is most beautifully bottled. Almost every one of the *grands parfums* reflects so much thought, taste, imagination, and fineness of materials and textures that picking the best would be like selecting the best painting in the Louvre.

Today every color of the rainbow has been used in designing the flacon and its carton: from clear through pink to cobalt and black. Experiments have been made with bottle tops of cast metal (Niki de St. Phalle), with housings of lacquerlike plastic (Armani, Opium), and

The dramatic flacon for Coque d'Or (Guerlain, 1937) in gold and cobalt blue—one of the most successful and original perfume bottles of all time. The identifying label, which was so pronounced in the bottles of the nineteenth century, has been condensed to a simple name incorporated into the glass itself. The title means "Golden Shell," and the perfume was created by Jacques Guerlain. Courtesy of Guerlain, Inc.

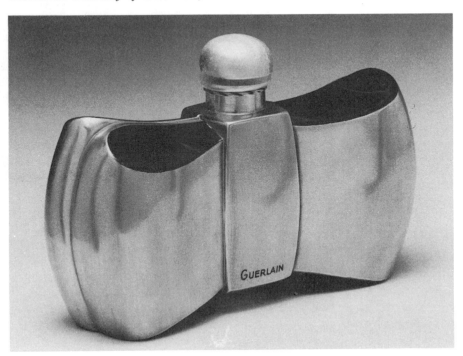

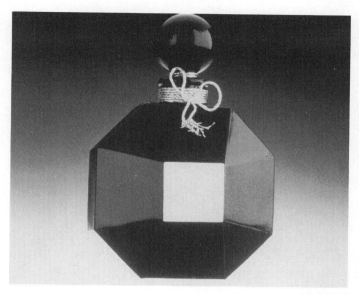

Like a cut gem, this dramatic flacon appeared in 1924, done by the firm Isabey for its Le Lys Noir and Le Dandy. Courtesy of Marylène Delbourg-Delphis

with surface emblems of real gold (Polo, Zen). These materials—as well as the beautiful paper stock and strong inks in the cartons and labels—are a significant determinant of the price of the finished product, and often they are many times more costly than the costly oils they hold. And yet this is not "just" packaging but a true decorative art that is alive and well today, although its roots go clear back to pharaonic Egypt.

Like the perfumer, the identity of the package designer is usually hidden behind that of the couturier or designer. But within the industry, certain names are synonymous with great artistry in package creation. In Paris, Serge Mansau has designed Vivre, Septième Sens, Infini, and Oscar de la Renta, and Pierre Dinand of Paris and New York has designed Ivoire, Van Cleef and Arpels, Coriandre, Kouros, J. L. Sherrer, Opium, and Magie Noire. Although René Lalique died shortly after World War II, his atelier continues to produce beautiful flacons, as does the illustrious House of Baccarat. Today the major implemen-

Flacons for Mon Ame by the firm of Ybry, Paris, 1926. Courtesy of Mary-lène Delbourg-Delphis

ters of fragrance-bottle designs are the firms of St. Gobain-Desjonquères, Pochet et du Courval, and Verreries Brosse—each in France. Although American perfumers are as numerous as their French counterparts, the American glass industry to date has shied away from the demands of this field of art glassware. However, there are talented package designers in the United States: Marc Rosen of Elizabeth Arden (who did KL and Burberry's), Ira Levy of Estée Lauder, and Joseph Messina of Max Factor.

It must be said that the fragrances that coruscate in their crystal containers on every perfume counter are rarely seen for the artistry they represent. Although this is a blind spot among consumers, who take the art of making the perfume and its package for granted, this is not so within the industry. Roudnitska writes that such a beautiful thing can become a "symbol of moral good," for "the aesthetic is the highest point to which the human spirit can rise."[7] Admiration for the skill entailed in perfume and package creation has taken some concrete forms. In 1980 Georges Vassallo, Mayor of Grasse, announced the opening of an International Museum of Perfumery, headed by the

Bottles created by the C. et J. Viard Company in the early twenties.

curator M. Georges Vindry. Although not yet fully completed, this project has already amassed an enormous collection of antique stills, classical labware of alchemy and early chemistry, distillers' handbooks and perfumers' manuals, art flacons, and poster art reflecting the images of beauty proposed over the centuries by leaders of fashion. The collection will be housed in the old factory of Hugues Aîné in Grasse, retaining the old facade with its bas-relief of twin stills but completely modernized within and crowned with a greenhouse for displaying the plants of perfumery.

Another important project has been the funding by St. Gobain-Desjonqueres of a data bank of French perfumery, presenting on an Apple III computer display terminal all the facts known about the six thousand perfumes marketed in France from 1889 on and presenting on an adjacent series of slide screens the package as advertised in the contemporary press. Marylène Delbourg-Delphis, a philosopher-turned-historian of contemporary culture, did the research, and M. Christian Marchandise suggested using the computer and provided the patronage for the project.

Perfume Research

Several companies have also been conspicuous for their support of research into the industry as a whole. International Flavors and Fragrances contributed in part to the enormous research work done by perfumer-author Steffen Arctander, whose volumes have been referred to in the section of this book on natural and synthetic materials. The Vetlesen Foundation of Mr. Henry Walters, Chairman of the Board of that corporation, and the National Endowment for the Humanities backed up my own research in this field at the New York Botanical Garden.

The Dragoco corporation has sponsored publication of a journal distributed gratis throughout the industry in German, French, English, Spanish, and Italian, which discusses *all* aspects of perfumery: history, perfume creation, botany, advertising and marketing, and new synthetics. Fritszche Dodge and Olcott Inc. helped to finance the publication of the six-volume set of Dr. Ernest Geunther's *The Essential Oils*, and Roure Bertrand Dupont has published *Recherches*, a handsome magazine embracing agriculture, olfactory physiology, and extensive studies of the constituents of essential oils. The same company runs one of the few schools for perfumery, located in Grasse. The only other school, also at Grasse, is directed by the firm of Charabot.

The American industry created the Fragrance Foundation in New York City in 1948. Headed by Annette Green, it serves to disseminate information about the products of perfumery and the faculty of olfaction both within the industry and to the general public. It sponsors lectures and awards for excellence in fragrance and package creation. A similar federation was organized in Paris, led by M. Robert Leduc.

In the United States as well as in France, various schools have begun to devote courses of instruction into this field, notably the Fashion Institute of Technology and Fairleigh Dickinson University.

Month-by-month developments in the industry are noted in the American *Perfumer and Flavorist*, and *Beauty Fashion Magazine*, and several European industry publications.

In Spain, the Museum of Perfumery has been organized in Barcelona to give recognition to the art of flacon design; in a quiet way (there is not even a catalog) the lawyer Ramón Planas has assembled four thousand pieces for display to the public.

14

Recent History:
Trade and Trends

What are the trends within the present-day fragrance industry? The story of perfumery today is exciting and complex—linked to trends in both high fashion and popular culture, to developments both in France, the traditional producer and market of fragrances, and in the United States, the newer rival.

Never before in history have so many products made use of fragrance. This has been the achievement of the United States industry—vinyl chairs, rubber tires, hair dyes, furniture polishes, lavatory bowl cleansers, and toys of every description. Since the War, men have been encouraged to use deodorants, and women warned of the danger of "feminine odor" and the need for "hygiene deodorants." Personal soaps, shampoos, mouthwashes, and detergents have become more fragranced than ever.

The great increase in sensory awareness that was one of the results of the hippie culture of the sixties has left a growing interest in the fragrance within the environment. Sachets, potpourris, scented candles, and shelf papers have made scent nearly as important to the "feel" of an interior as color. Even plant hybridists pay attention to the scent of flowers in breeding cultivars today, whereas once color and form alone were important.

The youth rebellion helped create the woman's consciousness movement of the seventies, and Charles Revson saw his most enormous success with the launch of Charlie (1973) which built upon this trend. Charlie wore the blue jeans of the sixties and yet was interested in fashion and elegance. The image used in the marketing of this fragrance was one of an independent woman, not one who was angling somehow for a man. Even the name of the perfume was masculine (Revson's own). The perfume was made quite strong (taking a leaf from the book of Estée Lauder) and the cologne was three times the concentration of aromatics found in an average cologne. The fragrance, which was very high in synthetics, was the object of innumerable arguments and discussions within Revlon, but once launched, it showed that Revson had succeeded in gauging the tenor of the times. In the first year sales exceeded ten million dollars, and since then have approached almost the fifty million dollar figure.

In 1975, still sensitive to the need to work with the trends generated from within the world of the consumer, Revson launched Jontue, with an appeal to a softer, more feminine and romantic personality. Magazine ads were hazy and atmospheric, and television commercials were shot in the Loire valley. This scent with its tuberose note proved to be another milestone in perfume marketing.

The seventies turned out to be the decade of the designers. Just as Revson did, these fashion authorities endeavored to work with the complexities of the consumer's desires, perfect and render them more elegant, and then present them back to the consumer with the stamp of an expert. This innovation, begun with Cardin and others in Paris, proliferated in the United States as well. And each designer brought forth a fragrance as one of the most important items in his or her line. Geoffrey Beene, Halston, Ralph Lauren, Oscar de la Renta, Diane von Furstenberg have become almost household words, and their fragrances have been among their greatest promoters.

In 1975, the French industry became alarmed at the loss of sales to

Grasse today—city of flowers, and mecca of world perfumery.

the beauty houses such as Lauder and Revlon, and the growing list of American designers, and made a response that has been epochal. In this year, the French couturier-designer Yves St. Laurent launched Opium.

Opium was a perfume that attempted to build upon the designer prestige, the strength of fragrance that had become popular in America, and what St. Laurent perceived to be a mood within the contemporary market. And although the fragrance was conceived in France it was aimed at the lucrative American consumer.

The fragrance was made extremely potent, rich in essential oils; the genre was oriental—like Shalimar, Tabu, and Youth Dew—a type rich in incense resins, spices, and florals. The package was designed in the form of a Japanese *inro* with a spray of Chinese bamboo and a tassel attached to suggest its use as an accessory. St. Laurent felt that it was for the woman "who wanted to be feminine again," so while it imitated Youth Dew in certain ways, it was the opposite of the go-getter Charlie. The name suggested the orientalism of the Second Empire, with overtones of wickedness and hedonism. The ads read, "for those who are addicted to Yves St. Laurent." The Opium model was a languorous odalisque, her eyes closed as she lay backwards upon a divan.

The name was considered by many to be scandalous—glamorizing drug use—and the price, criminal—$150 an ounce. But crime paid and paid well. Sales of $3,000,000 were realized within the first four months of Opium's American debut in September of 1978.

Opium sold so well that it set a trend of its own. Lancôme, the French cosmetic house, brought out Magie Noire, with a package covered with arcane alchemical symbols and an ambiance of the mysterious, arcane, and exotic. The House of Dior promoted Dioressence—*Dior barbare*—with a poster designed by Gruau illustrating a woman lounging on oriental cushions in the manner of Sarah Bernhardt.

Yves St. Laurent had declared that his Opium was "the sesame which opens the gate of dreams." Indeed it was, as French fashion leaders began to have pleasant dreams of regaining markets that had been crumbling since the sixties. Yves St. Laurent's royalties pay $35,000,000 per annum; the House of Cardin has a gross income of $21,000,000, and the designer Karl Lagerfeld draws $1,200,000 per year from his popular Chloë alone. Today, a perfume may generate as much as 70% of the income of a French fashion house.

Designer perfumes today, both from French and American names,

René Prinet's The Kreutzer Sonata *was first exhibited in Paris in 1901. The painting was later acquired by the Spanish firm of Dana, and was used to advertise its perfume Tabu, developed by Javier Serra in Barcelona in 1932. The theme of the work of art and the name ("taboo") evoke the dreams of forbidden but exciting terrain opening up to the user. Romance and voyages are recurring themes in fragrance advertizing—promising departures from the ordinary world in return for a few inhalations. Tabu is one of the classic "orientals"—rich in patchouli, oak moss, musk, and amber— and the prototype of the trend-setting American fragrance, Estée Lauder's* Youth Dew. *Courtesy of Dana Perfumes Corporation*

account for forty percent of sales, and the trend to hitch the perfume wagon to an illustrious star continues.

The few fragrances that are manufactured by purely fragrance houses continue to make a good showing. Guerlain lost some sales when it refused to adjust to American sales techniques such as giving the salesperson a commission, using television commercials, and sampling. Its Nahema, which received thirty-one percent of its advertising budget in 1980 and was packaged in a bottle adorned with a drop (the first essence to come from the distiller's retort), is generally considered too avant-garde for the American market. It has not caught on yet, and the company has equalized promotion to all of its perfumes. Guerlain has also adjusted to American ways now and has even won an Andy from the Advertising Club of New York. Parfums Caron has created a sumptuous parfumerie on Avenue Montaigne, presenting each of its many products in Louis XV-style Baccarat crystal flasks that release the essence at the turn of the spigot. Houbigant has decided to tap the mass market, somewhat the reverse response to the *défie Américaine*. In Spain the Houses of Myrugia and Puig continue to produce a variety of quality fragrances.

All retailers of fragrance make use of a variety of means to encourage sales. "GWP" has become industry slang for the presentation of a gift with the purchase of a fragrance. "PWP" is the abbreviation for a (discounted) purchase with the purchase of such an item. Perfumery has become the patron of a host of luxury crafts—jewelry, silk scarves, porcelain jars, candles, luggage, and many other accessories.

Since Charlie had proven that great profits could be made from the change in the self-image of women, market researchers constantly wonder about the selling of masculine toilet articles. Will there be a departure from the traditionally reluctant male consumer—will he begin to use scent with a wider range of notes more freely? Would men begin to use a "wardrobe of fragrances" as women have begun doing, using a brisk cologne in the morning and a softer scent for a dinner date? And would men actually purchase fragrances, instead of letting their wives or girlfriends do this for them? Some predicters saw a sudden change in both these areas, but the male market has had no sudden leaps forward. Although there may be no dramatic changes, it does seem that men will begin using scents with more interest and awareness than in recent history. Certainly the historical record indicates that men have always enjoyed and valued aromatics.

Nahema is one of the more avant-garde perfumes—an oriental type with notes of fruit fragrances. The bottle exhibits a drop in the center, an elegant allusion to the alembic as the source of so many fragrant essences. Courtesy of Guerlain, Inc.

Do analysts of trends foresee new markets overseas? Japan has certainly become dazzlingly prosperous. However, this has not brought unrestrained riches to producers in Paris and New York, for Japan has its own perfume companies and the Japanese woman continues to decline the level of fragrance use habitual in the United States and France. Hong Kong, Singapore, and Taiwan are obviously fertile fields for fragrance; China itself has returned to its traditional fondness for scents, and millions could be made if only a fraction of that market were to be tapped.

Unfortunately there has been no Marshall Plan extended to Latin America, Africa, or Southeast Asia, and thus vast legions of potential consumers remain, by and large, only harried producers of primary materials. Brazil, India, and Argentina are something of exceptions to this pattern. The Arab world has become suddenly wealthy, but the richest of the oil nations are very low in population. The Soviet Union has begun to renew its pre-1917 infatuation with fragrance and beauty; Poland is a major producer of cosmetics. What will be the on-going story of this ancient industry? No one can read trends so well that the future can be foretold. But we can pick out some of the principal patterns, and all evidence indicates that the global industry will expand and grow, although at a steady, not a death-defying, rate; sales within the American industry are presently approaching the two-billion-dollar mark.

Sensory awareness has emerged as one of the great features of contemporary life. We can be assured that mankind's long association with the beauty and variety of the universe of smells will continue to grow in extent and in fineness of perception. There will be a greater need than ever for more of the botany, chemistry, technology, physiology, style, art marketing, and imagination that have all been a part of the story of perfumery. Tomorrow's men and women, like their ancestors, will continue to breathe the "Aha!" of delight when a fine fragrance from the outside world passes through the nostrils, over the sensing cells, and strikes a responsive chord in the centers of consciousness in the brain.

Notes

INTRODUCTION

1. *Science and Civilization in China*, Cambridge University Press, Volume 4, p. 128.

CHAPTER 2

1. Quoted in "Sex and Smell" by James Hassett, *Psychology Today*, March 1978, p. 45.
2. "Sense and Sensibility," *The Century Magazine*, LXXXV, February 1908, pp. 573–577.
3. *Harpers Bazaar*, April 1979, p. 152.
4. "Annals of Medicine," *New Yorker*, p. 97, September 1977, by Berton Roueché.
5. Quoted in Paolo Rovesti, *In Search of Perfumes Lost*, Blow-up Press, Venice, 1980, p. 57.
6. Referred to in R. W. Moncrieff's *Odor Preferences*, Wm. Wiley, N.Y., 1966.
7. Rovesti, *op. cit.*, p. 54.
8. *"La Chevelure," Les Fleurs du Mal*, 1857, Edwin Morris, translator.
9. Quoted in M. Guillot, "On the Evocative Power of Perfumes," #3, *Recherches*, Roure Bertrand, Dupont. Paris, 1953, pp. 2–3.
10. *A la Recherche du Temps Perdu. Du Côté de Chez Swann*. T. I. de l'edition N.R.F. in-octavo, p. 67, Edwin Morris, translator.
11. *Paroles pout l'autre*, cited in G. Bachelard, *The Poetics of Space*, Beacon Press, Boston, Mass., 1969, p. 26.

CHAPTER 3

1. Groom, N., *Frankincense and Myrrh*, Longman, London and New York, 1981, p. 22.
2. Cf. F. Anderson, "A Flower for Eternity," *Garden* Magazine, N.Y. Botanical Garden, N.Y., Jan./Feb., 1983, pp. 8–13.

3. *Natural History*, XII, 42.
4. The Song of Solomon, 3:6(KJV), *The Jerusalem Bible*, Reader's Edition, Doubleday, N.Y., p. 868.
5. The Song of Solomon, 4:13–16, The Jerusalem Bible, p. 870.
6. Judith 10:3–5, The Jerusalem Bible, p. 548.

CHAPTER 4

1. Quoted in Paolo Rovesti, *In Search of Perfumes Lost*, p. 181.
2. Theophrastus, *Enquiry into Plants*, Book 9, ch. 4, secs. 2–3.
3. Groom, N., *Frankincense and Myrrh*, p. 233.
4. Festugière, A., *La Revelation d'Hermiès Trimegiste*. Vol. I, Paris, Gabalda, 1950, pp. 41–2.
5. *Ibid*, p. 242.
6. Forbes, R., *A Short History of Distillation*, p. 54.
7. Lopez, R. and Raymond, I., *Medieval Trade in the Mediterranean World*, Columbia University Press, N.Y., p. 25.
8. Schimmel, Annemarie, "The Celestial Garden in Islam," pp. 13–39, in *The Islamic Garden*, Dumbarton Oaks, Washington, D.C., 1976, p. 29.
9. *Ibid*, p. 36.

CHAPTER 5

1. De Bary, W. (general editor), *The Sources of Indian Tradition*, Columbia University Press, N.Y., 1970, Vol. 1, p. 255.
2. Thierry, Solange, "L'Inde et les Parfums," pp. 93–95, in *3000 Ans de Parfumerie*, Grasse, *Musée d'Art et d'Histoire*, 1980.
3. Gode, P.K., "Indian Science of Cosmetics and Perfumery," *Diamond Jubilee Special Number of Ratna-deepa*, Bombay n.d.; see also Gode, P.K., *Journal of the Bombay University*, September 1945, pp. 44–52.
4. Crowe, S., Haywood, S., Jellicoe, S., Patterson, G., *The Gardens of Mughul India*, Thames & Hudson, London, 1972, p. 191.
5. Rovesti, Paolo, *In Search of Perfumes Lost*, Blow-up Press, Venice, 1980, p. 170.
6. *The Wealth of India*, New Delhi, Dr. S. Bhatnagar et al. General Editorial Board, 1948.
7. Quoted in Goodrich, Carrington, *A Short History of the Chinese People*, 3rd ed. Harper and Row, paper, N.Y. 1963, p. 151.
8. Schaefer, Edward, *The Golden Peaches of Samarkand*, U. of California Press, Berkeley and Los Angeles, p. 155.
9. Needham, Joseph. *Science and Civilization in China*, vol. V:2, Cambridge University Press, p. 130.

10. Needham, Joseph, *op. cit.*, p. 150.
11. *Ibid.*, p. 151.
12. Bedini, Silvio A., "The Scent of Time," *Transactions of the American Philosophical Society*, The American Philosophical Society, Philadelphia, August, 1963, p. 24.
13. Schaefer, Edward, *The Golden Peaches of Samarkand*, University of California Press, Berkeley and Los Angeles, 1963, p. 140.
14. Swingle, Walter T., in *Report of the Librarian of Congress*, Washington, D.C., 1926–1927, p. 256.
15. Quoted in Hudson, Geoffrey, *Europe and China*, Beacon Press, Boston, n.d., p. 162.
16. Marco Polo, *The Description of the World*, edited by Moule, A.C., and Pelliot, Paul; London, 1938, p. 326.
17. Hudson, Geoffrey, *op. cit*, p. 163.

CHAPTER 6

1. Forbes, R., *A Short History of the Art of Distillation*, Brill, Leiden, 1948, p. 110.
2. Moore, F., *A History of Chemistry*, McGraw Hill, N.Y., 1939, p. 34.
3. Gildemeister, E., and Hoffman, F., *The Volatile Oils*, Pharmaceutical Review, Milwaukee, Minn., 1900, p. 26.
4. Lopez, R., Raymond, I., *Medieval Trade in the Mediterranean World*, Columbia University Press, N.Y., 1961, pp. 109–114.
5. Hudson, Geoffrey, *China and Europe*, Beacon Press, Boston, Mass., n.d., pp. 182–183.
6. Hudson, Geoffrey, op. cit, p. 186.
7. Rovesti, Paolo, *In Search of Perfumes Lost*, Blow-up Press, Venice, 1980, p. 200.
8. Quoted in Thompson, C.J.S., *The Mystery and Lure of Perfume*, J. P. Lippincott Company, Philadelphia, Pa., 1927, p. 112.
9. Quoted in Genders, Roy, *Perfumes Through the Ages*, G. P. Putnam's, N.Y., 1972, p. 162.

CHAPTER 7

1. Naves, Y., and Mazuyer, G., *Natural Perfume Materials*, Reinhold Publishing Company, N.Y., 1947, p. 14.

CHAPTER 8

1. Parry, Ernest, *Parry's Cyclopedia of Perfumery*, Vol. I, Blakiston, Philadelphia, Pa., 1925, p. 202.

CHAPTER 9

1. I am indebted to Marylène Delbourg-Delphis for this note as well as other observations about the twenties that appear on the Data Bank of French Perfumery (1889–1983), Saint Gobain-Desjonquères.
2. Batterberry, Michael and Ariane, *Mirror, Mirror, A Social History of Fashion*, Holt, Rinehart and Winston, N.Y., 1977, p. 348.

CHAPTER 11

1. Naves, Y., and Mazuyer, G., *Natural Perfume Materials*, Reinhold Publishing Corporation, N.Y., 1947, p. 201.
2. Arctander, Steffen, *Perfume and Flavor Materials of Natural Origin*, Elizabeth, N.J., 1960 (Published by the author) p. 509.
3. *Ibid.*, p. 509.
4. Dorland, Wayne, and Rogers, James A., Jr., *The Fragrance and Flavor Industry*, Dorland Company, Mendham, N.J., 1977, p. 168.

CHAPTER 12

1. Cf. "Steam Distillation of the Superficial Essential Oils: Hypotheses from Studies with Lavenders and Mints," E.F.K. Denny, *Perfumer and Flavorist*, Vol. 4, Oct./Nov., 1979, pp. 14–23.

CHAPTER 13

1. Quoted in Kaufman, William, *Perfume*, Dutton, N.Y. 1974, p. 133.
2. Quoted in Kaplan, Edward, "Gaston Bachelard's Philosophy of Imagination: An Introduction," *Philosophy and Phenomenological Research*, Vol. XXXIII, No. 1, Sept. 1972, pp. 2,3.
3. *Ibid.*, p. 5.
4. Paris, Presses Universitaires de France, 1977.
5. Quoted in Kaufman, William, *op. cit.*, p. 150.
6. *Souvenirs et Parfums*, "The Naming of Perfumes," Plon, Paris, 1965.
7. Roudnitska, Edmond, *L'Esthétique en Question*, Presses Universitaires de France, Paris, 1977, pp. 205, 253.

Bibliography

General

DORLAND, WAYNE; and ROGERS, JAMES Jr. *The Fragrance and Flavor Industry.* Wayne E. Dorland Co., Mendham, N.J. 1977.

GUENTHER, ERNEST. *The Essential Oils*, Vol. 1–6. D. Van Nostrand Co., 1949–1952, New York.

ARCTANDER, STEFFEN. *Perfume and Flavor Materials of Natural Origin.* Published privately by the author. Elizabeth, N.J., 1960.

DELBOURG-DELPHIS, MARYLÈNE. *Le Sillage des Elégantes*, J. C. Lattès, Paris, 1983.

JESSEE, JILL. *Perfume Album.* Robert E. Krieger, Huntington, N.Y. 1951. GILDEMEISTER, E.; and HOFFMAN, F. "The Volatile Oils," *Pharmaceutical Review.* Milwaukee, 1900.

POUCHER, WILLIAM. *Perfumes, Cosmetics and Soaps.* D. Van Nostrand and Co., N.Y., 1926.

NAVES, Y.; and MAZUYER, G. *Natural Perfume Materials.* Reinhold Publishing Corporation, N.Y., 1947.

KAUFMAN, WILLIAM. *Perfume.* E. P. Dutton, N.Y., 1974.

KENNETT, FRANCES. *History of Perfume.* Harrap, London, 1975.

COLA, FELIX. *Le Livre du Parfumeur.* Casterman, Paris, 1934.

BILLOT, M.; AND WELLS, F. *Perfume Technology.* John Wiley and Co., N.Y., 1975.

ROVESTI, PAOLO. *In Search of Perfumes Lost.* Blow-up Press, Venice, 1980.

VINDRY, GEORGES et al. *3000 Ans de Parfumerie, Parfums, Savons, Fards et Cosmétiques, de l'Antiquité à nos jours*, Exhibition Catalogue. Grasse, *Musée d'Art et d'Historie*, 1980.

PARRY, ERNEST. *Parry's Cyclopedia of Perfumery*, Vol. I–II. Blakiston, Philadelphia, 1925.

GENDERS, ROY. *Perfume Through the Ages.* Putnam, N.Y., 1972.

THOMPSON, C. *The Mystery and Lure of Perfumes.* J. B. Lippincott Co., Philadelphia, 1927.

LE GALLIENNE, RICHARD. *The Romance of Perfume.* R. Hudnut, N.Y., n.d.

VERRILL, A. H. *Perfumes and Spices.* L. C. Page and Co., Boston, 1940.

WALL, FLORENCE E. *The Principles and Practice of Beauty Culture.* Keystone Publications, N.Y., 1960.

ROSENGARTEN, F. JR. *The Book of Spices.* Livingston Publishing Co., Wynnewood, Pa., 1969.

CLAIR, C. *Of Herbs and Spices.* Abelard-Schuman, London, 1961.

Journals

Perfumer and Flavorist, Allured Publishing Corp., Wheaton, Ill.

Dragoco Report, Dragoco Corp., Totowa, N.J.

Recherches, Roure Bertrand Dupont S.A., Paris.

Parfums, Cosmetiques, Arômes. Societé d'Expansion Technique et Economique S.A., Paris.

Rivista Italiana delle Essenze, Profumi e delle Piante Officinali. Milano.

Drug and Cosmetic Industry. Allured Publishing Corp., Wheaton, Ill.

Cosmetic World. New York, N.Y.

Beauty Fashion Magazine. N.Y.

Economic Botany. New York Botanical Garden, N.Y.

The Materials of Perfumery

KESTERSON, J. W.; HENDERSON, R.; and BRADDOCK, R. *"Florida Citrus Oils."* University of Florida Press, Gainesville, Technical Bulletin #749.

HAMPTON, S. *The Scent of Flowers and Leaves.* London, Dulau & Co., 1925.

JAEGER, PAUL. *The Wonderful Life of Flowers.* E.P. Dutton, N.Y. 1961.

ROBINSON, TREVOR. *The Organic Constituents of Higher Plants.* Burgess, Minneapolis, 1963.

CROTEAU, RODNEY (ed.). *Fragrance and Flavor Substances.* D. & PS. Verlag, Pattensen, W. Germany, 1980.

KULKA, KURT. "The Chemistry of Essential Oils." *Perfumery and Essential Oil Record.* London, March, 1962.

TYLER, VARRO; BRADY, L.; ROBBERS, J. *Pharmacognosy.* Lea and Febiger, Philadelphia, 1976.

HOFFMANN, HENRI. "Naturals, Isolates, Derivatives and Synthetics." Class notes (unpublished).

SINGH, A. K., et al. "Fungitoxic Activity of Some Essential Oils." *Economic Botany*, 34(2), pp. 186–90. New York Botanical Garden, New York, 1980.

Olfaction

MONCRIEFF, R. W. *The Chemical Senses.* Leonard Hill Ltd., London, 1951.

GUILLOT, M.; and MME. S. GUILLOT-ALLEGRE. "On the Evocative Power of Perfumes." *Recherches*, #3, 1953. Roure Bertrand Dupont, Paris, pp. 2–9.

GUILLOT, M.; and MME. S. GUILLOT-ALLEGRE. "Proust and Sensory Recollection." *Recherches*, #5, June, 1955, pp. 16–23.

CALDINI, O.; and LORI, M. "Paeans to Perfume, Literary Praise of Perfume in Life and Art." *Dragoco Report*, 7/8, 1982, pp. 117–129.

AMOORE, JOHN. "The Stereochemical Theory of Olfaction." *Proceedings of the Scientific Section of the Toilet Goods Association* 37 (supplement), pp. 1-12, 1962.

WILENTZ, JOAN. *The Senses of Man.* Crowell, N.Y., 1968.

WRIGHT, R. H. *The Science of Smell.* Basic Books, N.Y., 1964.

BRODY, JANE. "Sense of Smell Proves to Be Surprisingly Subtle." *The New York Times*, Feb. 22, 1983.

SOBEL, DAVA. "Your Individual Scent Signature." *Vogue, Beauty Health Guide*, Spring/Summer, 1979, p. 22.

"Men's Fragrances: The Sexual Message." *Harper's Bazaar*, April, 1979, p. 152.

HASSETT, JAMES. "Sex and Smell," *Psychology Today*, March, 1979, pp. 40–45.

AMOORE, JOHN. *The Molecular Basis of Odor.* Charles Thomas, Springfield, 1970.

BURTON, ROBERT. *The Language of Smell.* Routledge and Kegan Paul, London, 1976.

GELDARD, FRANK. *The Human Senses.* John Wiley, N.Y., 1953.

MOSKOWITZ, HOWARD. "Odors in the Environment: Hedonics, Perfumery and Odor Abatement," *Handbook of Perception*, Vol. X, Academic Press, N.Y., 1978, pp. 307–47.

WINTER, RUTH. *The Smell Book.* Lippincott Co., Philadelphia, 1976.

GUILLOT, M. "Rotatory Power and Olfaction." *Recherches*, No. 5, June, 1955, pp. 24–31.

GATTEFOSSÉ, R. M. *L'Aromathérapie.* Girardot et Cie., Paris, 1937.

REDDET, M "Colloque d'Aromathérapie." *La France et ses Parfums*, Vol. VI, No. 36, Dec., 1963.

THIEMER, ERNST (ed.). *Fragrance Chemistry: The Science of the Sense of Smell.* Academic Press, N.Y., 1982.

HENKIN, ROBERT, M.D. "Medical Importance of Taste and Smell." *The Journal of the American Medical Assoc.*, Vol. 218, No. 11, Dec. 13, 1971.

Historical Development

Early History:

GROOM, NIGEL. *Frankincense and Myrrh.* Longman, London and New York, 1981.

HOWES, F. N. "Vegetable Gums and Resins." *Chronica Botanica*, Waltham, Mass., 1949.

PEYRON, LOUIS. "La Myrrhe, Aujourdh'hui et Hier." *Rivista Italiana EPPOS*, LX, No. 9, Sept., 1978, pp. 497–503.

FORBES, ROBERT JAMES. *A Short History of the Art of Distillation*. Brill, Leiden, 1948.

PAPADOPOULO, ALEXANDRE. *Islam and Muslim Art*. Abrams, N.Y., 1979.

MOLDENKE, HAROLD and ALMA. "Plants of the Bible." *Chronica Botanica*, Waltham, Mass., 1952.

BROVARSKI, E.; DOLL, S.; and FREED, R. *Egypt's Golden Age: The Art of Living in the New Kingdom 1558–1085 B.C.* Museum of Fine Arts, Boston, 1982.

ANDERSON, FRANK. "A Flower for Eternity." *Garden Magazine*, Jan./Feb., 1983, pp. 8–13.

VANDIER D'ABBADIE, J. "Ancient Egyptian Ointment Spoons." Roure Bertrand Dupont, Paris, *Recherches*, Oct., 1952, No. 2, pp. 20–29.

ABRAHAMS, HAROLD. "Onycha, Ingredient of the Ancient Jewish Incense; An Attempt at Identification." *Economic Botany*, 33(2), 1979, pp. 233–36.

CHANEY, W.; and BASBOUS, M. "The Cedars of Lebanon." *Economic Botany*, 32: pp. 118–23, April/June, 1978.

THEOPHRASTUS. *Enquiry into Plants*, Vol. II. Sir Arthur Hort (trans.) W. Heinemann, London, 1916

PLINY, THE ELDER. *Natural History*, Vol. 4. H. Rackham (trans.) Harvard University Press, Cambridge, Mass., 1945.

MAW, GEORGE. *A Monograph on the Genus Crocus*. Dulan and Co. London, 1886.

STEWART. *Early Islam*. Time-Life Books, N.Y., 1967.

HITTI, PHILIP. *History of the Arabs*. St. Martin's Press, N.Y., 1970.

MORRIS, EDWIN. "Roots, The Earliest History of the Essential Oil Industry." *Perfumer and Flavorist*, Vol. 6, Feb./March, 1981.

MORRIS, EDWIN T. "The Gum Resins, Mankind's First Perfumes." *Dragoco Report*, Dragoco Corp., Totowa, N.J., in press.

The Aromatic East

BHATNAGAR, S. S., et al. *The Wealth of India*. New Delhi, 1948, Volumes 1–11.

BURKILL, I. H. *A Dictionary of the Economic Products of the Malay Peninsula*. London, 1935.

LAUFER, BERTHOLD. *Sino-Iranica, Chinese Contributions to the History of Civilization in Ancient Iran*. Field Museum of Natural History, Chicago, Ill., 1919.

YAMADA, KENTARO. *Tozai Koyaku Shi (A History of Aromatics in the East)*. Tokyo, 1956.

Chau Ju-Kua: His Work on the Chinese and Arab Trade in the Twelfth and Thirteenth Centuries (Chu-fan-chi). Translated and annotated by FRIE-

DRICH HIRTH and W. W. ROCKHILL. Imperial Academy of Sciences, St. Petersburg, 1911 (reprinted, Paragon, N.Y., 1966).

FENNELL, T. A. "For Southern Gardens—Hedychiums." *The National Horticultural Magazine*, Oct., 1954, pp. 238–43.

GODE, P. K. "Studies in the History of Indian Cosmetics and Perfumery, The Gandhayukti Section of the Visnudharmottara." *Ganganath Jha Research Institute Journal*, Vol. III, Parts 3–4, May/Aug., 1946.

GODE, P. K. "Indian Science of Cosmetics and Perfumery." *Ratna-Deepa*, Rajapur (not dated).

GODE, P. K. "Studies in the History of Indian Cosmetics and Perfumery, The Campaka Oil and its Manufacture (between A.D. 500 and 1850)." *Bharatiya Vidya*, Vol. VI, Nos. 7 and 8, July/Aug., 1945.

GODE, P. K. "The Royal Bath." *The International Perfumer*, Vol. II, No. 8. (not cited on reprint) Lesquire, East Molesey, England, Aug. 1977.

PEYRON, LOUIS. "Odeurs et Parfums en Inde, Hier et Aujourd'hui." *Rivista Italiana Essenze, Profumi, Piante Officinali*.

BEDINI, SILVIO, "The Scent of Time, A Study of the Use of Fire and Incense for Time Measurement in Oriental Countries." *Transactions of the American Philosophical Society*, Vol. 53, Part 5, Aug, 1963, Philadelphia.

NEEDHAM, JOSEPH. *Science and Civilization in China*. Vol. V:2, 1974; Vol. V:4, 1980, Cambridge University Press, Cambridge.

SCHAFER, EDWARD. *The Empire of Min*. Charles Tuttle, Rutland, Vt., 1954.

LI CH'IAO-P'ING. *The Chemical Arts of Old China*, 1948.

BASHAM, A. L. *The Wonder That Was India*. Taplinger Publishing Co., N.Y., 1967.

GOODRICH, L. CARRINGTON, *A Short History of the Chinese People*. Harper Torchbook Edition, 1963.

SMITH, F. PORTER, M.D.; STUART, G. A., M.D. *Chinese Medicinal Herbs*. Georgetown Press, San Francisco, 1973.

ROI, J., S. J. *Traité des Plantes Médicinales Chinoises*. Paris, Paul de Chevalier, 1955.

DE BARY, WILLIAM; BASHAM, A. L., et al. *Sources of Indian Tradition*, Volume I. Columbia University Press, N.Y., 1958.

SCHAFER, EDWARD. *The Vermilion Bird*. University of California Press, Berkeley and Los Angeles, 1967.

SWINGLE, WALTER. "Trees and Plants We Owe to China, II." *Asia and the Americas*, June, 1943, pp. 343–47. American Asiatic Association. N.Y.

LIN, T'IEN-WAI. *Sung-tai hsiang yao mao-yi shih kao* ("A History of the Fragrance Trade in the Sung Dynasty"), Hong Kong, Chung-kuo hsuëh she, 1960.

WATSON, ERNEST, *The Principal Articles of Chinese Commerce*. Shanghai, Kelly and Walsh, Ltd., 1923.

Koh-Do ("The Way of Fragrance") Publication of the Japan Koh-Do Association, Tokyo (undated).

MURASAKI LADY. *The Tale of Genji*, (Publisher-TK)

MORRIS, EDWIN T. "In the Fragrant Gardens of China." *Dragoco Report*, 11/12, 1981, pp. 235–47.

MORRIS, EDWIN T. "Romantic Sandalwood, Its History and Use." *Dragoco Report*, 4/5, 1982, pp. 106–16.

MORRIS, EDWIN T. "Patchouli, the Scent that Intrigues." *Dragoco Report*, May, 1983.

MORRIS, EDWIN T. "Vetiver, Gift of India." *Dragoco Report*, June, 1983.

Europe, the Metamorphosis of a Craft into an Industry

ROSETO, GIOVANNI. *Secreti Nobillissimi dell'Arte Profumatoria*. Reprint, 1968. Venice, 1678.

ANDERSON, FRANK. *An Illustrated History of the Herbals*, Columbia University Press, N.Y., 1977.

PARRY, JOHN. *Spices*, Volume I, "The Story of Spices." Chemical Publishing Co., N.Y., 1969.

LINDSAY, W. S. *History of Merchant Shipping and Ancient Commerce*. A.M.S. Press, N.Y., 1965.

GUERILLOT, L. GUYOT, L. *Les Epices, Presses Universitaires de France*, Paris, 1963.

PARTINGTON. J. R. *A Short History of Chemistry*. Harper and Row, N.Y., 1957.

MOORE, F. *A History of Chemistry*. McGraw-Hill, Inc., N.Y., 1939.

BATTERBERRY, MICHAEL and ARIANE. *Mirror, Mirror, A Social History of Fashion*, Holt, Rinehart, Winston, N.Y., 1977.

LAUNERT, EDMOND. *Scent and Scent Bottles*. Barry and Jenkins, London, 1974.

URDANG, GEORGE. "Quintessence, the Story of Extracts." *What's New*, Abbot Laboratories, North Chicago, Ill., Spring, 1944, Pharmacy Ed., pp. 6–19.

LACH, DONALD F. *Asia in the Making of Europe*, Vol. I, "The Century of Discovery." University of Chicago Press, Chicago, Ill., 1965.

LOPEZ, RAYMOND. *Medieval Trade in the Mediterranean World*. Columbia University Press, N.Y., 1961.

HANNA, WILLARD A. "The Unsavory Saga of the Nutmeg Islands." *Asia*, May/June, 1978, pp. 15–23.

CROFTON, R. H. *A Pageant of the Spice Islands*, London, J. Bale and Sons, 1936.

FURBER, HOLDEN. *Rival Empires of Trade in the Orient, 1600–1800*. University of Minnesota Press, 1976.

MILLER, RUSSELL; eds., Time-Life Books. *The East Indiamen*. Time-Life Books, Alexandria, Va., 1980.

HUDSON, GEOFFREY F. *Europe and China, A Survey of Their Relations from the Earliest Times to 1800.* Beacon, Boston, paperback #114 (not dated).

BLOOM, HERBERT. *The Economic Activity of the Jews of Amsterdam.* Kenikat Press, Port Washington, N.Y., 1937.

FLAUMENHAFT, EUGENE and MRS. EUGENE. "Asian Medicinal Plants in Seventeenth-century French Literature." *Economic Botany,* 36(2), 1982, N.Y. Botanical Gardens, N.Y., pp. 147–62.

TOUW, MIA. "Roses in the Middle Ages." *Economic Botany,* 36(1) 1982, N.Y. Botanical Gardens, N.Y., pp. 71–83.

BAYLE, VICTOR. *L'Amateur de Parfums.* Raoul Solar, Paris, 1953.

The Twentieth Century

La Parfumerie Française et l'Art dans la Présentation. La Revue des Marques de la Parfumerie et de la Savonnerie, Paris, 1925.

BERENDT, JOHN. "The Amazing World of Caswell-Massey." *Cosmopolitan,* N.Y. 1982.

JESSEE, JILL. "Historic Highlights of the American Fragrance Industry." *Dragoco Report,* Jan., 1983.

TOBIAS, ANDREW, *Fire and Ice, The Charles Revson/Revlon Story.* William Morrow and Co., Inc. N.Y., 1976.

BILLOT, MARCEL. "Seventy-five Years of Perfume Creations." *American Perfumer and Cosmetician,* April, 1966.

Lalique and Company. *Lalique Glass.* Dover, N.Y., 1981.

SCHIAPARELLI, ELSA. *Shocking Life.* Dutton, N.Y., 1954.

POIRET, PAUL. *My First Fifty Years,* Gollancz, London, 1934.

DIOR, CHRISTIAN. *Dior by Dior.* The Autobiography of Christian Dior, Penguin, 1954. London, Weidenfeld and Nicholson.

BALMAIN, PIERRE. *My Years and Seasons.* Doubleday, 1965.

The Modern Industry: Supplies and Materials

ARCTANDER, STEFFEN. *Perfume and Flavor Chemicals,* 2 vol. Published privately by the author, Oliphant, Pa., 1969.

BEDOUKIAN, PAUL Z. *Perfumery and Flavoring Synthetics.* Elsevier Publishing Co., N.Y., 1960.

BEDOUKIAN, PAUL Z. *Perfumery and Flavoring Materials, Annual Review Articles,* 1945–1982. Allured Publishing Corp., Wheaton, ILL., 1982.

FENAROLI, GIOVANNI. *Handbook of Flavor Ingredients,* 2 vol. Chemical Rubber Co., Cleveland, Oh., 1975.

ATAL, C. K.; KAPUR, B. *Cultivation and Utilization of Aromatic Plants.* Regional Research Laboratory, Jummu-Tawi, India, 1982.

MARGARIS, N. (ed.). *Aromatic Plants.* Martinus Nijhoff/Dr. W. Junk Publishers, The Hague, Netherlands, 1982.

SIEVERS, A. F. "Methods of Extracting Volatile Oils from Plant Material and the Production of Such Oils in the United States." *U.S.D.A. Technical Bulletin* 16, Jan., 1928, Washington, D.C.

Annales Techniques (Technical Data). VIIIth International Congress of Essential Oils, Cannes-Grasse, Oct., 1980, Fedarom, Grasse, 1982.

HOOD, S. C.; TRUE, R. H. "Camphor Cultivation in the United States.", *USDA Yearbook, 1910,* pp. 449–60, Washington, D.C.

The Contemporary Industry

ROUDNITSKA, EDMOND. *L'Esthétique en Question. Presses Universitaires de France,* Paris, 1977.

FOSTER, KATE. *Scent Bottles.* Connoisseur, London, 1966.

EWING, ELIZABETH. *A History of Twentieth-century Fashion.* Charles Scribner's Sons, N.Y., 1974.

WERIGUIN, CONSTANTIN. *Souvenirs et Parfums.* Plon, Paris, 1965.

LAVER, JAMES. *The Concise History of Costume and Fashion.* Charles Scribner's Sons, N.Y., 1969.

JELLINEK. PAUL *The Practice of Modern Perfumery,* Interscience, N.Y., 1954.

VEREY, ROSEMARY. *The Scented Garden.* Van Nostrand Reinhold, N.Y., 1982.

GENDERS, ROY. *Scented Flora of the World.* Robert Hale Ltd., London, 1977

FOX, HELEN MORGENTHAU. *Gardening with Herbs for Flavor and Fragrance.* Dover, N.Y., 1970.

TAYLOR, NORMAN. *Fragrance in the Garden.* Van Nostrand Reinhold, N.Y., 1953.

FRIEDMAN, JANE. "France vs. U.S.: War of the Noses." *The New York Times,* Aug. 5, 1979.

LIPPA, SI; SHEINMAN, MORT; McCARTHY, PATRICK. "The Rich Designers." *Women's Wear Daily,* May 7–14, 1982, pp. 4–6.

MOTTUS, ALLAN. "Ritz/Lauder Tassle Tussle Spices Season." *Cosmetics and Fragrance Retailing,* Nov., 1978, pp. 42–3, 53.

NEMY, ENID. "Chinese-Americans Join Other Groups in Campaign Against Opium Perfume." *The New York Times,* Apr. 24, 1979, p. C13.

Index